W9-BMP-818

COMPUTER
BOOK SERIES
FROM IDG

Photoshop® 4 For Macs For Dummies®, 2nd Edition

Cheat Sheet

Selection Tricks

Note: All selection tricks performed with selection tools. (There's a shocker.)

Draw straight lines	Option-click with lasso tool
Add to selection outline	Shift-drag
Deselect specific area	Option-drag
Deselect all but intersected area	Shift-Option-drag
Deselect entire image	⌘-D
Select everything	⌘-A
Hide selection outlines	⌘-H
Delete floating selection	Delete
Move selection outline only	Drag or press an arrow key

Moving Selections

Note: Use the move tool to perform the following tricks. Or press ⌘ and use any other tool except the hand or pen tool.

Nudge selection one pixel	arrow key
Nudge selection ten pixels	Shift-arrow key
Clone selection	Option-drag

Toolbox Shortcuts

M	V
M again	W
C	B
L	Y
L again	U
A	O
E	O again
S	O again
R	T
R again	T again
P	G
N	I
K	Z
H	
	X
D	
F	

Layer Tricks

Convert floating selection to layer	⌘-Shift-J
Clone selection to a new layer	⌘-J
Cut selection to a new layer	⌘-Shift-J
Change opacity of floater or layer	1, ... , 9, 0
Activate layer that contains specific image	Control-Option-click with move tool
Activate next layer up	Option-]
Activate next layer down	Option-[
Hide all layers but one	Option-click on eyeball
Select the contents of active layer	⌘-click on layer name in Layers palette

...For Dummies: #1 Computer Book Series for Beginners

Photoshop® 4 For Macs® For Dummies®, 2nd Edition

Cheat Sheet

Palette Shortcuts

Brushes palette	F5
Color palette	F6
Layers palette	F7
Info palette	F8
Options palette	Return
All palettes and toolbox	Tab
Just palettes	Shift-tab
Raise value in option box	up arrow
Lower value in option box	down arrow

More Fun with Selections

Fill selection with foreground color	Option-Delete
Fill selection with background color	⌘-Delete
Display Fill dialog box	Shift-Delete
Cut selection	⌘-X
Copy selection	⌘-C
Paste image last cut or copied	⌘-V
Reapply last filter	⌘-F
Reapply filter and change settings	⌘-Option-F
Adjust brightness and contrast	⌘-L

Navigation Tricks

Scroll image	spacebar-drag
Zoom in	⌘-spacebar-click
Zoom in and change window size	⌘-plus
Zoom out	Option-spacebar-click
Zoom out and change window size	⌘-minus
Zoom to 100%	Double-click zoom tool

Daily Activities

Cancel operation	⌘-period
Close image	⌘-W
General preferences	⌘-K
Open image	⌘-O
Print image	⌘-P
Quit Photoshop	⌘-Q
Save image to disk	⌘-S
Undo last operation	⌘-Z

Painting and Editing Tricks

Increase brush size	]
Select largest brush size	Shift-]
Decrease brush size	[
Select smallest brush size	Shift-[
Change opacity of tool in 10% increments	1, ... , 9, 0
Paint or edit in straight lines	click, Shift-click
Change eraser style	E
Reveal saved image with eraser	Option-drag
Finger paint with smudge tool	Option-drag

IDG BOOKS WORLDWIDE

Copyright © 1996 IDG Books Worldwide, Inc. All rights reserved.

Cheat Sheet $2.95 value. Item 0039-2

For more information about IDG Books, call 1-800-762-2974.

...For Dummies: #1 Computer Book Series for Beginners

Readers Rave about Previous Editions of Photoshop For Dummies:

"Easy to use, simple language, starts from scratch. Not just tips and tricks. I bought it to have on hand for those I train."
— Carolyn Boyle, Orlando, Florida

"Simple, straightforward, good beginner overview (with which to start) and eventual development of more advanced details."
— Allen J. Monczyk, Brooklyn, New York

"Great book to start learning a complex program . . . I laughed, I cried."
— Robert G. Kopp, Plano, Illinois

"It broke down all of the complicated jargon into simple English. It allowed me to use my program to the fullest extent."
— Jesse Stenbak, Keene, New Hampshire

"The manual that came with Photoshop was so boring and long winded that reading this book was a pleasure."
— Marlene Colon, Highlands, New Jersey

"I loved it being so down to earth, and no 'nerd speak'."
— Caron Green, Campbell, California

"This is fun and easy enough to read that I can read it on it's own rather than using it only as a reference to solve problems while at the computer."
— Roberta Brenner, Van Nuys, California

"It's actually interesting and enjoyable to read from cover to cover as well as informative. I learned Photoshop 3.0 in no time at all!"
— Daniel Timiraus, Miami, Florida

"Of all the IDG books I have, this one has to be the champion. I thoroughly enjoyed it. It is far easier to understand than Photoshop 3 manuals."
— Seif Jaiwaji, Edmonton, Alberta

"Sense of humor is right up my alley . . . funnier than Don Rickles at his best moments on the old *Tonight Show.*"
— Ken Funk, New York, New York

References for the Rest of Us!®

COMPUTER BOOK SERIES FROM IDG

Are you intimidated and confused by computers? Do you find that traditional manuals are overloaded with technical details you'll never use? Do your friends and family always call you to fix simple problems on their PCs? Then the *...For Dummies*® computer book series from IDG Books Worldwide is for you.

...For Dummies books are written for those frustrated computer users who know they aren't really dumb but find that PC hardware, software, and indeed the unique vocabulary of computing make them feel helpless. *...For Dummies* books use a lighthearted approach, a down-to-earth style, and even cartoons and humorous icons to diffuse computer novices' fears and build their confidence. Lighthearted but not lightweight, these books are a perfect survival guide for anyone forced to use a computer.

> *"I like my copy so much I told friends; now they bought copies."*
>
> **Irene C., Orwell, Ohio**

> *"Quick, concise, nontechnical, and humorous."*
>
> **Jay A., Elburn, Illinois**

> *"Thanks, I needed this book. Now I can sleep at night."*
>
> **Robin F., British Columbia, Canada**

Already, millions of satisfied readers agree. They have made *...For Dummies* books the #1 introductory level computer book series and have written asking for more. So, if you're looking for the most fun and easy way to learn about computers, look to *...For Dummies* books to give you a helping hand.

IDG BOOKS WORLDWIDE™

5/97

PHOTOSHOP® 4
FOR
MACS®
FOR
DUMMIES®

2ND EDITION

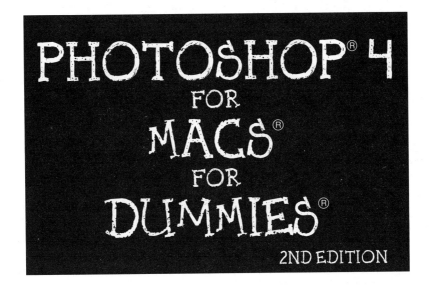

PHOTOSHOP® 4
FOR
MACS®
FOR
DUMMIES®
2ND EDITION

by Deke McClelland

Revised by
Julie King

IDG Books Worldwide, Inc.
An International Data Group Company

Foster City, CA ♦ Chicago, IL ♦ Indianapolis, IN ♦ Southlake, TX

Photoshop® 4 For Macs® For Dummies®, 2nd Edition

Published by
IDG Books Worldwide, Inc.
An International Data Group Company
919 E. Hillsdale Blvd.
Suite 400
Foster City, CA 94404
www.idgbooks.com (IDG Books Worldwide Web site)
www.dummies.com (Dummies Press Web site)

Copyright © 1996 IDG Books Worldwide, Inc. All rights reserved. No part of this book, including interior design, cover design, and icons, may be reproduced or transmitted in any form, by any means (electronic, photocopying, recording, or otherwise) without the prior written permission of the publisher.

Library of Congress Catalog Card No.: 96-77699

ISBN: 0-7645-0039-2

Printed in the United States of America

10 9 8 7 6 5 4 3

2B/RR/QT/ZY/IN

Distributed in the United States by IDG Books Worldwide, Inc.

Distributed by Macmillan Canada for Canada; by Transworld Publishers Limited in the United Kingdom; by IDG Norge Books for Norway; by IDG Sweden Books for Sweden; by Woodslane Pty. Ltd. for Australia; by Woodslane Enterprises Ltd. for New Zealand; by Longman Singapore Publishers Ltd. for Singapore, Malaysia, Thailand, and Indonesia; by Simron Pty. Ltd. for South Africa; by Toppan Company Ltd. for Japan; by Distribuidora Cuspide for Argentina; by Livraria Cultura for Brazil; by Ediciencia S.A. for Ecuador; by Addison-Wesley Publishing Company for Korea; by Ediciones ZETA S.C.R. Ltda. for Peru; by WS Computer Publishing Corporation, Inc., for the Philippines; by Unalis Corporation for Taiwan; by Contemporanea de Ediciones for Venezuela; by Computer Book & Magazine Store for Puerto Rico; by Express Computer Distributors for the Caribbean and West Indies. Authorized Sales Agent: Anthony Rudkin Associates for the Middle East and North Africa.

For general information on IDG Books Worldwide's books in the U.S., please call our Consumer Customer Service department at 800-762-2974. For reseller information, including discounts and premium sales, please call our Reseller Customer Service department at 800-434-3422.

For information on where to purchase IDG Books Worldwide's books outside the U.S., please contact our International Sales department at 650-655-3200 or fax 650-655-3295.

For information on foreign language translations, please contact our Foreign & Subsidiary Rights department at 650-655-3021 or fax 650-655-3281.

For sales inquiries and special prices for bulk quantities, please contact our Sales department at 650-655-3200 or write to the address above.

For information on using IDG Books Worldwide's books in the classroom or for ordering examination copies, please contact our Educational Sales department at 800-434-2086 or fax 817-251-8174.

For press review copies, author interviews, or other publicity information, please contact our Public Relations department at 650-655-3000 or fax 650-655-3299.

For authorization to photocopy items for corporate, personal, or educational use, please contact Copyright Clearance Center, 222 Rosewood Drive, Danvers, MA 01923, or fax 978-750-4470.

LIMIT OF LIABILITY/DISCLAIMER OF WARRANTY: AUTHOR AND PUBLISHER HAVE USED THEIR BEST EFFORTS IN PREPARING THIS BOOK. IDG BOOKS WORLDWIDE, INC., AND AUTHOR MAKE NO REPRESENTATIONS OR WARRANTIES WITH RESPECT TO THE ACCURACY OR COMPLETENESS OF THE CONTENTS OF THIS BOOK AND SPECIFICALLY DISCLAIM ANY IMPLIED WARRANTIES OF MERCHANTABILITY OR FITNESS FOR A PARTICULAR PURPOSE. THERE ARE NO WARRANTIES WHICH EXTEND BEYOND THE DESCRIPTIONS CONTAINED IN THIS PARAGRAPH. NO WARRANTY MAY BE CREATED OR EXTENDED BY SALES REPRESENTATIVES OR WRITTEN SALES MATERIALS. THE ACCURACY AND COMPLETENESS OF THE INFORMATION PROVIDED HEREIN AND THE OPINIONS STATED HEREIN ARE NOT GUARANTEED OR WARRANTED TO PRODUCE ANY PARTICULAR RESULTS, AND THE ADVICE AND STRATEGIES CONTAINED HEREIN MAY NOT BE SUITABLE FOR EVERY INDIVIDUAL. NEITHER IDG BOOKS WORLDWIDE, INC., NOR AUTHOR SHALL BE LIABLE FOR ANY LOSS OF PROFIT OR ANY OTHER COMMERCIAL DAMAGES, INCLUDING BUT NOT LIMITED TO SPECIAL, INCIDENTAL, CONSEQUENTIAL, OR OTHER DAMAGES. FULFILLMENT OF EACH COUPON OFFER IS THE RESPONSIBILITY OF THE OFFEROR.

Trademarks: All brand names and product names used in this book are trade names, service marks, trademarks, or registered trademarks of their respective owners. IDG Books Worldwide is not associated with any product or vendor mentioned in this book.

is a trademark under exclusive license to IDG Books Worldwide, Inc., from International Data Group, Inc.

About the Author

Deke McClelland is the author of more than 30 books about desktop publishing and graphics programs for the Mac and for Windows, including IDG Books Worldwide's bestselling *Macworld Photoshop 3 Bible, CorelDRAW! 6 For Dummies, Photoshop 3 For Macs For Dummies,* and *Macworld FreeHand 4 Bible,* and he is the coauthor of *PageMaker 6 For Windows For Dummies,* 2nd Edition.

He is also contributing editor to *Macworld* magazine and frequently pops up in *Publish* and *PC World.* He received the Ben Franklin award for the Best Computer Book in 1989 and won prestigious Computer Press Awards in 1990, 1992, and 1994. When he isn't writing, he hosts the television series *Digital Gurus* for the Jones Computer Network. In his few minutes of spare time, Deke lives with his wife and aging cat in Boulder, Colorado.

ABOUT IDG BOOKS WORLDWIDE

Welcome to the world of IDG Books Worldwide.

IDG Books Worldwide, Inc., is a subsidiary of International Data Group, the world's largest publisher of computer-related information and the leading global provider of information services on information technology. IDG was founded more than 25 years ago and now employs more than 8,500 people worldwide. IDG publishes more than 275 computer publications in over 75 countries (see listing below). More than 60 million people read one or more IDG publications each month.

Launched in 1990, IDG Books Worldwide is today the #1 publisher of best-selling computer books in the United States. We are proud to have received eight awards from the Computer Press Association in recognition of editorial excellence and three from *Computer Currents'* First Annual Readers' Choice Awards. Our best-selling *...For Dummies®* series has more than 30 million copies in print with translations in 30 languages. IDG Books Worldwide, through a joint venture with IDG's Hi-Tech Beijing, became the first U.S. publisher to publish a computer book in the People's Republic of China. In record time, IDG Books Worldwide has become the first choice for millions of readers around the world who want to learn how to better manage their businesses.

Our mission is simple: Every one of our books is designed to bring extra value and skill-building instructions to the reader. Our books are written by experts who understand and care about our readers. The knowledge base of our editorial staff comes from years of experience in publishing, education, and journalism — experience we use to produce books for the '90s. In short, we care about books, so we attract the best people. We devote special attention to details such as audience, interior design, use of icons, and illustrations. And because we use an efficient process of authoring, editing, and desktop publishing our books electronically, we can spend more time ensuring superior content and spend less time on the technicalities of making books.

You can count on our commitment to deliver high-quality books at competitive prices on topics you want to read about. At IDG Books Worldwide, we continue in the IDG tradition of delivering quality for more than 25 years. You'll find no better book on a subject than one from IDG Books Worldwide.

John Kilcullen
CEO
IDG Books Worldwide, Inc.

Steven Berkowitz
President and Publisher
IDG Books Worldwide, Inc.

Eighth Annual Computer Press Awards ➤ 1992

Ninth Annual Computer Press Awards ➤ 1993

Tenth Annual Computer Press Awards ➤ 1994

Eleventh Annual Computer Press Awards ➤ 1995

IDG Books Worldwide, Inc., is a subsidiary of International Data Group, the world's largest publisher of computer-related information and the leading global provider of information services on information technology. International Data Group publishes over 275 computer publications in over 75 countries. Sixty million people read one or more International Data Group publications each month. International Data Group's publications include: **ARGENTINA:** Buyer's Guide, Computerworld Argentina, PC World Argentina; **AUSTRALIA:** Australian Macworld, Australian PC World, Australian Reseller News, Computerworld, IT Casebook, Network World, Publish, Webmaster; **AUSTRIA:** Computerwelt Osterreich, Networks Austria, PC Tip Austria; **BANGLADESH:** PC World Bangladesh; **BELARUS:** PC World Belarus; **BELGIUM:** Data News; **BRAZIL:** Annuário de Informática, Computerworld, Connections, Macworld, PC Player, PC World, Publish, Reseller News, Supergamepower; **BULGARIA:** Computerworld Bulgaria, Network World Bulgaria, PC & MacWorld Bulgaria; **CANADA:** CIO Canada, Client/Server World, ComputerWorld Canada, InfoWorld Canada, NetworkWorld Canada, WebWorld; **CHILE:** Computerworld Chile, PC World Chile; **COLOMBIA:** Computerworld Colombia, PC World Colombia; **COSTA RICA:** PC World Centro America; **THE CZECH AND SLOVAK REPUBLICS:** Computerworld Czechoslovakia, Macworld Czech Republic, PC World Czechoslovakia; **DENMARK:** Communications World Danmark, Computerworld Danmark, Macworld Danmark, PC World Danmark, Techworld Denmark; **DOMINICAN REPUBLIC:** PC World Republica Dominicana; **ECUADOR:** PC World Ecuador; **EGYPT:** Computerworld Middle East, PC World Middle East; **EL SALVADOR:** PC World Centro America; **FINLAND:** MikroPC, Tietoverkko, Tietoviikko; **FRANCE:** Distributique, Hebdo, Info PC, Le Monde Informatique, Macworld, Reseaux & Telecoms, WebMaster France; **GERMANY:** Computer Partner, Computerwoche, Computerwoche Extra, Computerwoche FOCUS, Global Online, Macwelt, PC Welt; **GREECE:** Amiga Computing, GamePro Greece, Multimedia World; **GUATEMALA:** PC World Centro America; **HONDURAS:** PC World Centro America; **HONG KONG:** Computerworld Hong Kong, PC World Hong Kong, Publish in Asia; **HUNGARY:** ABCD CD-ROM, Computerworld Szamitastechnika, Internetto online Magazine, PC World Hungary, PC-X Magazin Hungary; **ICELAND:** Tolvuheimur PC World Island; **INDIA:** Information Communications World, Information Systems Computerworld, PC World India, Publish in Asia; **INDONESIA:** InfoKomputer PC World, Komputek Computerworld, Publish in Asia; **IRELAND:** ComputerScope, PC Live!; **ISRAEL:** Macworld Israel, People & Computers/Computerworld; **ITALY:** Computerworld Italia, Macworld Italia, Networking Italia, PC World Italia; **JAPAN:** DTP World, Macworld Japan, Nikkei Personal Computing, OS/2 World Japan, SunWorld Japan, Windows NT World, Windows World Japan; **KENYA:** PC World East African; **KOREA:** Hi-Tech Information, Macworld Korea, PC World Korea; **MACEDONIA:** PC World Macedonia; **MALAYSIA:** Computerworld Malaysia, PC World Malaysia, Publish in Asia; **MALTA:** PC World Malta; **MEXICO:** Computerworld Mexico, PC World Mexico; **MYANMAR:** PC World Myanmar; **NETHERLANDS:** Computer! Totaal, LAN Internetworking Magazine, LAN World Buyers Guide, Macworld Netherlands, Net, WebWereld; **NEW ZEALAND:** Absolute Beginners Guide and Plain & Simple Series, Computer Buyer, Computer Industry Directory, Computerworld New Zealand, MTB, Network World, PC World New Zealand; **NICARAGUA:** PC World Centro America; **NORWAY:** Computerworld Norge, CW Rapport, Datamagasinet, Financial Rapport, Kursguide Norge, Macworld Norge, Multimediaworld Norge, PC World Ekspress Norge, PC World Nettverk, PC World Norge, PC World ProduktGuide Norge; **PAKISTAN:** Computerworld Pakistan; **PANAMA:** PC World Panama; **PEOPLE'S REPUBLIC OF CHINA:** China Computer Users, China Computerworld, China InfoWorld, China Telecom World Weekly, Computer & Communication, Electronic Design China, Electronics Today, Electronics Weekly, Game Software, PC World China, Popular Computer Week, Software Weekly, Software World, Telecom World; **PERU:** Computerworld Peru, PC World Profesional Peru, PC World SoHo Peru; **PHILIPPINES:** Click!, Computerworld Philippines, PC World Philippines, Publish in Asia; **POLAND:** Computerworld Poland, Computerworld Special Report Poland, Cyber, Macworld Poland, Networld Poland, PC World Komputer; **PORTUGAL:** Cerebro/PC World, Computerworld/Correio Informático, Dealer World Portugal, Mac*In/PC*In Portugal, Multimedia World; **PUERTO RICO:** PC World Puerto Rico; **ROMANIA:** Computerworld Romania, PC World Romania, Telecom Romania; **RUSSIA:** Computerworld Russia, Mir PK, Publish, Seti; **SINGAPORE:** Computerworld Singapore, PC World Singapore, Publish in Asia; **SLOVENIA:** Monitor; **SOUTH AFRICA:** Computing SA, Network World SA, Software World SA; **SPAIN:** Communicaciones World España, Computerworld España, Dealer World España, Macworld España, PC World España; **SRI LANKA:** Infolink PC World; **SWEDEN:** CAP&Design, Computer Sweden, Corporate Computing Sweden, Internetworld Sweden, it.branschen, Macworld Sweden, MaxiData Sweden, MikroDatorn, Nätverk & Kommunikation, PC World Sweden, PCaktiv, Windows World Sweden; **SWITZERLAND:** Computerworld Schweiz, Macworld Schweiz, PCtip; **TAIWAN:** Computerworld Taiwan, Macworld Taiwan, NEW VISiON/Publish, PC World Taiwan, Windows World Taiwan; **THAILAND:** Publish in Asia, Thai Computerworld; **TURKEY:** Computerworld Turkiye, Macworld Turkiye, Network World Turkiye, PC World Turkiye; **UKRAINE:** Computerworld Kiev, Multimedia World Ukraine, PC World Ukraine; **UNITED KINGDOM:** Acorn User UK, Amiga Action UK, Amiga Computing UK, Apple Talk UK, Computing, Macworld, Parents and Computers UK, PC Advisor, PC Home, PSX Pro, The WEB; **UNITED STATES:** Cable in the Classroom, CIO Magazine, Computerworld, DOS World, Federal Computer Week, GamePro Magazine, InfoWorld, I-Way, Macworld, Network World, PC Games, PC World, Publish, Video Event, THE WEB Magazine, and WebMaster; online webzines: JavaWorld, NetscapeWorld, and SunWorld Online; **URUGUAY:** InfoWorld Uruguay; **VENEZUELA:** Computerworld Venezuela, PC World Venezuela; and **VIETNAM:** PC World Vietnam.   3/24/97

Publisher's Acknowledgments

We're proud of this book; please register your comments through our IDG Books Worldwide Online Registration Form located at: http://my2cents.dummies.com.

Some of the people who helped bring this book to market include the following:

Acquisitions, Development, and Editorial

Project Editor: Jennifer Ehrlich

Assistant Acquisitions Editor: Gareth Hancock

Permissions Editor: Joyce Pepple

Copy Editor: Michael Bolinger

Technical Editor: Ben Barbante

Editorial Manager: Kristin A. Cocks

Editorial Assistant: Chris H. Collins

Production

Project Coordinator: Debbie Stailey

Layout and Graphics: E. Shawn Aylsworth, Linda M. Boyer, Elizabeth Cárdenas-Nelson, J. Tyler Connor, Dominique DeFelice, Angela F. Hunckler, Jane E. Martin, Drew R. Moore, Mark C. Owens, Anna Rohrer, Brent Savage, Kate Snell, Michael A. Sullivan, Ian A. Smith

Proofreaders: Melissa D. Buddendeck, Michelle Croninger, Joel K. Draper, Nancy Price, Carrie Voorhis, Karen York

Indexer: David Heiret

General and Administrative

IDG Books Worldwide, Inc.: John Kilcullen, CEO; Steven Berkowitz, President and Publisher

IDG Books Technology Publishing: Brenda McLaughlin, Senior Vice President and Group Publisher

Dummies Technology Press and Dummies Editorial: Diane Graves Steele, Vice President and Associate Publisher; Mary Bednarek, Director of Acquisitions and Product Development; Kristin A. Cocks, Editorial Director

Dummies Trade Press: Kathleen A. Welton, Vice President and Publisher; Kevin Thornton, Acquisitions Manager

IDG Books Production for Dummies Press: Beth Jenkins Roberts, Production Director; Cindy L. Phipps, Manager of Project Coordination, Production Proofreading, and Indexing; Kathie S. Schutte, Supervisor of Page Layout; Shelley Lea, Supervisor of Graphics and Design; Debbie J. Gates, Production Systems Specialist; Robert Springer, Supervisor of Proofreading; Debbie Stailey, Special Projects Coordinator; Tony Augsburger, Supervisor of Reprints and Bluelines; Leslie Popplewell, Media Archive Coordinator

Dummies Packaging and Book Design: Patti Crane, Packaging Specialist; Kavish + Kavish, Cover Design

♦

The publisher would like to give special thanks to Patrick J. McGovern, without whom this book would not have been possible.

♦

Dedication

To Elizabeth, who came home from a low-brow evening of bingo to cart her klutz of a husband off to the hosipital. That's just the kind of loving person she is.

Acknowledgments

Thanks to the many folks who loaned me products and support, including John Leddy and Mark Hamburg at Adobe; Charles Smith at Digital Stock; Tom Hughes at PhotoDisc; and the helpful folks at Palmer's.

Thanks also to Diane Steele for providing advice and support, to Beth Jenkins and the art department for their expertise and cooperation, to Ben Barbante for keeping an eye out for the technical foibles, and to Jennifer Ehrlich for keeping the whole shebang on track and in good shape. Finally, special thanks to Julie King for the excellent job of revising this edition to bring things up to date.

Contents at a Glance

Cartoons at a Glance

By Rich Tennant

The 5th Wave By Rich Tennant

ATTEMPTING TO SAVE MONEY ON FAMILY PHOTOS, THE DILBRANTS SCAN THEIR NEWBORN INTO A PHOTO IMAGING PROGRAM WITH PLANS OF JUST DITHERING THE CHILD INTO ADOLESCENCE.

"Nope! She must have moved again! Run the scanner down her once more."

page 291

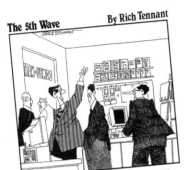

The 5th Wave By Rich Tennant

"...AND TO ACCESS THE PROGRAM'S 'HOT KEY,' YOU JUST DEPRESS THESE ELEVEN KEYS SIMULTANEOUSLY. HERB OVER THERE HAS A KNACK FOR DOING THIS THAT I THINK YOU'LL ENJOY—HERB! GOT A MINUTE?"

page 7

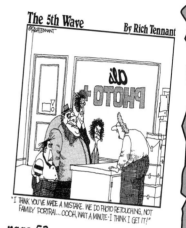

The 5th Wave By Rich Tennant

"I THINK YOU'VE MADE A MISTAKE. WE DO PHOTO RETOUCHING, NOT FAMILY PORTRAI....OOOH, WAIT A MINUTE-I THINK I GET IT!"

page 53

The 5th Wave By Rich Tennant

NATIONAL ENQUIRER PHOTO IMAGING WORKSHOP

"Remember, your Elvis should appear bald and slightly hunched—nice Big Foot, Brad—keep your two-headed animals in the shadows and your alien spacecrafts crisp and defined."

page 109

The 5th Wave By Rich Tennant

GRIB INC
KODA
UFO INVESTIGATION TEAM

"I'VE GOT SOME IMAGE EDITING SOFTWARE, SO I TOOK THE LIBERTY OF ERASING SOME OF THE SMUDGES THAT KEPT SHOWING UP AROUND THE CLOUDS. NO NEED TO THANK ME."

page 167

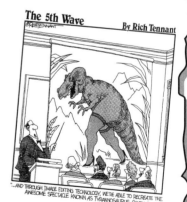

The 5th Wave By Rich Tennant

"...AND THROUGH IMAGE EDITING TECHNOLOGY, WE'RE ABLE TO RECREATE THE AWESOME SPECTACLE KNOWN AS TYRANNOSAURUS GWEN."

page 217

Fax: 978-546-7747 • E-mail: the5wave@tiac.net

Table of Contents

Introduction

●●

*W*hy in the world is Photoshop such a popular program? Normally, graphics software is about as much of a hit with the general public as a grunge rock band is with the senior-citizen set. And yet Photoshop — a program that lets you correct and modify photographs on your computer screen — has managed to work its way into the hearts and minds of computer users from all walks of life. What gives?

Wouldn't you know it, I just happen to have a couple of theories. First, when you work in Photoshop, you're not drawing from scratch, you're editing photos. Sure, it can be a little intimidating to tamper with a photograph, but it's nothing like the chilling, abject fear that seizes your soul when you stare at a blank screen and try to figure out how to draw things on it. Simply put, a photograph inspires you to edit it in precisely the same way that an empty piece of paper does not.

Second, after Photoshop hooks you, it keeps you interested with a depth of capabilities that few pieces of software can match. Unlike so many programs that have caught on like wildfire over the years but are actually a pain in the rear to use — I won't name any, but I bet you can think of a few — Photoshop is both powerful and absorbing. After several years with the program, I am continually discovering new things about it, and I've enjoyed nearly every minute of it. (Okay, so a couple of stinky minutes sneak themselves in every once in a while, but that's to be expected. Photoshop is a computer program, after all, and we all know that computers are cosmic jokes whose only reason for being is to mock us, ignore our requests, and crash at the least opportune moments. In fact, considering that it's a computer program, Photoshop fares remarkably well.)

Why a Book . . . For Dummies?

Just because Photoshop is a pleasure to use doesn't mean that the program is easy to learn. In fact, it's kind of a bear. A big, ornery, grizzly bear with about 17 rows of teeth and claws to match. There's so much to the program that it honestly takes months of earnest endeavor to sift through it all. By yourself, that is.

When you go into battle armed with this book, however, Photoshop sucks in its teeth, retracts its claws, and lies down like a lamb. In fact, studies show that if you just hold the book up to the computer screen, Photoshop behaves 50 percent better, even if you never read a single page.

If you do read a page or two, Photoshop not only behaves, it makes sense. The truth is, I wrote this book with the following specific goals in mind:

- ✔ To show you what you need to know at the precise pace you need to know it.
- ✔ To teach you how to do the right things in the right way, right off the bat.
- ✔ To distract you and shove little facts into your head when you're not looking.
- ✔ To make the process not only less painful, but a real adventure that you'll look back on during your Golden Years with a wistful tear in your eye. "Oh, how I'd like to learn Photoshop all over again," you'll sigh. "Nothing I've done since — whether it was winning the lottery that one time or flying on the inaugural commuter shuttle to the moon with the original cast of *Star Trek* — seemed quite so thrilling as sifting through Photoshop with that crazy old ...*For Dummies* book."

Okay, maybe that's an exaggeration, but prepare yourself for a fun time. In a matter of days, you'll be doing things that'll make your jaw hang down and dangle from its hinges. And don't worry, it's all perfectly legal throughout the 50 states as well as Puerto Rico, the Virgin Islands, and Guam.

Don't You Have Another Photoshop Book?

I must admit, this is not my first book on Photoshop. In fact, if you insist on counting, this is my second. (Well, if you want to be completely technical, this is the second edition of my second book. The first edition covered Version 3 of Photoshop. But I digress.) My first Photoshop book, *Macworld Photoshop 4 Bible* (IDG Books Worldwide, Inc.), is an 800-page tome that covers just about everything there is to know.

But some folks get a little worried when they see an 800-page book. They look forward to reading the 800 pages with the same dread anticipation they normally reserve for eating 800 pieces of dry toast. As people who have read the *Bible* know, the pages are anything but dry and laborious; in fact, they're more like 800 tasty cookies. "Make it fatter, and throw in a free forklift so I can tote it around my house," is the typical response I get. But even so, the *Bible* is something that this book is not. It's exhaustive. It assumes that you just can't get enough Photoshop knowledge.

Photoshop 4 For Macs For Dummies — like its predecessor, *Photoshop 3 For Macs For Dummies* — looks at things from a different angle. It points out the features you need to know and shows you exactly how to use them. You don't want to make Photoshop your life — not yet, anyway — but you don't want the thing to just sit there and beep at you while completely destroying your photograph, either. You'd like to reach a certain satisfying level of comfort, like the one you've recently achieved with your cat now that it's no longer clawing the furniture apart. Becoming comfortable and productive with Photoshop is what this book is all about.

What's in This Book?

This book comprises a bunch of independent sections designed to answer your questions as they occur. Oh, sure, you can read the book cover to cover, and it will make perfect sense. But you can also read any section completely out of context and know exactly what's going on.

To help you slog through the information, I've broken up the book into six major parts. Each of these parts contains three or four chapters, and these chapters are divided into sections and subsections. Graphics abound to illustrate things that would take 1,000 words to explain, and there are even two sets of glorious color plates — 16 pages in all — to show off special issues related to color. As it just so happens, the previous edition of this book, *Photoshop 3 For Macs For Dummies,* was the first *...For Dummies* book to feature color.

To give you an overview of the kind of information you're likely to find in these pages, here's a quick rundown of the six major parts.

Part I: What the . . . ? Aagh, Help Me!

The first stage of using any computer program is the worst. You don't know what you can do, you don't know how good the program is, you don't even know how to ask a reasonably intelligent question. These first three chapters get you up and running in record time.

Chapter 1 introduces you to image editing, explains where to find images to edit, and provides a quick glimpse of what's new in Version 4 of Photoshop. Chapters 2 and 3 take you on a grand tour of the Photoshop interface and image window and give you all the information you need to navigate both.

Part II: The Care and Feeding of Pixels

Before you can edit a digital photograph, you have to know a few things about the nature of the beast. What's a pixel, for example, and why is it so dangerous to get rid of one? What's the difference between a color image and a grayscale image — other than the obvious? And how do you save or print your image after you finish editing it? I answer all these questions and many more in Chapters 4 through 7.

Part III: Tiptoe through the Toolbox

Photoshop offers fewer tools — pencils, paintbrushes, and the like — than most graphics programs. But these tools are remarkably capable, allowing you to perform pages and pages of tricks while expending minimum effort. Learn how to smear colors, get rid of dust specks, erase mistakes, and do a whole lot more in Chapters 8 through 11.

Part IV: Select Before You Correct

The selection tools let you cordon off the portion of the photograph you want to edit. Select the face, for example, and Photoshop protects the body, no matter how randomly you drag or how spastic your brushstrokes. Chapters 12 through 14 help you understand how selections work and how to use them to your advantage.

Part V: So, You Say You're Serious about Image Editing

Now we step into the really incredible part of the Photoshop playground. In Chapter 15, I introduce you to layers, a Photoshop feature that adds flexibility, creative opportunity, and security to your image-editing life. In Chapter 16, you find out how to create text effects and add them to your image. And in Chapters 17 and 18, I show you the commands that professionals use to sharpen focus, change brightness and contrast, correct colors, and generally make an image look three times better than it did when you started. Very exciting stuff.

Part VI: The Part of Tens

Chapters 19 through 21 contain the ultimate Photoshop Top Ten lists. Find out the most essential Photoshop shortcuts, the most amazing special-effects tricks, and the answer to that age-old question, "Now that I've finished mucking up my image in Photoshop, what do I do with it?"

What's with All the Margin Icons?

When you're driving, road signs are always warning you about bad things. Slow, Detour, Stop, Dip — these are all signs that I, for one, hate to see. I mean, you never see good signs like Go Ahead and Speed, No Traffic This Way, or Free Money Up Ahead.

This book isn't like that. Using friendly little margin icons, I highlight good things and bad things, and the good things even outnumber the bad. For example, you'll find several times more Tip icons than Warning icons. So don't shy away from the road signs in this book; welcome them into your reading ritual with open arms. Here's your field guide to icons:

I hate computer jargon as much as the next red-blooded American. But sometimes, I have to use it because there's no word for this stuff in normal, everyday, conversational English. It's a crying shame, I know, but at least I warn you that something nerdy is coming your way with this icon.

Photoshop has very few obvious shortcuts and a ton of hidden ones. That's where the Tip icon comes in. It says, "Hey, whoa there, here's a juicy one!"

This icon calls your attention to special little reminders of things I've mentioned in the past or things I want you to bear in mind for the future.

Photoshop is a kind and gentle program. But every once in a while, it pays to be careful. The Warning icon tells you when to keep an eye out for trouble.

This icon points out features or commands that have changed or are new in Version 4. If you're upgrading to Version 4 from an earlier version of Photoshop, pay attention to this road sign, because lots of things are different now.

Now and then, I feel compelled to share something with you that has nothing whatsoever to do with your learning Photoshop or any other computer program. It's just my way of showing that I care.

Where Do I Go Now?

When I was in grade school, I don't think that a year went by that our teacher didn't show us how to handle our new books. Open the book once in the center and then open the first quarter and the last quarter, each time gently creasing the spine. Never fold the pages or roll them so that they won't lie flat. And be sure to read the words from the beginning to end, just as the author meant them to be read. A book, after all, is a Special Thing to Be Treasured.

Well, I'll tell you what, this isn't your teacher's book and it isn't my book either. This is your book, so you treat it and read it any way you please.

- ✔ Break the spine first thing out. The pages lie flatter that way.
- ✔ When you have a question, look it up in the index. Feel free to shut the book and get on with your life when you're done (though I'll do my best to snag you and make you read longer).
- ✔ If you're just curious about what the book has to offer, look up whatever topic interests you in the table of contents and read a few pages.
- ✔ If you want to find out everything the book has to offer in what I consider the optimum order, turn the next page and start reading at your own pace.
- ✔ If you come across something important, don't hesitate to fold the page, slap a sticky note on it, circle the text with a highlighter pen, or rip out the page and tack it to the wall.
- ✔ And when you've gleaned everything there is to glean, house-train your new puppy with the pages or use them for kindling.

I just want you to know that you have my permission to learn in any way that suits you. Respecting a book is a waste of energy; respecting yourself and your needs is what counts.

How to Bug Me

Want to send me a line of congratulations or complaint? Fill out the registration card in the back of this book, and the folks at IDG Books will pass it along to me. Or send me an e-mail at either of these addresses:

America Online: DekeMc

Internet: DekeMc@InternetMCI.com

I'm not very regular about checking my mail, mind you — I do it once a week if I'm feeling particularly diligent, less frequently otherwise. But I never fail to answer, eventually.

Part I
What the . . . ? Aagh, Help Me!

The 5th Wave   **By Rich Tennant**

"...AND TO ACCESS THE PROGRAM'S 'HOT KEY,' YOU JUST DEPRESS THESE ELEVEN KEYS SIMULTANEOUSLY. HERB OVER THERE HAS A KNACK FOR DOING THIS THAT I THINK YOU'LL ENJOY—HERB! GOT A MINUTE?"

In this part . . .

A lot has been written, spoken, and tapped out in Morse code about the value of information. To hear some folks tell it, information is now the top commodity in the industrialized world. Well, I don't know if that's true or not — personally, you can give me money over information any day of the week. "There's always more room in my billfold than my head," is my saying. But being dumb on any subject is no fun. I mean really dumb — as in, you don't even know what questions to ask in order to get answers.

Well, I've been this dumb myself, and frankly, I remain this dumb about all kinds of subjects. If you're not sure how to ask an intelligent question about Photoshop, take heart. These first three chapters answer that most impossible of all questions to express, "What the . . . ? I mean . . . ? You know, if the . . . ? Aagh, help me!" For example, you find out what Photoshop is, take a quick, all-expenses-paid jaunt through its tools and commands, and learn how to open and view images.

By the end of Chapter 3, you won't know everything there is to know about Photoshop — otherwise, I could have dispensed with the 18 chapters that follow it — but you will know enough to phrase a few intelligent questions. And please remember that as you read these chapters, there's no shame in being a dummy. I mean, it must be more than coincidental that the initials for *Photoshop For Dummies* are Ph.D.

Chapter 1

Meet Dr. Photo and Mr. Shop

- -

- -

*P*hotoshop is arguably the most comprehensive and most popular photo editor around. In fact, I don't know a single computer artist who doesn't use Photoshop on an almost daily basis, regardless of what other programs he or she may also use.

I assume that you've at least seen Photoshop before, if not used the program, and that you have a vague idea of what it's all about. But just so that we're all clear on the subject, the primary purpose of Photoshop is to make changes to photographic images that you somehow managed to get on disk. (For some clever ideas on acquiring such images, see the section "Where Do I Find Images to Abuse?" in this chapter.)

If you've only used Photoshop for a week or so, you may have mistaken it for a fairly straightforward package. Certainly, on the surface of the program, Photoshop comes off as rather friendly. But lurking a few fathoms deep is another, darker program, one that is distinctly unfriendly for the uninitiated but wildly capable for the stout of heart. My analyst would no doubt declare Photoshop a classic case of a split personality. It's half man, half monster; half mild-mannered shoeshine boy, half blonde-grabbing, airplane-swatting King Kong; half kindly old gent with white whiskers chewing on a pipe, half green-gilled invader from another planet chewing on your . . . well, perhaps you don't want to know. In short, Photoshop has a Dr. Jekyll-and-Mr. Hyde thing going, only it's way scarier.

As you may recall from the last time you saw *Abbott and Costello Meet Dr. Jekyll and Mr. Hyde* — indisputably the foremost resource of information on this famous tale — this Jekyll character (not to be confused with the similarly named cartoon crow) is normally your everyday, average, nice-guy scientist. Then one day, he drinks some potion or gets cut off in traffic or something and changes into his ornery alter ego, known at every dive bar in town by the surname Hyde. Photoshop behaves just the same way, except that no magical transformation is required to shift between the program's Jekyll half and its Hyde half. Both personalities coexist simultaneously in what you might call harmony.

This chapter explores both sides of the Photoshop brain. It also introduces you to the personality changes found in the latest incarnation of the program, Version 4. Finally, I get you started on the road to image-editing bliss by explaining where to find images to edit in the first place.

The Bland but Kindly Dr. Photo

To discover the benevolent Dr. Jekyll half of Photoshop, you need look no further than the standard painting and editing tools. Shown in Figure 1-1, these tools are so simple, they're practically pastoral, the kind of household appliances your great-grandmother would have been comfortable with. The eraser erases, the pencil draws hard-edged lines, the airbrush sprays a fine mist of color, and so on. These incredibly straightforward tools attract new users just as surely as a light attracts miller moths (except new users don't give off quite so much dust when you squish them).

But you quickly discover that on their own, these tools aren't super-duper exciting, just like the boring Dr. Jekyll. They don't work much like their traditional counterparts — a line drawn with the pencil tool, for example, doesn't look anything like a line drawn with a real pencil — and they don't seem to be particularly applicable to the job of editing images. Generally speaking, you have to be blessed with pretty major hand-eye coordination to achieve good results using these tools.

The Ghastly but Dynamic Mr. Shop

When the standard paint and editing tools don't fit the bill, you try to adjust the performance of the tools and experiment with the other image controls of Photoshop. Unfortunately, that's when you discover the Mr. Hyde half of the program. You encounter options that have meaningless names such as Dissolve, Multiply, and Difference. Commands such as Image Size and Canvas Size — both of which sound harmless enough — seem to damage your image. And clicking on icons frequently produces no result. It's enough to drive a reticent computer artist stark raving insane, as illustrated in Figure 1-2.

Figure 1-1:
Many of the Photoshop tools have an old-world rustic charm that's sure to warm the cockles of the most timid technophobe.

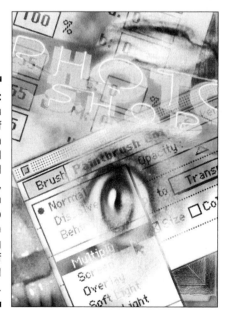

Figure 1-2:
When you tire of playing with the standard painting and editing tools, you run smack dab into a terrifying collection of options and commands.

The net result is that many folks return broken and frustrated to the under-equipped and boring but nonthreatening painting and editing tools that they've come to know. It's sad, really. Especially when you consider all the wonderful things that the more complex Photoshop controls can do. Oh sure, the controls have weird names and they may not respond as you think they should at first, but after you come to terms with these slick puppies, they perform like you wouldn't believe.

In fact, the dreaded Mr. Hyde side of Photoshop represents the core of this powerful program. Without its sinister half, Photoshop is just another rinky-dink piece of painting software whose most remarkable capability is keeping the kids out of mischief on a rainy day.

The Two Phunctions of Photoshop

Generally speaking, the two halves of Photoshop serve different purposes. The straightforward Jekyll tools mostly concentrate on *painting,* and the more complex Hyde capabilities are devoted to *image editing.* Therefore, to tackle this great program, you may find it helpful to understand the difference between the two terms.

Painting without the mess

Painting is just what it sounds like: You take a brush loaded with color and smear it all over your on-screen image. You can paint from scratch on a blank canvas or you can paint directly on top of a photograph. The first option requires lots of talent, planning, and a few dashes of artistic genius; the second option requires an opposable thumb. Okay, that's a slight exaggeration — some lemurs have been known to have problems with the second option — but most people find painting on an existing image much easier than creating an image from scratch.

Take Figure 1-3, for example. Here's a rather drab fellow drinking a rather drab beverage. (Though you may guess this man to be Dr. Jekyll armed with the secret potion, most scholars consider it highly doubtful that even Jekyll was this goofy.) I introduce this silly person solely to demonstrate the amazing functions of Photoshop.

Were you to paint on our unsuspecting saphead, you might arrive at something on the order of the image shown in Figure 1-4. I invoked all these changes using a single tool — the paintbrush — and just two colors — black and white. Suddenly, a singularly cool dude emerges. No planning or real talent was involved; I simply traced over some existing details in the image. Better yet, I haven't permanently damaged the image, as I would if I tried the same thing using a real-life paintbrush. Because I saved the original image to disk (as explained in Chapter 6), I can restore details from the original image at whim (the subject of Chapter 11).

Figure 1-3:
The unadorned "I Love My Libation" poster boy of 1948.

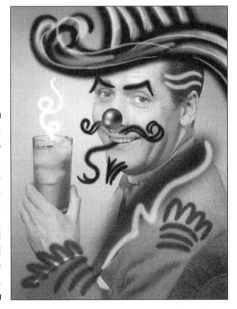

Figure 1-4:
A few hundred strokes of the paintbrush result in a party animal to rival Carmen Miranda.

Editing existing image detail

The remade man in Figure 1-4 is the life of the party, but he's nothing compared to what he could be with the aid of some image editing. When you edit an image, you distort and enhance its existing details. So rather than painting with color, you paint with the image itself.

Figure 1-5 demonstrates what I mean. To achieve this grotesque turn of the visual phrase, I was obliged to indulge in a liberal amount of distortion. First, I flipped the guy's head and stretched it a little bit. Well, actually, I stretched it a lot. Then I further exaggerated the eyes and mouth. I rotated the arm and distorted the glass to make the glass meet the ear. Finally, I cloned a background from a different image to cover up where the head and arm used to be. The only thing I painted was the straw (the one coming out of the guy's ear). Otherwise, I lifted every detail from one of two photographs. And yet, this man's very own mother wouldn't recognize him, were she still alive today.

Mind you, you don't have to go quite so hog-wild with the image editing. If you're a photographer, for example, you may not care to mess with your work to the point that it becomes completely unrecognizable. Call you weird, but you like reality the way you see it. Figure 1-6 shows a few subtle adjustments that affect neither the form nor composition of the original image. These changes merely accentuate details or downplay defects in the image.

Figure 1-5:
Image
editing has
no respect
for
composition,
form, or
underlying
skeletal
structure.

Figure 1-6:
If Figure 1-5 is a little too disgusting for your tastes, you can apply more moderate edits to your image.

Just for the record, here are a few common ways to edit photographs in Photoshop:

- ✔ You can *sharpen* an image to make it appear in better focus, as in the first image in Figure 1-6. Generally, sharpening is used to account for focus problems in the scanning process, but you can sometimes sharpen a photograph that was shot out of focus.

- ✔ If you want to accentuate a foreground image, you can blur the focus of the background. The image on the right side of Figure 1-6 is an example.

- ✔ If a photograph is too light or too dark, you can fix it in a flash through the miracle of color correction. You can change the contrast, brighten or dim colors, and actually replace one color with another. Both of the images in Figure 1-6 have been color corrected.

- ✔ Using the Photoshop selection and move tools, you can grab a chunk of your image and physically move it around. You can also clone the selection, stretch it, rotate it, or copy it to a different image.

And that's only the tip of the iceberg. The remaining chapters of this book explore Photoshop as both a painting program and an image editor. Most chapters contain a little bit of information on both topics, but as a general rule, the first half of the book stresses painting, and the second half spends more time on image editing. Rip the book in half and you may very well have the makings of a late-night horror flick.

It's New! It's Improved!

Evidently, the folks at Adobe read the earlier edition of this book (the one that covered Version 3) and were inspired by my colorful dual-personality analogy. Why else would Version 4 be one part helpful, unbelievably great upgrade and one part exercise in frustration?

On one hand, Version 4 includes some incredibly useful new features. On the other, Version 4 trashes some time-honored shortcuts and techniques used in earlier versions of the program, a development that is sure to confuse and annoy veteran Photoshop users.

Mind you, Adobe didn't set out purposely to aggravate Photoshop fans; the company is simply trying to make Photoshop behave similarly to its Adobe cousins — PageMaker and Illustrator, to name two. The thinking is that after you get acquainted with one Adobe program, you'll find it easy to use others. To bring Photoshop in line with the rest of the family, some keyboard shortcuts and tools were altered in Version 4. (The Cheat Sheet at the front of this book provides a handy reference to the new shortcuts, by the way.)

The good news is that Version 4's good side more than compensates for its bad side. So in the interest of focusing on the positive, here are just some of the improvements Version 4 brings you:

- ✔ The new Navigator palette, discussed in Chapter 3, gives you a faster and more convenient way to zoom in and out on an image and view different areas of the image.

- ✔ Speaking of zooming, you can now zoom in and out with greater flexibility. Whereas previous versions of Photoshop let you zoom only in preset increments determined by the program, Version 4 lets you specify any zoom ratio you want. Chapter 3 zooms in on the topic further.

- ✔ Grids and guides, long offered in page-layout programs, are now offered in Photoshop, too. Covered in Chapter 3, grids and guides serve as handy tools for lining things up within an image.

- ✔ A new text mask tool makes it easy to use type as a selection outline. If that sounds like Greek to you, don't panic; Chapter 16 explains all.

- ✔ The Float command, a popular editing device in earlier versions, is gone. Photoshop now automatically creates a new layer for you when you perform certain actions, such as adding text to an image or cutting and pasting one part of an image into another. Version 4 also brings you adjustment layers, which enable you to color correct all the layers in an image in one fell swoop — and in a way that takes the risk out of color correction. Chapters 15 and 18 have the details.

✔ Following the latest software trend, Photoshop now offers context-sensitive menus. To translate that into English, you can press Control together with the mouse button to quickly display a list of commands related to whatever it is you're trying to accomplish at the moment. See Chapter 2 for the lowdown.

✔ On top of all these goodies, Photoshop 4 also offers improved gradient (blend) capabilities, as discussed in Chapter 14 and provides you with a ton of new filters, as discussed in Chapter 17.

If you're used to working in Photoshop 3, some of these changes may confuse you at first, but they make the editing process much easier after you get the hang of things. Of course, if you've never used Photoshop before, you won't even be aware of Version 4's bad side — ignorance is bliss, as they say.

Where Do I Find Images to Abuse?

Recapping this book's top news so far: Photoshop is first and foremost an image editor. Although you can paint images from scratch, you're more likely to use the program to edit photographs that have been captured to disk.

Herein resides the problem. We all know how to turn photographs from our cameras into colorful pieces of paper that we can then slap into albums or frames for public display. (In other words, we all know how to get our film processed.)

But few of us have scanned a photograph to disk. You can't go to the local Piggly Wiggly, for example, and say, "Pardon me, I'd like to process this roll of film to disk so that I can open it up on my Mac." The cashier would look at you as if you had popped out of the pages of the *Sun*. "Blood Sucking Vampire from Outer Space Requests Film-to-Disk Transfer!" reads the headline in her mind. "Top Scientists Baffled by Implications!"

Now that I've mentioned the *Sun,* I would be delinquent if I failed to acknowledge this proud publication's contributions to the field of image editing. In the last few years of grocery shopping, I have yet to see a front page item in the *Sun* that was not edited to the fullest extent possible. Whether it's featuring an image of a 400-pound baby, a housewife with fingers growing out of her ears, or a real-life alien that looks enough like E.T. to be a hand puppet, the *Sun* can't be beat for ghoulish manipulation of everyday photos. Its motto — "We will let no image go unmolested" — tugs at the heartstrings of old hacks and burgeoning image editors alike. We salute you, *Sun!*

Anyway, when it comes to finding images to edit in Photoshop, grocery stores are out. But you can still find plenty of affordable options if you look in the right places:

- ✔ You can purchase collections of photos on CD-ROM. These collections range in price from less than 25 cents to several dollars per image. Some of my favorite image vendors are PhotoDisc (phone 206-441-9355); Digital Stock (619-794-4040); and ColorBytes (303-989-9205). Most of the images in this book come from these vendors, in fact (see Appendix B for specific image credits). Figure 1-7 shows two vintage images taken from Volume 13, "Italian Fine Art, Prints, and Photographs" from PhotoDisc.

- ✔ If you're hooked into the Internet or an online service such as CompuServe or America Online, you can find zillions of photos to download. The problem is, most of these images are of dubious quality and/or porno-graphic. If you want high-quality, general-purpose images, you have to subscribe to a specialized service such as PressLink Online/MediaStream (800-717-2206); Comstock (212-353-8600); and The Picture Exchange (800-579-8737). Unfortunately, these services are extremely expensive. They charge hourly online and download fees in addition to the cost of the photos themselves.

- ✔ You can take your own photo into your local Kinko's or some other copy shop or service bureau and scan the image to disk — assuming, of course, that you aren't lucky or rich enough to have a scanner available in your own office. Kinko's charges $9.95 per image.

Figure 1-7:
Two PhotoDisc images from an era when little kids were encouraged to climb on the furniture and barbers forgot to remove their hats.

✔ A better (and cheaper) method for scanning images is to scan them to a Photo CD, which costs between $1 to $3 a shot plus the price of the CD itself, which is usually in the neighborhood of $10. One CD can hold about 100 images, and you don't have to worry about scanning all 100 images at the same time. You can scan just a few and then keep adding to the CD as needed. To find a place where you can scan images to Photo CD, look in the Yellow Pages under "Photo Finishing–Retail." Be sure to shop around; prices vary widely from vendor to vendor. Also, be aware that having your images scanned to CD may take a few days, so plan ahead.

Chapter 2

Canvassing the On-Screen Canvas

* *

In This Chapter

▶ Launching Photoshop

▶ Taking some first, tentative looks at the Photoshop interface

▶ Switching between Photoshop and the Finder

▶ Defining mouse terminology

▶ Choosing commands

▶ Using dialog boxes and palettes

▶ Picking up tools from the toolbox

* *

*I*f you're brand new to Photoshop — and/or to computers in general — this is the chapter for you. It explains the basic stuff you need to know before you can begin using the program to distort the faces of all your family members.

Even if you're already familiar with the basic interface of Photoshop, give this chapter the once-over to get acquainted with new features in Version 4 and to make sure that we're speaking the same language. Here is where we calibrate brains, so to speak.

Giving Photoshop the Electronic Breath of Life

Before you can use Photoshop, you have to start up — or *launch* — the program. Here's how:

1. **Start your Mac.**

   After your computer comes alive, you find yourself at the Mac's central way station, known as the Finder. The Finder is where you can fumble around with the contents of your hard drive.

2. Locate and activate the Adobe Photoshop 4.0 folder.

That famous Adobe eyeball icon is on the folder to let you know what lurks inside the folder. (If you can't find the folder, see the next section for some help.) Use the mouse to move the arrow-shaped cursor over the icon and then press the mouse button. Then choose File⇨Open from the menu bar or press ⌘-O. A window labeled Adobe Photoshop should open, containing another eyeball icon and some other icons.

If choosing File⇨Open requires too much effort, you can launch Photoshop using a couple of shortcuts. Either double-click — press the mouse button twice in rapid-fire succession — on the program icon or press ⌘-down arrow.

In case you recently jumped ship from the Microsoft Windows platform — hey, welcome aboard! — you should know that the Enter key does not launch files on the Mac.

3. Double-click on the eyeball icon in the Adobe Photoshop window.

This icon is the one that actually launches the program.

4. Enter your name, company name and serial number

You need to take this step only the first time you start Photoshop. You can find the serial number for your copy of Photoshop on your product registration card.

5. Hope it works.

If you see the Photoshop splash screen — a kind of billboard that provides garish graphics and some copyright information — you're in business. If a message appears saying "Insufficient memory to open this application" or something equally disappointing, scream loudly and hope that the resident computer expert is in close proximity. You need help.

After your computer stops making little shicka-shicka noises and your screen settles down, you arrive at the Photoshop desktop, which is where all the action takes place in this amazing program. You can tell that Photoshop is launched and ready to go by the appearance of a toolbox and one or more palettes, as shown in Figure 2-1. The menu bar at the top of your screen changes to resemble the one in Figure 2-1 as well. (I cover the toolbox, palettes, and menu bar later in this chapter.)

Don't freak out and start running around the room in a frenzy if you're a little fuzzy on what I mean by *click, menu, dialog box,* and a few other terms. I cover all this stuff in fairly hefty detail, in short order, and in this very same chapter.

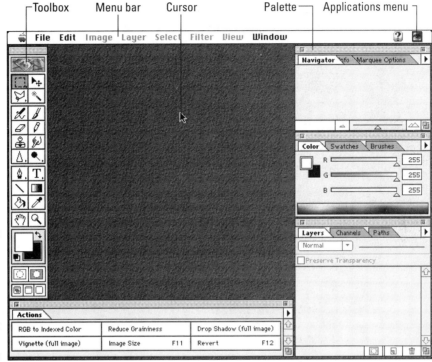

Toolbox   Menu bar   Cursor   Palette   Applications menu

Figure 2-1:
The
Photoshop
desktop
makes
its first
appearance.

Tracking down a lost eyeball

Can't find the Photoshop eyeball icon to start the program? Here are a few
suggestions:

- ✔ If you're not sure where Photoshop is located on your hard drive, choose
  File⇨Find from the menu bar (or press ⌘-F). Then type the word
  Photoshop and whack the Return key. If you're using System 7.1.2 or
  earlier, a folder opens, displaying a file that has *Photoshop* in its name. Or a
  message appears saying that the file is on the desktop. If the file displayed
  isn't the program, choose File⇨Find Again or press ⌘-G to search for the
  next occurrence of *Photoshop.*

- ✔ If you're using System 7.5, your Mac lists every file that contains the word
  Photoshop in the Items Found dialog box. Click on the Photoshop program
  in the top list to display the location of the file in the bottom list. Choose
  File⇨Open Enclosing Folder or press ⌘-E to open the folder and access the
  program icon.

- ✔ If repeated pressing of ⌘-G or thorough searching of the Items Found
  dialog box doesn't turn up the Photoshop program, cry in anguish and
  beat your monitor with something soft and squishy. Or see Appendix A in
  this book for installation instructions — whichever option you find more
  personally satisfying.

Why does Photoshop give your computer Alzheimer's?

If your computer says that it's out of memory, it just means that a part of the machine is filled to capacity. Memory — known in computer dweeb circles as *RAM* (pronounced *ram,* like the goat) — allows your computer to run programs. Photoshop needs lots of RAM — it requires a minimum of 12 to 16MB, depending on your system, and prefers to have even more. If you can't launch Photoshop because of a memory error, you have three options:

✔ Free up RAM by quitting all other programs that are currently running. Then try to launch Photoshop again.

✔ Restart your computer by choosing Special⇨ Restart at the Finder and then try to launch Photoshop after the Finder reappears.

✔ Buy and install more RAM.

If you've never tried to upgrade the RAM in your machine before, seek out expert advice from your local computer guru.

Switching between Photoshop and the Finder

In back of the myriad desktop elements of Photoshop, you can probably see the icons and open windows from the Finder. (I hid these in Figure 2-1 just to make the picture less confusing.) If you click on a Finder element or on the desktop pattern, you're taken back to the Finder, and the Photoshop toolbox and palettes disappear. If you have an image open, however, the image window remains visible.

✔ If you inadvertently click yourself out of Photoshop, choose Photoshop from the list of running programs in the Applications menu, which is the icon on the far right side of the menu bar (refer to Figure 2-1). Or just click on the Photoshop image window. The toolbox and palettes return to the screen to show you that Photoshop is back in the game.

✔ You may be wondering why in the heck this program-switching happens. No, it's not just to irritate you. The Finder is a piece of software, just like Photoshop. The only difference is that the Finder has to be running the entire time you use your Mac. This means that all the time you're using Photoshop, the Finder is working away in the background. When you click on the desktop or some other Finder element, the Finder comes to the foreground, and Photoshop goes to the background. But both programs continue to operate until you quit Photoshop or shut down your computer.

✔ When using Photoshop, if the clutter from the Finder gets too distracting, choose the Hide Others command from the Applications menu to hide every Finder element except the icons.

✔ If your Mac is equipped with System 7.5, you can hide the icons by choosing Apple⇨Control Panels⇨General Controls. (If you don't know how to choose things from menus, see the section "Maneuvering through Menus," in this chapter.) Inside the General Controls dialog box, click on the Show Desktop When in Background check box to deselect it. Then close the dialog box. Bye-bye go the icons. (Note that you can't click on the background to switch to the Finder if you choose this option; you have to use the Applications menu to switch between programs.)

✔ Remember that you can always tell where you are just by looking at the Applications menu icon in the upper-right corner of your screen. It always shows a miniature version of the foreground program icon. If you're at the Finder, the icon is a little computer — one of those single-piece computers like the Classic or the old Macintosh Plus. If the icon is some variation on an eyeball, you know you're in Photoshop. Other icons vary. A little *W* means Microsoft Word. A little *X* means Excel. A little Krusty the Clown means Bart Simpson has been using your computer (you lucky devil, you).

Making Sense of the Mouse and the Cursor

Ever hung around one of those lopsided couples — the kind made up of one person who says "Jump" and another who says "How high?" Well, your mouse and the cursor — that little arrow that moves around on-screen (caught in the act in Figure 2-1) — have this same dynamic going on. In fact, the cursor's only goal in life is to emulate everything the mouse does. If the mouse moves, the cursor moves. If the mouse stops, the cursor stops. The little guy has no mind of its own. It's kind of sad, actually. You want to grab the cursor and say, "Take hold of your life, man, and quit being such a victim!"

But the cursor is the cursor. There's no sense in trying to change it, so you may as well exploit it. By taking advantage of this skewed relationship, you can control the way Photoshop and other Macintosh programs behave. Throughout this book, I ask you to do certain things with the cursor, but you perform these actions using your mouse. For example, if I instruct you to move the cursor, you move the mouse, which makes the cursor move in kind.

Here's a quick look at some other things I ask you to do with the mouse that the cursor has no choice but to go along with:

✔ To *click* is to press the button on top of the mouse and immediately release it without moving the mouse. For example, you click on an icon in the top portion of the toolbox to select a tool.

✔ To *double-click* is to press and release the button twice in rapid succession without moving the mouse. As I mentioned earlier, you can open a program by double-clicking on its icon.

✔ To *press and hold* is to press the button and hold it down for a moment without moving the mouse. This action is sometimes called *mousing down*, although I think this sounds too much like an aerobic exercise. I refer to this operation very rarely — for example, when some item takes a moment or two to display.

✔ To *drag* is to press the button and hold it as you move the mouse. You then release the button to complete the operation. In Photoshop, for example, you drag with the pencil tool to draw a free-form line.

✔ To *crush* the mouse is to set it on the floor and stack heavy rocks on it. You'll almost never be called on to perform this technique. In fact, I only recommend crushing to very desperate performance artists, and then only if swinging the mouse around by the cord and shouting, "Somebody's going to lose an eye!" fails to get a rise.

You can also use the keyboard and mouse in tandem. For example, in Photoshop, you can draw a perfectly horizontal line by pressing the Shift key while dragging with the line tool. Or you can press Option and click on the rectangular marquee tool in the upper-left corner of the toolbox to change it to the elliptical marquee tool. Such actions are so common that you'll see key and mouse combinations joined into compound verbs, such as Shift-dragging, Option-clicking, or Shift-Option-crushing.

Maneuvering through Menus

As do all Macintosh programs, Photoshop sports a single menu bar at the top of its desktop (it's labeled in Figure 2-1). Each word in the menu bar — File, Edit, Image, and so on — represents a menu, which is simply a list of commands that you can use to open and close images, manipulate selected portions of a photograph, hide and display palettes, and initiate all kinds of mind-boggling sophisticated procedures.

I explain the most essential Photoshop commands throughout the course of this book. But before I send you off to cope with a single one of them, I feel compelled to provide some background information on how to work with menus.

✔ To choose a command from a menu, you press and hold on the menu name, drag down to the command name, and release the mouse button at the desired command. (After a few repetitions, it becomes reflexive, I promise.)

✔ Some commands bring up additional menus called *submenus*. For example, if you choose File⇨Preferences, you display a submenu offering still more commands. If I ask you to choose File⇨Preferences⇨General, you choose the Preferences command under the File menu to display the submenu and then choose the General command from the submenu, all in one, beautiful, continuous movement. When you do it just right, it's like something out of *Swan Lake*.

✔ In many cases, you can choose a command by using a keyboard equivalent instead of mousing around the menus. For example, to initiate the File⇨Open command, you can just press ⌘-O — that is, press and hold the ⌘ key, press the O key, and then release both keys.

✔ Most keyboard equivalents are listed along the right side of a menu. Some keyboard equivalents select tools and perform other functions. Either way, I keep you apprised of them throughout this book. If you take the time to memorize a few here and there, you'll find yourself saving a heck of a lot of time and effort. (For the most essential shortcuts, read Chapter 19. Also, tear out the Cheat Sheet at the front of this book and tape it up somewhere within easy ogling distance.)

✔ Version 4 offers you yet another way to access some commands. If you press the Control key and hold down the mouse button inside an image window, you display a *context-sensitive menu*. In nongeek-speak, a context-sensitive menu is a mini-menu that contains commands related to the current tool, palette, or image, as shown in Figure 2-2.

Context-sensitive menu

Figure 2-2:
To access context-sensitive menus, press Control and hold down the mouse button.

| Select None |
| Select Inverse |
| Layer Via Copy |
| Layer Via Cut |
| Feather... |
| Last Filter |
| Free Transform |
| Numeric Transform |
| Fill... |
| Stroke... |
| Make Work Path... |
| Save Selection... |

Talking Back to Dialog Boxes

Photoshop reacts immediately to some menu commands. But for other commands, the program requires you to fill out a few forms before it processes your request. If you see an ellipsis (three dots, like so . . .) next to a command name, that's your clue that you're about to see such a form, known in computer clubs everywhere as a *dialog box.*

Figure 2-3 shows a sample dialog box. As the figure demonstrates, a dialog box can contain any or all of six basic kinds of options. The options work as follows:

✔ A box in which you can enter numbers or text is called an *option box.* Double-click in an option box to highlight its contents and then replace the contents by entering new stuff from the keyboard.

✔ Some option boxes come with *slider bars.* Drag the triangular slider to the left or right to lower or raise the associated numerical value. All without hydraulics, mind you.

✔ You can select only one circular *radio button* from any gang of radio buttons. To select a radio button, click on the button or on the option name that follows it. The selected radio button is filled with a black dot; all deselected radio buttons are hollow.

Slider bar Pop-up menu Option box Button

Figure 2-3:
The
anatomy of
a dialog box.

Radio button   Check box

✔ Although you can select only one radio button at a time, you can select as many *check boxes* as you want. Really, go nuts. To select a check box, click on the box or on the option name that follows it. An X fills the check box to show that it's selected. Clicking on a selected check box turns off the option.

✔ To conserve space, some multiple-choice options appear as *pop-up menus.* Press and hold on the down-pointing arrow to display a menu of option choices. Drag to the desired option in the menu and release to choose it, just as if you were choosing a command from a standard menu. As with radio buttons, you can select only one option from a pop-up menu at a time.

✔ Not to be confused with the radio button, the normal, everyday variety of *button* allows you to close the current dialog box or display others. For example, click on the Cancel button to close the dialog box and cancel the command. Click on OK to close the dialog box and execute the command according to the current settings. Clicking on a button with an ellipsis (such as Load . . . and Save . . .) displays yet another dialog box.

As you can with menus, you can select options and perform other feats of magic inside dialog boxes from the keyboard. The following shortcuts work in most dialog boxes: To advance from one option box to the next, press the Tab key. To back up, press Shift-Tab. Press Return to select the button surrounded by a heavy outline (such as OK in Figure 2-3). Press ⌘-period to select the Cancel button.

In addition, you can press the up-arrow key to raise an option box value by one; press the down-arrow key to decrease the value by one. Pressing Shift-up arrow and Shift-down arrow raises and lowers the value by ten, respectively. (You can also use this technique inside palettes, which are discussed in the next section.)

If you change your mind about choices you make in a dialog box, you can quickly return things to the settings that were in force when you opened the dialog box. In most dialog boxes, pressing the Option key magically changes the Cancel button to a Reset button. Click on the Reset button to bring back the original values.

Playing Around with Palettes

Photoshop 4 offers free-floating *palettes* that you can hide or leave on-screen at whim. The palettes, which are basically dialog boxes that can remain on-screen while you work, provide access to options that affect the performance of tools, change the appearance of an image, and otherwise assist you in your editing adventures. I cover the specifics of using the options in the most popular palettes in chapters to come, but here's a brief introductory tour of how palettes work:

✔ As illustrated by the palette shown in Figure 2-4, palettes may contain the same kinds of options as dialog boxes — pop-up menus, option boxes, and so on. For information on using these options, see the preceding section.

✔ Each palette is actually a collection of palettes sharing the same palette window. To switch to a different palette in a palette window, click on its tab.

✔ Click on the close box on the left side of the title bar to — guess what — close the palette. (To make the palette come back, choose the desired palette from the Window menu.)

✔ You can hide or display the currently open palettes and the toolbox by pressing Tab. Press Shift-Tab if you want to hide or display all the palettes but leave the toolbox as is. Note that this trick doesn't work if an option box inside a palette is active — that is, if the option box is highlighted or if the cursor is blinking inside it. In this case, pressing Tab and Shift-Tab moves you from option to option throughout all open palettes. To de-activate the option box, just click outside it or press Return to make the option box value take effect. You can then use the Tab/Shift-Tab shortcuts to hide and display palettes.

✔ You can also hide and display individual palettes by pressing their key-board shortcuts: F5 for the Brushes palette; F6 for the Color palette; F7 for the Layers palette; and F8 for the Info palette.

✔ Some palettes contain icons, just like the toolbox. Click on an icon to perform a function, such as changing the brush size or deleting a selected image.

✔ Drag the title bar at the top of the palette to move the palette around on-screen.

✔ Shift-click on a title bar to snap the palette to the nearest edge of the screen. For example, if the palette is near the right side of the screen, Shift-clicking on its title bar moves it all the way over to the right, giving you more space to view your image on-screen.

Figure 2-4: The many elements of a healthy palette.

✔ Click on the zoom box on the right side of the title bar to collapse the palette so that only the most essential options at the top of the palette are visible. Click on the zoom box again to bring all of the options into full view.

✔ Option-click on the zoom box to hide all but the title bar and the palette tabs. Or double-click on a palette tab. The advantage is that you free up screen space without closing the palettes altogether.

✔ Some palettes have a size box, as labeled in Figure 2-4. You can drag the box to resize the palette. Click on the zoom box to return to the default palette size.

✔ You can break any palette off into its own window by dragging the palette tab out of the current window, as shown in Figure 2-5. You can also combine palettes into a single palette window by dragging a tab from one palette into another.

✔ Want to know my favorite application of this technique? Drag the Swatches palette out of the Color/Swatches/Brushes palette window to create a separate Swatches palette. Then close the Swatches palette altogether. See, the Swatches palette isn't very useful, so you may as well get it off the screen. Now you can drag the Options palette into the same palette window as the Color and Brushes palette, enabling you to access all three of these very vital palettes while using up a minimum of on-screen space.

✔ Press and hold on the right-pointing arrowhead on the right side of the palette, just below the title bar — phew, I need a breather — to display the palette menu. Here's yet another place to find commands, just in case you manage to master all of the others. Yeah, right.

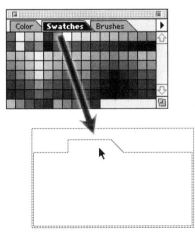

Figure 2-5: Drag the palette tab (left) to break the palette off into its own little palette apartment

As you can in a dialog box, you can raise or lower the value in a palette option box by pressing the arrow keys. Press the up-arrow key to raise the value by one; press down arrow to lower the value by one. Press Shift-up arrow and Shift-down arrow to raise or lower the value by ten, respectively.

Opening Up Your Toolbox

I think that you're ready to move on to the tempestuous world of the toolbox. As shown in Figure 2-6, the items in the toolbox fall into three basic categories — tools, color controls, and icons. Future chapters explain in detail how to use the various gizmos in the toolbox, but here's a basic overview of what's in store:

- ✔ The top two-thirds or so of the toolbox is devoted to an assortment of tools that you can use to edit images, just as you might use an assortment of pencils and paintbrushes to paint a picture. To select one of these tools, click on its icon. Then use the tool by clicking or dragging it inside your image.

- ✔ A tiny, right-pointing triangle in the bottom-right corner of a tool icon indicates that more tools are hidden away on a *flyout* menu behind that icon. To display the flyout menu and reveal the hidden tools, press and hold the mouse button on the icon. Drag across the row of tools until your cursor is hovering over the tool you want to use and then release the mouse button.

- ✔ You can also Option-click on a tool icon to cycle through all the tools hidden beneath it.

- ✔ The bottom third of the toolbox contains color selection options and other icons. These icons respond immediately when you click on them.

- ✔ If you've been clicking away on the toolbox icons and haven't seen any results, don't panic. Your copy of Photoshop isn't broken; the icons just don't do anything unless you have an image open. To find out how to open images, see Chapter 3.

- ✔ Actually, one of the icons in the toolbox does do something with no image on-screen. If you click on the very top icon in the toolbox — the one with the ghostly looking eyeball in it — you display a splash screen that contains a scrolling list of the names of the people who developed the program.

- ✔ If you have Netscape Navigator or another Web browser installed on your computer, clicking on the Adobe icon in the top left corner of the splash screen launches your browser and displays an Adobe Web page that resides on your hard drive. The page includes links that you can use to access Adobe's actual Web site after you log on to the Internet.

- ✔ When you get bored with playing with the splash screen, press Return to put it away.

✔ For an even more entertaining time-waster, ⌘-click on the eyeball. You see a screen with a big black cat on it — a leftover from the development stages of the program. ⌘-click on the cat's nose to make it belch. See, computer programmers are fun people after all. Press Return to send the cat back from whence it came.

✔ You can also access all the tools and icons and two of the color controls from the keyboard. For example, to select the blur tool, you just press the R key. To select the sharpen tool, which shares the flyout menu with the blur tool, you press R again. Other keyboard equivalents are shown in Figure 2-6.

✔ One exception to the preceding tip: Choosing tools from the flyout menu in the top-left corner of the toolbox, which contains marquee tools and the crop tool, actually involves two shortcut keys. Press M to switch between the rectangular and elliptical marquee tools, but press C to select the crop tool. You can't select the single-row and single-column marquee tools from the keyboard.

✔ If you can't remember the name of a particular tool, pause your cursor over its icon for a second or two. A little label appears to tell you the name of the tool and its keyboard equivalent.

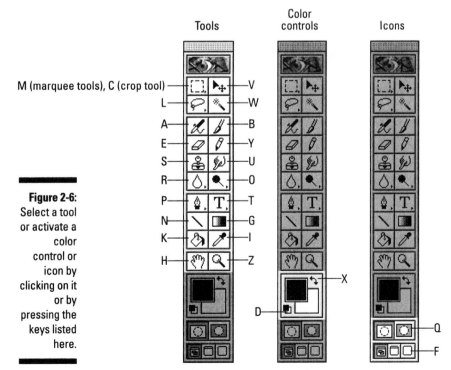

Figure 2-6:
Select a tool or activate a color control or icon by clicking on it or by pressing the keys listed here.

Chapter 3
Now the Fun Really Begins

. . . .

In This Chapter

▶ Opening and closing images

▶ Creating a new, blank image

▶ Mastering your windows

▶ Moving around your image

▶ Zooming in and out

▶ Changing views

▶ Turning on grids and guides

. . . .

*W*hen you first start Photoshop, you're presented with a plethora of tools, menus, and palettes, as illustrated in Chapter 2. Until you open up an image, those contraptions are intriguing, yet ultimately worthless — it's like having an easel, a full set of brushes, and a whole paintbox full of paints, but no canvas. And with Photoshop, you can't even amuse yourself by creating a political mural on your neighbor's garage door, as you can with traditional paint. No, if you want to become a digital Picasso (or Rembrandt, or Monet, or whatever artistic legend you choose), you need to open an image.

This chapter explains how to open existing images and also how to create a new, blank canvas for an image you want to paint from scratch. Then it explains the myriad ways you can display your image on-screen in order to view your masterpiece from just the right perspective.

Don't Just Sit There, Open Something

If you're a longtime computer buff, you might expect opening an image to be a relatively straightforward process. You just choose File➪Open or press ⌘-O and select the image file you want to display, right?

Well, opening files in Photoshop involves a little complication: You need to know whether the image you want to open is a Photo CD image or not. The steps for opening a Photo CD image are different than the steps for opening images saved in other formats. The following sections give you the lowdown on opening both types of images.

The term *Photo CD image* can be a little confusing; it refers to images saved in the Kodak Photo CD file format, not simply to images that come from a CD. A Photo CD image has the letters *PCD* tagged onto the end of its filename.

Opening a non-Photo CD image

To open an image that's stored in any format except the Kodak Photo CD format, walk this way:

1. **Choose File⇨Open.**

   If choosing the commands from the menu is too much work — and it is — just press ⌘-O. The Open dialog box rears its useful head, as shown in Figure 3-1.

2. **Go to the Desktop level.**

   Click on the Desktop button or press ⌘-D to see everything that you can see at the Finder. The scrolling list in the center of the dialog box shows you all the folders and images that are strewn loose on the desktop. At the top of the list are the names of the hard drives, floppy disks, and other disks currently available to you.

3. **Select the disk that contains your image.**

   Assuming that your image isn't lying about on the desktop, select the disk name that contains the image you want to open. (It's also possible that the image is inside a folder on the desktop, in which case you should stay at the desktop level.)

4. **Open the desired folder in the central list.**

   Double-click on a folder name to open the folder. The list then displays all folders and images inside that folder. Double-click on another folder if you need to open it, and so on.

Figure 3-1:
This dialog box lets you locate and open images on your hard drive or some other disk.

5. **Select the image you want to open.**

   After you locate your image, click on its name in the list to select it. A preview of the image appears on the left side of the dialog box so that you can see what it looks like. (If no preview appears, make sure that the Show Thumbnail check box is selected. Also see the "Where's my preview?" sidebar, in this chapter.)

6. **Click on the Open button.**

   Or press the Return key or press ⌘-O.

That's all there is to it. Your image is now open and ready to abuse. But before you have at it in earnest, here are a few additional notes on opening images:

✔ To close a folder and view the contents of the folder that contains it, click on the disk name in the upper-right corner of the Open dialog box. (The disk name is DekeMC in Figure 3-1.)

✔ You can also press ⌘-up arrow to advance up a folder. Or you can drag on the folder bar to display a pop-up menu of folders that contains the current folder. For example, if the items in the pop-up menu read Elephant, Digestive Systems, Food-Processing Enzymes, then the Food-Processing Enzymes folder resides inside the Digestive Systems folder, which is on the Elephant disk.

✔ In addition to double-clicking on a folder to open it, you can press ⌘-down arrow.

✔ The keyboard equivalents ⌘-left arrow and ⌘-right arrow let you switch from one disk to another.

Where's my preview?

You wouldn't think that a little thing like a preview icon would deserve its own sidebar, but about 50 things can go wrong with it. Here's some stuff to keep in mind:

✔ If no preview appears, you may be able to create one by clicking on the Create button. Unfortunately, this button only works if the image was saved in the PICT format. If the image was saved in some other format, the button appears grayed out, or dimmed, which means that it's useless in this instance.

✔ "What the heck are you talking about?" you ask. Well, the PICT format is one of the ways you can save an image. The file format for a selected image is always listed near the bottom of the Open dialog box (as labeled in Figure 3-1). If it says anything but PICT (it says JPEG in the figure), forget about the Create button. For more information on file formats, read Chapter 6.

✔ If there isn't room on the left side of the dialog box for a preview, you don't have Apple's QuickTime system extension loaded. Tell the resident computer experts — who were probably the people who got rid of QuickTime — to take care of this grave problem. If they say, "You don't need QuickTime, it's not important," explain that I told you it was very important when using Photoshop. If the computer experts respond, "Deke? Never heard of the guy," go ahead and punch 'em.

✔ Use the preview to help identify images. For example, if you or someone you work with name an image TRX33.Feb 24-William (or something equally meaningless), you can click on it and view a small version of the image that may or may not be identifiable. But, hey, it's better than nothing.

✔ If you can't find a file in a certain folder, it may be because Photoshop doesn't think it can open the file. To see all files in a folder, whether Photoshop can open them or not, select the Show All Files check box. If the file appears, go ahead and try to open it. It may not work, but it's worth a try.

✔ If you can't find an image, you can use the Find button to hunt it down. Click on the Find button (or press ⌘-F) to display another dialog box that contains a single option box. Enter the name of the image and press Return. You don't have to enter the complete filename — a partial name will do. For example, if you enter *super,* your computer finds any files that have *super* in them, including Super Bowl, supersonic, Superman, and others.

✔ If the first search doesn't find the file, click on the Find Again button or press ⌘-G to keep looking.

Opening a Kodak Photo CD image

As mentioned earlier, opening a Kodak Photo CD image involves a different process than opening other types of images. Here's the scoop:

1. **Choose File⇨Open or press ⌘-O.**

   Make sure to choose this command from inside Photoshop.

2. **Locate the Photo CD disc.**

   This task will probably involve a press or two of ⌘-right arrow. The disc will have some meaningless machine-assigned name like PCD0196.

3. **Open the PHOTO_CD folder.**

   Inside, you find several weirdly named files.

4. **Open the IMAGES folder.**

   Here's where the real images live. They all have dumb names like IMG0001.PCD;1 and so on. Luckily, every Photo CD disc comes with two or three sheets of tiny thumbnail printouts so that you know which image is associated with each file name.

5. **Double-click on the image you want to open.**

   After what may seem like an interminable amount of time — don't give up and think that your computer has crashed — the dialog box shown in Figure 3-2 appears.

6. **Click on the Source button.**

   Here's the tricky part. The Photo CD interpreter built into Photoshop wants more than anything to make sure that the colors in the image are correctly converted from the disk to your screen. Therefore, you have to tell Photoshop a source and destination for the image. It's kind of weird, but just do as I tell you and you won't go wrong.

Figure 3-2: This dialog box rears its pesky head when you try to open a Photo CD file from the IMAGES folder.

Image: IMG0001.PCD;1

Resolution: 1024 by 1536 ▼

File Size: 4.50M

☒ Landscape (faster)

Source   Kodak Photo CD

Destination   Adobe Photoshop RGB

Image Info   Cancel   OK

7. Select the proper film type.

If the image you want to open was scanned from a 35mm slide, select the Universal Ektachrome option. If it came from a film negative, select the Photo CD Color Negative option. (If you're opening an image from a commercial CD, such as one from Digital Stock, you can assume that the Source option should be set to Universal Ektachrome because the images undoubtedly originated from slides.)

Press Return to go back to the dialog box shown in Figure 3-2.

8. Click on the Destination button.

It's right there below Source.

9. Select Adobe Photoshop RGB from the pop-up menu.

This choice converts the scan to a standard color Photoshop image. Press the Return key when you finish.

10. Select an option from the Resolution pop-up menu.

The option you select depends on the amount of memory available to your computer. I would suggest starting with 1024 by 1536. If that gives your computer fits after the next step, try selecting the 512 by 768 option, which creates an image that's roughly big enough to fill a 17-inch monitor. The smallest option, 128 by 192, results in an image that's too tiny for even an ant to edit.

11. Press Return or click on the OK button.

Photoshop opens the Photo CD image. If you get an out-of-memory error, try opening the image again and selecting a smaller resolution option, as described in the preceding step.

If an image opens up lying on its side, you can shift it to an upright position by rotating it. Choose Image➪Rotate Canvas➪90° CW (clockwise) if the image is resting on its left side; choose Image➪Rotate Canvas➪90° CCW (counter-clockwise) if the image is taking a nap on its right side. (The latter is more common.) If the image turns upside-down, choose Edit➪Undo and then choose the command that you didn't choose the first time.

After you open an image for the first time, the Source and Destination options remain set. This means that you can skip Steps 6 through 9 when opening future Photo CD images.

I Want to Start from Scratch!

To create a new image instead of opening an existing one, choose File➪New or press ⌘-N. Photoshop displays the New dialog box. There, you can name your file; specify the width, height, and resolution (as discussed in Chapter 4); and set the color mode (as discussed in Chapter 5). However, you'll probably have little reason to create a new image unless you just want to play around with the painting tools. Photoshop is, after all, made primarily for editing existing images.

Behold the Image Window

After you open up an image, Photoshop displays the image on-screen inside a new image window. The window contains several new elements of its own, as labeled in Figure 3-3.

Windows are a staple of the Macintosh working environment. In fact, every element labeled in the figure except the page preview box and the magnification box (and the odd-looking creature with the goggles, of course) is found in all windows across the board. Here's your chance to learn everything about windows — that's windows with a small *w* — in one convenient bulleted list:

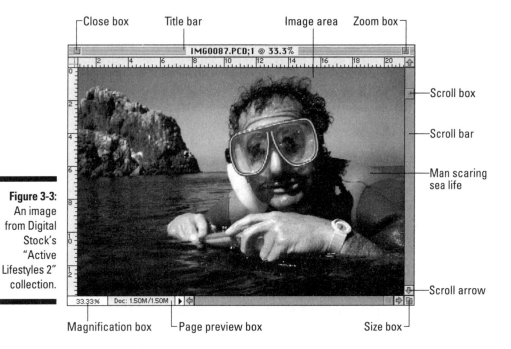

Close box   Title bar   Image area   Zoom box

IMG0087.PCD;1 @ 33.3%

Scroll box

Scroll bar

Man scaring
sea life

Figure 3-3:
An image
from Digital
Stock's
"Active
Lifestyles 2"
collection.

Scroll arrow

33.33%   Doc: 1.50M/1.50M

Magnification box   Page preview box   Size box

▸ The *title bar* lists the title of your image, hence the name. The added bonus of the title bar is that you can drag on it to move the window to a different location on-screen. Just like a palette title bar. Easy stuff.

✔ Click on the *close box* to close the image window. Alternatively, you can choose File⇨Close or press ⌘-W. You know, W as in *hasta la vista, window*. (If you've made some changes to the image, Photoshop asks you whether you want to save the new and improved image, a process explained in great detail in Chapter 6.)

✔ Drag the *size box* in the lower-right corner of the image window to change the size of the window. The image remains the same; you're just changing the size of the window that holds the image. Give it a try and see what I mean.

✔ Click on the *zoom box* to collapse or expand the window to match the exact size of the image. If the image is too big for the screen to hold it, the window expands to hold as much of the image as possible.

✔ The *page preview box* in the lower-left corner of the window shows how much memory your image is consuming, measured in digital chunks called *bytes*. The first number is the size of the image as it would be sent to the printer; the second number reflects the size of the image with layer information included. I discuss file size and resolution and all those other thorny issues in Chapter 4 and explain layers in Chapter 15. For the time being, don't worry about the preview box too much. I just didn't want to leave you wondering, "What in the Sam Hill is this thingie here?"

✔ If you click and hold the mouse button down on the page preview box, Photoshop displays a window that shows you where the image will appear on the page when you print the image. The big X indicates the image in the preview.

✔ Hold down Option as you click on the page preview box, and Photoshop displays a box showing the height, width, resolution, and number of channels in the image. (Channels are discussed in Chapter 5.)

✔ The scroll bars let you navigate around and display hidden portions of the image inside the window. Photoshop offers two scroll bars, one vertical bar along the right side of the image and one horizontal bar along the bottom.

✔ If you click on a scroll arrow, you nudge your view of the image slightly in that direction. For example, if you click on the right-pointing scroll arrow, an item that was hidden on the right side of the photograph slides into view. Click in the gray area of a scroll bar to scroll the window more dramatically. Drag a scroll box to manually specify the distance scrolled.

✔ Using the scroll arrows isn't the only way to move around your image; in fact, it's probably the least efficient method. For some better options, check out the techniques presented in the section "The Screen is Your Digital Oyster," coming up next.

✔ The area inside the title bar and scroll bars is the image area. This is where you paint and edit and select details and otherwise have at your image. Obviously, we look at the image area a lot throughout the many pages of this book.

You can open as many images on-screen as your computer's memory and screen size allow. But only one image is active at a time. To make a different window active, just click on it or choose its name from the bottom of the Window menu.

The Screen Is Your Digital Oyster

The Photoshop toolbox includes two navigation tools: the hand tool, which lets you scroll the image inside the window with much more ease than the silly scroll bars afford, and the zoom tool, which lets you move closer to or farther away from your image. The hand tool and the zoom tool are called *navigation tools* because they don't change the image, they merely move your view of the image so that you can get a better look-see.

Version 4 offers a new, additional navigation aid, appropriately called the Navigator palette. The palette gives you a super-convenient way to zoom and scroll your image; in fact, after you become familiar with the palette, you may not use the hand and zoom tools at all. But in the interest of fair play, I present all of your various options for moving around in your image in the upcoming sections.

Using the hand tool

If you're familiar with other Macintosh or Windows programs, you need to know something about Photoshop: The scroll bars are useless. Keep away from them. I want you to promise me you'll always use the hand tool or the new Navigator palette (explained shortly) instead. Promise? Good. As for you new users, I don't worry about you because I'm going to show you the right way.

Consider the following example: Figure 3-4 shows another Digital Stock image — this time from the "Children and Teens" collection. The top view in the figure shows a young lad in obvious distress. The problem is that the picture is wider than my screen, so I can't see what's causing him such grief.

To view the rest of the scene, I select the hand tool by clicking on its icon in the toolbox. Then I position my Photoshop hand over the hand in the picture, as shown in the top example in Figure 3-4, and drag to the left. The image moves with the hand cursor, as shown in the bottom example, and reveals the source of the boy's torment.

Dragging with the hand tool is like turning your head to view a new part of your surroundings. You can drag at any angle you please — up, down, sideways, or diagonally.

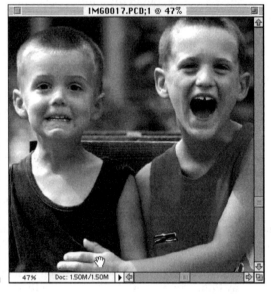

—Hand cursor

Figure 3-4:
Dragging with the hand tool reveals that a bad haircut isn't the only thing a kid has to worry about.

You can also select the hand tool by pressing the H key. To temporarily access the hand tool when another tool is selected, press the spacebar. As long as the spacebar is down, the hand tool is available. Releasing the spacebar returns you to the selected tool.

Using keyboard shortcuts

As in most other programs, you can also move about your image by using keyboard shortcuts. Press Page Up or Page Down to scroll up or down an entire screen. Press Shift-Page Up or Shift-Page Down to scroll in smaller increments. Press Home to go to the upper-left corner of the image and press End to move to the lower-right corner.

If you're working on a PowerBook and the keyboard doesn't have Page Up and Page Down keys, use these keyboard shortcuts instead: Press Control-K to scroll up one screen; Control-L to scroll down one screen; Control-Shift-K or Control-Shift-L to nudge your view up or down just a little, respectively; Control-A to go the upper-left corner of the image; and Control-D to go to the lower-right corner.

Zooming in and out on your work

When you first open an image, Photoshop displays the entire image so that it fits on-screen. But you may not be seeing the details in the image as clearly as you'd like. The first view is sort of like being far away from the image. If you want to inspect it in more detail, you have to step closer.

Photoshop gives you several ways to zoom in and out on your work, as described in these next few sections.

Zooming doesn't change the size at which your image prints. It just affects the size at which you see the image on-screen. It's like looking at some eentsey-teentsey life-form under a microscope. The creature doesn't actually grow and shrink as you vary the degree of magnification, and neither does your image.

The zoom tool

Using the zoom tool is one avenue for changing your view of an image. Every time you click with the tool, you magnify an image to a larger size. Here's an example of how it works:

1. **Select the zoom tool.**

   Click on the zoom tool in the toolbox. It's the one that looks like a magnifying glass. You can also press the Z key to grab the zoom tool.

2. **Click in the image area.**

   Photoshop magnifies the image to the next preset zoom size (the increments are set by Photoshop), as demonstrated in the second example of Figure 3-5. The program centers the magnified view about the point at which you click. In Figure 3-5, for example, I clicked between the girl's eyes.

3. Repeat.

To zoom in farther still, click again with the zoom tool, as demonstrated in the bottom example of Figure 3-5.

Figure 3-5:
Clicking with the zoom tool magnifies your image in preset increments.

A setting in the Zoom Tool Options palette determines whether Photoshop resizes your image window to match the image when you zoom with the zoom tool. To display the palette, select the zoom tool and press Return. If you want your image windows to be resized when you zoom, select the Resize Windows to Fit option. The only hitch comes when the window bumps into a palette — when the window hits a palette that's anchored to the side of the screen (as opposed to floating in the middle of the screen), it thinks that it's hit some sort of wall and stops zooming. To get around the problem, press Tab to hide all the palettes and the toolbox and then zoom. Press Tab again to bring back the palettes and the toolbox. Here's some other zoom tool stuff you'll want to tuck away for future reference:

- ✔ Option-click with the zoom tool to zoom out on your image.

- ✔ You can also zoom in and out from the keyboard: Press ⌘-+ (the Command key followed by the plus-key) to zoom in; press ⌘- –(Command-minus) to zoom out. Note that Photoshop zooms your window in and out to match the image size when you use this shortcut, regardless of the setting in the Zoom Tool Options palette. If you don't want the window to resize, press ⌘-Option-+ or ⌘-Option- –to do your zooming from the keyboard.

- ✔ As you zoom, Photoshop displays the *zoom factor* in the title bar. A zoom factor of 100 percent shows you one screen pixel for every pixel in your image. (Pixels are explained thoroughly in the Chapter 4.)

Keep in mind that a 100 percent zoom ratio doesn't necessarily correspond to the printed size of your image, as you might expect. If you want to view your image at its printed size, use the Print Size command, explained in the next section.

- ✔ To magnify just one section of an image, drag with the zoom tool to surround the area with a dotted outline. Photoshop fills the image window with the area you surrounded.

- ✔ To temporarily access the zoom tool while another tool is selected, press ⌘-spacebar. Press ⌘-Option-spacebar to get the zoom out cursor. In either case, releasing the keys returns you to the previously selected tool.

The View commands

Version 4's new View menu offers some more ways to change the magnification of your image. The first two zoom commands on the menu, Zoom In and Zoom Out, aren't of much interest; they do the same thing as clicking and Option-clicking with the zoom tool, except that you can't specify the center of the new view as you can with the zoom tool. But you may find the other three View commands helpful at times:

- ✔ Choose View➪Actual Pixels or press ⌘-Option-0 (zero) to return to the 100 percent zoom ratio. This view size shows you one pixel on your monitor for every pixel in the image, which is the most accurate way to view your image. (For background information on all this pixel stuff, read Chapter 4.)

✔ Choose View⇨Fit on Screen or press ⌘-0 (zero) to display your image at the largest size that allows the entire image to fit on-screen.

✔ You can also choose the Actual Pixels view by double-clicking on the zoom tool icon in the toolbox. Double-click on the hand tool icon to change to Fit on Screen view.

✔ Choose View⇨Print Size to display your image on-screen at the same size that it will print. Note that Photoshop just provides an approximation of the print size; your actual printed piece may be slightly smaller or larger.

The magnification box

The zoom tool and View commands are great when you want to zoom in or out to one of the preset Photoshop zoom ratios. But what if you want more control over your zooming? The answer awaits in the magnification box in the lower-left corner of the image window.

To enter a zoom ratio, just double-click on the magnification box and type in the zoom ratio you want to use. If you know exactly what zoom ratio you want, press Return to make Photoshop do your bidding. But if you want to play around with different zoom ratios, press Shift-Return instead. That way, Photoshop zooms your image but keeps the magnification box active so that you can quickly enter a new ratio if the first one doesn't work out. Press the up- and down-arrow keys to raise or lower the magnification value in .01 percent increments. Press Shift-up arrow or Shift-down arrow to raise or lower the value in .1 percent increments. When you're satisfied, press Return.

When you use the magnification box, the image window size doesn't change as you zoom, regardless of the setting in the Zoom Tool Options palette.

To make the image window grow or shrink so that the image fits exactly in the window, click on the zoom box in the upper-right corner of the title bar.

Navigating by palette

The Navigator palette, shown in Figure 3-6, is one of the handiest additions to Version 4. To display the palette, choose Window⇨Show Navigator. Or press F8 to display the Info palette and then click on the Navigator palette tab. To make the palette smaller or larger, drag on its size box in the lower-right corner.

The palette provides a handy, all-in-one tool for scrolling and zooming. It's especially useful when you're working on a large image that won't fit entirely on-screen when you're zoomed in for detail work. Here are the how-tos for using the palette:

✔ In the center of the palette, you see a thumbnail view of your image, as in Figure 3-6. The palette shows your entire image, even if it's not all visible in the main image window.

✔ See the box that surrounds a portion of the thumbnail? That's called the view box. The area within the box corresponds to the portion of your image that's visible in the main image window. As you drag the box, Photoshop scrolls your image in the main image window to display the area that's surrounded by the box. You can also click on an area in the thumbnail to move the view box over that portion of the image.

View box

Figure 3-6:
The new
Navigator
palette
provides a
nifty way to
zoom and
scroll your
image.

Magnification box   Zoom out⌐   Zoom slider   Zoom in⌐

✔ Press and hold ⌘, and the cursor in the palette changes to a zoom cursor. If you drag the view box with the cursor (keep pressing ⌘), you resize the view box, which in turn zooms the image in the image window.

✔ The palette also contains a magnification box, as labeled in the figure. The box works just like the one in the image window; just enter a zoom factor and press Return.

✔ To zoom in or out in the preset Photoshop increments (as with the zoom tool), click on the zoom in or zoom out buttons, labeled in Figure 3-6.

✔ You can also zoom by dragging the Zoom slider — drag left to zoom out and drag right to zoom in.

If you don't like the color of the view box, you can change it. Click on the right-pointing arrow in the upper-right corner of the palette and choose the Palette Options command. Then choose a new color from the Color pop-up menu.

Filling up the screen with your image

One more thing about changing the way you view stuff on-screen; then I'll let you move forward. The three icons at the bottom of the toolbox enable you to change the way the window fills the screen. These icons appear labeled in Figure 3-7.

Figure 3-7: Those weird little icons at the bottom of the toolbox change your on-screen landscape.

Image fills entire screen

Menu bar only

Normal window

✔ Click on the leftmost icon to view the window normally, with scroll bars and title bar and all that stuff. This is the default setting.

✔ Click on the center icon to eliminate the scroll bars and title bar and fill the screen with the image. All background programs are hidden, as is the desktop pattern. Any portions of the screen that aren't consumed by the image appear gray. The toolbox, palettes, and menu bar remain visible.

✔ If you want to take over still more screen real estate, click on the rightmost icon to hide the menu bar. Now any portions of the screen that don't contain image are black. The only desktop elements that remain available are the palettes and the toolbox.

✔ As covered in Chapter 2, you can press Tab to hide the toolbox and all the palettes; press Tab again to redisplay them. To hide and redisplay the palettes only, press Shift-Tab.

You can cycle through the different screen modes by pressing the F key instead of clicking on the toolbox icons if you prefer. Press F once to select the second icon, press F again to select the third icon, and press F a third time to return to the first icon.

Tools for the Terribly Precise

If you've ever used a page layout program such as PageMaker or QuarkXPress, you're no doubt familiar with the concept of *grids* and *guides,* which are new to Photoshop 4. Shown in Figure 3-8, grids and guides are on-screen devices that help you align elements in your image. For example, in the figure, I used a guide to position my text exactly 2 inches from the left edge of the image and 11 inches from the top of the image.

In addition to grids and guides, Photoshop also offers rulers that run across the top and left sides of the image window. Grids, guides, and rulers come in handy when you're feeling the urge to be especially precise with your work.

Guide   Move guide cursor   Ruler   Grid line

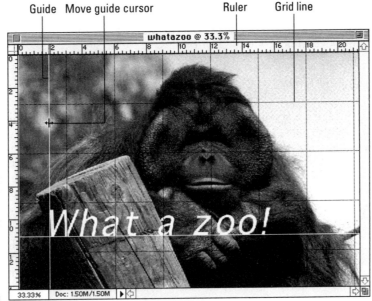

Figure 3-8:
Our furry
friend isn't
really
fenced in;
he's just
covered
with grid
lines and
guides.

Switching on the rulers

To display rulers, choose View⇨Show Rulers or press ⌘-R. To hide the rulers, choose View⇨Hide Rulers or press ⌘-R again.

By default, the rulers use inches as their unit of measurement. But if you want to use some other unit — say, picas — choose File⇨Preferences⇨Units & Rulers. Or just double-click on a ruler. In the Rulers section of the dialog box that appears, select a new unit of measure from the Units pop-up menu.

Guides are horizontal and vertical lines that you create to help you align elements in your image. Guides don't print; they're creatures of the on-screen world only. You can create as many guides as you need.

Before you can create a guide, you have to display the rulers by choosing View⇨Show Rulers or pressing ⌘-R. Then drag from one of the rulers to "pull out" a guide. Drag from the horizontal ruler to create a horizontal guide; drag from the vertical ruler to create a vertical guide.

Here are some more guides to using guides:

- After you create a guide, you can reposition it. First, select the move tool (it's the top right tool in the toolbox) by clicking on its icon in the toolbox. Then place the cursor over the guide until you see the double-headed arrow, as in Figure 3-8, and drag the guide to its new home. Alternatively, you can ⌘-drag the guide with any other tool except the hand or pen tool. (Pressing ⌘ temporarily accesses the move tool when any tool but the hand or pen tool is selected.)

- To remove a guide, drag it out of the image window using the move tool or ⌘-drag with any other tool but the pen or hand tool. To get rid of all guides, choose View⇨Clear Guides.

- To lock a guide in place, choose View⇨Lock Guides or press ⌘-Option-; (semicolon). To unlock the guides so that you can move them again, choose the command or press the shortcut again.

- Whenever you drag an image element near a guide, the element "snaps" into alignment with the guide — as if the guide had some sort of magnetic pull. If you don't want stuff to snap to guides, choose View⇨Snap to Guides or press ⌘-Shift-; (semicolon). Choose the command again to turn snapping back on. (A check mark next to the command name means that the feature is turned on.)

- To change the color of the guides, choose File⇨Preferences⇨Guides & Grid, double-click on a guide with the move tool or ⌘-double-click on the guide with any other tool but the hand or pen tool. In the Guides section of the dialog box that appears, you can choose a color and line style for your guides. Press Return to exit the dialog box and make your changes official.

Turning on the grid

Unlike guides, which you can position willy-nilly in the image window, the grid positions lines across your image in preset intervals. You can't move grid lines, but you can change the spacing and color of the lines.

To turn on the grid, choose View⇨Show Grid or press ⌘-" (quote). To change the spacing and appearance of the grid lines, choose File⇨Preferences⇨Guides & Grid. Photoshop presents you with a dialog box in which you can choose a color and line style for the grid lines; specify how far apart you want to space the lines; and choose whether you want to subdivide the grid with secondary grid lines or not. You can also choose a unit of measurement for the grid.

Like guides, the lines of a grid have "snapping" capabilities — anything you drag near a grid line automatically snaps into alignment with that line. You turn snapping on and off by choosing View⇨Snap to Grid or by pressing ⌘-Shift-"(quote). A check mark next to the command name in the menu means that snapping is turned on.

Part II

The Care and Feeding of Pixels

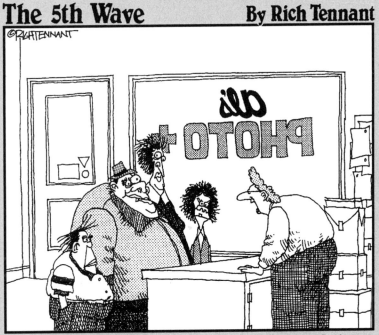

The 5th Wave   By Rich Tennant

"I THINK YOU'VE MADE A MISTAKE. WE DO PHOTO RETOUCHING, NOT FAMILY PORTRAI...OOOH, WAIT A MINUTE-I THINK I GET IT!"

In this part . . .

1 can't tell you how disappointed I was the first time I dissected a frog. Here we had been looking at all the cool pictures of the animal's colorful innards, and the moment we got the critter open, everything was various shades of pale beige. Where are the blue veins? And the red arteries? And the purple muscles and organs, and the bright yellow fat cells? Is my frog defective?

That's the problem with real life — it's never as interesting as the pictures. But an electronic image is different. It's not some natural miracle that tests the minds of our best scientists and absolutely baffles the brains of junior high school students; it's something designed by humans expressly to be understood by other humans. So you can be sure that the dissection that takes place in Chapters 4 through 7 looks the same on your computer screen as it does in my figures, except more colorful.

The chapters in this part tell you how to manage the colored specks — called *pixels* — that make up the image, how color and black-and-white images work, and how to save and print the image when you're done editing. These chapters aren't obscure experiments; they're straightforward journeys through features that you use every time you open Photoshop. Even better, you don't have to put up with the nauseating smell of formaldehyde.

Oh, and one more thing: The publisher wants me to tell you that no frogs were killed or inconvenienced in the making of this book. One parrot was made to take notation, but that's it.

Chapter 4
Sizing Up Your Image

. . . .

In This Chapter

▶ Taking a close look at the pixels in an image

▶ Using the Image Size dialog box

▶ Understanding resolution

▶ Matching the width of an image to page columns

▶ Changing the number of pixels in an image

▶ Resizing the canvas independently of the image

. . . .

*I*mages that you create and edit in Photoshop — or in any other image editor, for that matter — are made up of tiny squares called *pixels*. Understanding how pixels work in an image can be enormously confusing to beginning image editors. Unfortunately, managing your pixel population correctly is essential to turning out professional-looking images, so you really do need to come to grips with how pixels work before you can be successful with Photoshop.

This chapter explains everything you need to know to put pixels in perspective, including how the number of pixels in an image affect its quality, printed size, and size on disk. I also show you how to reduce or enlarge the size of the on-screen canvas on which all your pretty pixels perch. In other words, this chapter offers pages of particularly provocative pixel paragraphs, partner.

The Version 4 Image Size dialog box, which is Grand Central Station for controlling pixels, has some important differences from the one in earlier versions of Photoshop. Be sure to pay special attention to information marked with the Version 4 icon if you've upgraded from an earlier version.

Welcome to Pixeltown

Imagine, if you will, that you are the victim of a terrifying scientific experiment that has left you 1 millimeter tall. After recovering from the initial shock that such terrifying scientific experiments tend to produce on one's equilibrium, you discover that you are sitting on a square tile that's colored with a uniform shade of blue. Beyond your tile are eight other blue tiles, one to your right and one to your left, one in front and one behind, and four others in diagonal directions. In other words, the tiles are aligned in a perfect grid, just like standard floor tiles. You notice upon further inspection that each of the blue tiles differs slightly in shade and tone. As you slowly turn, it becomes evident that you're surrounded by these colored tiles for as far as your infinitesimally tiny, pinprick eyes can see.

You cry out in anguish and fling your dust-speck body about in the way that folks always do when plagued by these terrifying scientific experiments. As if in answer to your pitiful squeals, you start to grow. In a matter of moments, you increase in size to almost five centimeters tall. A bug that was considering devouring you has a change of mind and runs away. You can now see that you sit in the midst of a huge auditorium, and that all the tiles on its vast and unending floor are colored differently, gradually changing from shades of blue to shades of green, red, and yellow. You continue to grow: 10 centimeters, 20, 50, a full meter tall. The tiles start to blend together to form some kind of pattern. Two meters, five, ten. You've now grown several times beyond your normal height, reaching 20 meters tall. Your massive head bursts through the flimsy ceiling of the room.

When you reach the height of a 50-story building, your growth spurt comes to an end. You look down at the ruined auditorium, whose walls have been shredded to rubble by the great edges of your tremendous feet, and you notice a peculiar thing. You stand not on a floor, but on a picture, as rich in color and detail as any you've seen. The tiles, which now appear dot-sized to you, have merged together to create a seamless blend. You had expected the result to have the rough appearance of a mosaic — requiring a heavy dose of imagination to compensate for occasionally choppy transitions — but in fact it looks exactly like a continuous photograph.

The vision inspires you to claw at your temples, fling your arms about in circles, and shriek, "What's happening to me?!" The answer, of course, is nothing. Well, okay, your body may be stretched out of shape, but your eyes are working fine. You see, when you get far enough away from a perfect grid of colored tiles — whether via a terrifying scientific experiment or more conventional means — the tiles disappear, and an overall image takes shape.

What does this little trip down sci-fi lane have to do with Photoshop? Well, a lot, actually. Like the image on the auditorium floor, your Photoshop image is made up of a grid of colored squares. In this case, the squares are called *pixels*.

By now, you're probably thinking, "Fine, images are made up of a bunch of itsy-bitsy square pixels. So what? Who cares? Quit wasting my time, darn you." The truth is, these tiniest of image particles are at the heart of what makes Photoshop and your electronic images tick.

Every single painting and image-editing function in Photoshop is devoted to changing either the quantity or the color of pixels. That's all Photoshop does. I know, it sounds so simple that you figure I must be joking, exaggerating, or just plain lying. But as Salvador Dalí is my witness, it's the absolute truth. Photoshop is merely an extremely sophisticated pixel counter and colorer, nothing more.

Screen Pixels versus Image Pixels

Like the tiles in the preceding story, each pixel in a computer image is perfectly square, arranged on a perfect grid, and colored uniformly — that is, each pixel is one color and one color only. Put these pixels together, and your brain perceives them to be an everyday, average photograph.

The display on your computer's monitor is also made up of pixels. Like image pixels, screen pixels are square and arranged on a grid. A typical 13-inch monitor measures 640 screen pixels wide by 480 screen pixels tall. These screen pixels are kind of tiny, so you may not be able to make them out. Each one generally measures $1/72$ inch across.

To understand the relationship between screen and image pixels, open an image. After the image comes up on-screen, double-click on the zoom tool in the toolbox or choose View⇨Actual Pixels. The title bar on the image window lists the zoom ratio as 100 percent, which means that you can see one pixel in your image for every pixel displayed by your monitor.

To view the image pixels more closely, enter a value of 200 percent in the magnification box in the lower-left corner of the image window (double-click on the box to activate it). A 200 percent zoom factor magnifies the image pixels to twice their previous size, so that one image pixel measures two screen pixels tall and two screen pixels wide. If you change the zoom factor to 400 percent, Photoshop displays four screen pixels for every image pixel, giving you a total of 16 screen pixels for every image pixel (four screen pixels tall by four screen pixels wide). Figure 4-1 illustrates how different zoom factors affect the appearance of your image pixels on-screen.

Remember that the zoom factor has nothing to do with the size at which your image will print — it only affects how your image looks on-screen. If you want to see your image on-screen at its approximate print size, choose View⇨Print Size.

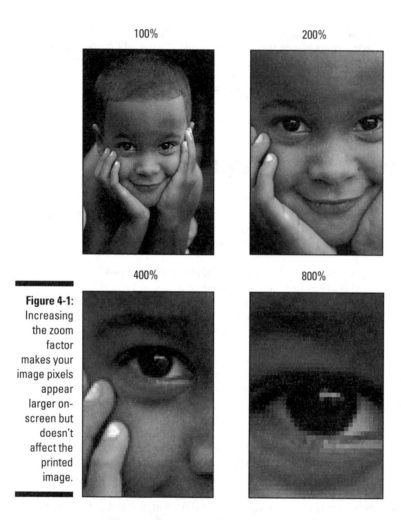

Figure 4-1:
Increasing the zoom factor makes your image pixels appear larger on-screen but doesn't affect the printed image.

Image Size, Resolution, and Other Tricky Pixel Stuff

A Photoshop image has three primary attributes related to pixels: file size, physical dimensions, and resolution, as explained in the following list. You control these attributes through the Image Size dialog box, shown in Figure 4-2. To display the dialog box, choose Image⇨Image Size.

If you just want to get a quick look at the dimensions and resolution of an image, press Option as you press and hold the mouse button on the page preview box in the lower-left corner of the image window. Photoshop displays a little box listing the dimensions, resolution, and other scary stuff.

Link icon ⌐

Figure 4-2:
You control
file size,
image
dimensions,
and
resolution
through the
Image Size
dialog box.

✔ The *file size* of the image is a measure of how many pixels the image contains. The image in Figure 4-1 is 256 pixels wide by 384 pixels tall, for a total of 98,304 pixels. Most of the images you create will contain hundreds of thousands or even millions of pixels.

✔ Photoshop refers to file size as *pixel dimensions.*

✔ The *resolution* of an image refers to the number of pixels that print per inch. For example, the resolution of the first image in Figure 4-1 is 180 pixels per inch (ppi). That may sound like an awful lot of pixels squished into a small space, but it's about average.

✔ Not to be confused with file size, the *dimensions* of an image are its physical width and height when printed, as measured in inches, centimeters, or your unit of choice. You can calculate the dimensions by dividing the number of pixels by the resolution. For example, the little boy in Figure 4-1 measures 256 pixels ÷ 180 pixels per inch = 1 $^3/_8$ inches wide, and 384 pixels ÷ 180 ppi = 2 $^1/_8$ inches tall. Measure him with a ruler and you see that this is indeed the case.

No problem, right? I mean, okay, this stuff is a little technical, but it's not like it requires an advanced degree in cold fusion to figure out what's going on. And yet, the Image Size dialog box may well be the most confusing Photoshop dialog box. You can even damage your image if you're not careful. So be extremely careful before you make changes in the Image Size dialog box (the upcoming sections tell you everything you need to know to stay out of trouble).

If you just want to reduce or enlarge an image for printing, you may be able to simply enter a percentage value into the Reduce or Enlarge option boxes in the Page Setup dialog box (choose File➪Page Setup). Photoshop then scales your image to the new size during the print cycle only. Your image isn't permanently altered as it is when you use the Image Size dialog box. For more information, see Chapter 7.

Resolving resolution

Although the Resolution option box is positioned unceremoniously toward the bottom of the Image Size dialog box, it's one of the most critical values to consider if you want your images to look good.

The Resolution value determines how tightly the pixels are packed when printed. It's kind of like the population density of one of those ridiculously large urban areas cropping up all over the modern world. Take Lagos, Nigeria, for example, which is a city of nearly 10 million souls — more than London, Paris, or Shanghai. Lagos, in case you're curious, is the fastest-growing major metropolitan area in the world, with an annual population explosion of 5 percent. (If that doesn't sound so bad, consider that it would put Lagos at 33 million people in the year 2020, which would be more than Tokyo, the current topper.) At roughly 150,000 people packed into each square mile (on average, that's 15 times as crowded as New York City), the population density of Lagos is second only to Hong Kong.

In order to increase the population density, you have to either increase the number of people in a city or decrease the physical boundaries of the city and scrunch everyone closer together. The same goes for resolution. If you want a higher resolution (more pixels per inch), you can either decrease the physical dimensions of the image or increase the file size (pixel dimensions) by adding pixels to the image. For example, the two images in Figure 4-3 have the same file size, but the smaller image has twice the resolution of the larger image — 180 pixels per inch versus 90 ppi.

Conversely, population density goes down as people die off or as the boundaries of the city grow. For example, if we were to mandate that Lagos spread out evenly over the entire 360,000 square miles of Nigeria, the population density would temporarily drop to 28 people per square mile (assuming, of course, that the other 110 million Nigerian residents happened to be on vacation at the time). Likewise, when you increase the dimensions of an image or delete some of its pixels, the resolution goes down.

Before you get the mistaken idea that this analogy is completely airtight, I should in all fairness mention a few key differences between a typical image and Lagos:

Figure 4-3:
Two images with the exact same number of pixels but subject to two different resolutions.

- Although I've never been there, I imagine that Lagos has its crowded spots and its relatively sparse areas. An image, by contrast, is equally dense at all points. Unlike population density, therefore, resolution is constant across the board.

- An image is always rectangular. Having misplaced my aerial map of Lagos, I can't swear to its shape, but I imagine that it's rather free-form.

- Population density is measured in terms of area — you know, so many folks per square mile. Resolution, on the other hand, is measured in a line — pixels per linear inch. So an image with a resolution of 180 pixels per inch contains 32,400 pixels per square inch. (That's 180 squared, in case you're wondering where I got the number.)

- The pixels in an image are absolutely square. The people in Lagos are shaped rather arbitrarily, with undulating arms and legs jutting out at irregular and unpredictable angles.

Yeah, okay, but what resolution should I use?

The Auto button in the Image Size dialog box is supposed to generate a perfect Resolution value based on the line screen that your printer will use. The only problem is, no one knows what a line screen setting is. Rather than bother with trying to explain this arcane bit of printing technology to you at this point — what with your head already spinning with Lagos population data — I decided to come up with both ideal and acceptable values for certain kinds of print jobs. See whether these work for you.

Type of Job	Ideal Resolution	Acceptable Setting
Full-color image for magazine or professional publication	300 ppi	225 ppi
Full-color slides	300 ppi	200 ppi
Color image for laser printing or overhead projections	180 ppi	120 ppi
Color images for multimedia productions and World Wide Web pages	72 ppi	72 ppi
Black-and-white images for imageset newsletters, flyers, etc.	180 ppi	120 ppi
Black-and-white images for laser printing	120 ppi	90 ppi

Keep in mind that there are no hard-and-fast rules about resolution settings. You can specify virtually any resolution setting between the ideal and acceptable settings and achieve good results. (If your commercial printer or service bureau tells you that you're getting bad results because your resolution doesn't match some exact ideal, consult a different company; this excuse is an example of a bad carpenter blaming his tools.) Even if you go with a Resolution value that's lower than the suggested acceptable setting, the worst that can happen is that you'll get fuzzy or slightly jagged results. But there is no wrong setting.

> ✔ You have total control over the size and resolution of an image. Like it or not, Lagos is entirely out of your hands.

Changing pixel dimensions

The top two option boxes in the Image Size dialog box enable you to change your image's pixel dimensions — the number of pixels wide by the number of pixels tall. (The number of pixels in your image is also known as the file size.) Unless you want to risk ruining your image — or you really, really know what you're doing when it comes to pixels — avoid these option boxes like the plague.

Lowering the Pixel Dimensions values can be dangerous because what you're really doing is throwing away pixels, and when you delete pixels, you delete detail. Figure 4-4 shows what I mean. The physical size of all three images is the same, but the detail drops off from one image to the next. The first image contains 64,000 pixels and is printed at a resolution of 140 ppi; the second contains $1/4$ as many pixels and is printed at 70 ppi. The third contains only 4,000 pixels and has a resolution of 35 dpi. Notice how details such as the shadows from the girl's eyelashes and the distinction between individual hairs in her eyebrows become less pronounced and more generalized as the pixel population decreases.

Increasing the file size (by raising the Pixel Dimensions values) isn't such a hot idea either because Photoshop can't generate image elements out of thin air.

Figure 4-4:
Three images, each of which contains fewer pixels and is printed at a lower resolution than the image above it.

When you raise the Pixel Dimensions values, Photoshop adds pixels by averaging the preexisting pixels in a way that may result in image softening and never results in the miraculous reconstruction of detail.

If changing the pixel dimensions is so dangerous, you may wonder why Photoshop gives you the option to do so at all. Well, although I don't recommend ever adding pixels to an image, you may need to lower the pixel dimensions on occasion. If your file size is really large — that is, your image contains a ton of pixels — you may want to toss some of the pixels overboard.

In an ideal world, you want as many pixels as possible, because more pixels means greater image detail. But the more pixels you have, the more disk space the image consumes, which can be a problem if you're working with limited computing resources. Large file sizes can also slow Photoshop down substantially. Also, if you're publishing your image on the Internet, you may want to reduce your file size so that users can download the image more quickly. Finally, you may need to lower the pixel dimensions in order to make an image print at the size you want.

Even when you dump pixels from an image, however, you shouldn't attack the job from the Pixel Dimensions options boxes; I show you a better way in the steps within the section "Using the Image Size dialog box safely."

In some particularly nerdy circles, changing the number of pixels in an image is called *resampling*. The idea is that you sample the photograph when you scan it — as if that makes a lick of sense — so any adjustment to the quantity of pixels after scanning is resampling. Photoshop uses the term resampling, but I prefer to call it resizing, because this gives folks a fighting chance of understanding what I'm talking about. But just be aware that there are computer aficionados out there who will gladly stick their noses high in the air, trade shocked stares with one another, and mutter pronouncements such as, "Don't tell me she has mouse privileges," or "Gad, did you hear what it said?" These things must be endured.

Changing the physical dimensions of the image

The Width and Height boxes in the Print Size portion of the Image Size dialog box reflect the actual printed size of your image and the approximate size of your image when distributed over the World Wide Web. (Because monitors can vary from user to user, the actual size of the image may change a little when viewed on different monitors.)

The pop-up menus next to the Width and Height options let you change the unit of measure displayed in the option boxes. For example, if you select Picas from the Print Size Width pop-up menu, Photoshop converts the Width value from

Matching images to columns

What is the meaning of the Columns option in the Print Size Width pop-up menu? Oh, man, you would ask that. All right (sigh), I suppose I'd better tell you.

You see, Photoshop is capable of precisely matching the width of an image to the columns in a printed document. So, for the sake of argument, let's say that you're working on an image that you eventually want to place into PageMaker. This specific PageMaker document happens to be a three-column newsletter. Each column is 2 inches wide, and the gutter between each column is ¼ inch wide.

To match Photoshop column settings to those in PageMaker, choose File⇨Preferences⇨Units &

Rulers and enter the column specs — in this case, 2 and .25 — into the Column Size option boxes, highlighted in the following figure. (Select Inches from the pop-up menus if you want to use inches.) From that point on, a Column in the Image Size dialog box conforms to your settings. One column, for example, would be two inches wide; 2 columns would be 4¼ inches wide — 4 inches for the two columns and the extra ¼ inch for the gutter.

Columns is not an option in the Height pop-up menu (inside the Image Size dialog box) because columns run up and down, not left to right. In other words, columns make no sense as a system of measurement for height.

inches to picas. (A pica is an obscure typesetting measurement equal to ⅙ inch.) The Percent option in the pop-up menu enables you to enter new Width and Height values as a percentage of the original values. Enter a value larger than 100 percent to increase the print size; enter a value lower than 100 percent to reduce the print size.

When you change the print size of the image, either the Resolution value or the number of pixels in the image automatically changes, too, which can affect the quality of your image. For more information, read the section, "Resolving resolution," earlier in this chapter. And for details on how to change the print size without ruining your image, see the section "Using the Image Size dialog box safely," later in this chapter.

Keeping things proportionate

Both pairs of Width and Height option boxes list the dimensions of your image in the current unit of measure. If you enter a different value into either option box and click on the OK button (or press Return), Photoshop resizes your image to the dimensions. Pretty obvious, eh?

But strangely, when you change either the Width or Height value, the other value changes, too. Are these twins separated at birth? Is there some new cosmic relationship between Width and Height that is known only to outer-space aliens and the checkout clerk at your local grocery store? No, it's nothing more than a function of the Constrain Proportions check box, which is turned on by default. Photoshop is simply maintaining the original proportions of the image.

If you click on the Constrain Proportions button and turn it off, Photoshop permits you — in a very generous spirit, I might add — to adjust the Width and Height values independently. Notice that the little link icon (labeled back in Figure 4-2) disappears, showing that the two options are now maverick independents with reckless disregard for one another. You can now create stretchy effects like the ones shown in Figure 4-5. In the first example, I reduced the Width value by a factor of two and left the Height value unchanged. In the second example, I did the opposite, reducing the Height value and leaving the Width value unaltered.

However, in order to deselect the Constrain Proportions check box, you must select the Resample Image check box. As explained in the section "Using the Image Size dialog box safely," when the Resample Image check box is selected, Photoshop either adds or deletes pixels from your image to compensate for the changes to the width and height of the image. Because adding pixels can make your image look like mud, never increase the width or height value with Constrain Proportions deselected. It's okay to decrease the width and height values, as long as the Resolution value stays in the acceptable range (see the sidebar "Yeah, okay, but what resolution should I use?" for recommended resolution values).

Using the Image Size dialog box safely

As mentioned in the section "Resolving resolution," you have three image attributes — size, resolution, and dimension — all vying for your attention and all affecting each other. These attributes, in fact, are like three points on a

Figure 4-5:
Known to
friends and
family as Kid
Squishums,
this
versatile
little tike is
the result of
deselecting
the
Constrain
Proportions
check box.

triangle. Change any one of the points, and at least one of the others has to change proportionately. If you decrease the file size (number of pixels), for example, either the physical dimensions (printed size) or resolution (number of pixels per inch) must also decrease. If you want to increase the physical dimensions, you have to increase the file size — add pixels, in other words — or decrease the resolution.

Thinking about all the possible permutations can drive you crazy, and besides, they aren't the least bit important. What is important is that you understand what you can accomplish with the Image Size dialog box and that you know how to avoid mistakes. So now that I've provided all the background you need, it's finally time for me to offer a modicum of fatherly advice:

✔ Changing the Pixel Dimensions (file size) values can be deadly, as explained in the section "Changing pixel dimensions." To avoid changes to file size, deselect the Resample Image check box at the bottom of the Image Size dialog box. When you deselect the option, the Image Size dialog box changes, and the Width and Height options in the Pixel Dimensions portion of the dialog box become unavailable to you. A link icon also connects the Width, Height, and Resolution option boxes, showing that changes to one value affect the other two values as well.

✔ To turn off Constrain Proportions option box, you must turn on the Resample Image option box. If you make changes to the image width and height values, Photoshop will resample the image. If you're lowering the width and height values, you'll probably be okay, but if you try to raise the width and height values, you're likely to muck things up.

✔ Want a surefire method to tell whether you've changed the file size? Your image looks different on-screen after you change the Resolution or Print Size values and exit the Image Size dialog box. As long as the file size remains unchanged, you won't see any difference — none, zilch, zippo — on-screen. On-screen, Photoshop just shows your image pixels with respect to screen pixels; resolution and dimension only enter into the equation when you print the image. Therefore, you want the image to look the same on-screen after you get done fiddling around with the Image Size command.

✔ If you manage to mess everything up and change one or more settings in the Image Size dialog box to settings you don't want to apply, you can return to the original settings by Option-clicking on the Cancel button. Pressing Option changes the word Cancel to Reset; clicking resets the options. Now you have your original settings back in place so that you can muck them up again. If you already pressed Return to exit the Image Size dialog box, choose Edit⇨Undo right away to undo your changes.

✔ Whatever you do, be sure to use the Bicubic setting in the Resample Image pop-up menu. I'd tell you what bicubic means, but you don't want to know. Suffice it to say, it keeps Photoshop running smoothly.

✔ If you want to change the unit of measure that displays by default in the Image Size dialog box pop-up menus, choose File⇨Preferences⇨Units & Rulers and select a different option from the Units pop-up menu.

After all the warnings I've given you so far, you may think that changing the image size is something that you never want to do. But as mentioned earlier, you may in fact want to reduce the image size on some occasions — to get the image to print at a certain size, to enable your computer to handle the image, or to make the image faster to download from the Internet. The following steps show you how to reduce your image size without turning your image into a worthless pile of goo.

Before you follow these steps, choose File⇨Save As to save a backup copy of your image. The steps result in Photoshop tossing away pixels, and after you delete pixels, you can't get them back. So always make a copy of the original in case things don't work out or you decide you want to use the original again at a later date.

1. **Open the image at the highest resolution possible.**

   For example, if you're opening a Photo CD image, select the 2048 by 3072 option from the Resolution pop-up menu. If that doesn't work — Photoshop may complain that you don't have enough memory to pull it off — try again and select the 1024 by 1536 option. Whatever works, go for it.

2. **Choose Image⇨Image Size to open the Image Size dialog box.**

3. **Note the values in the Pixel Dimensions Width and Height option boxes.**

   You may want to write 'em down — they're important.

4. **Enter your desired print width and height in the Print Size option boxes.**

   If you want Photoshop to retain the original proportions of your image, make sure that the Constrain Proportions option box is checked.

5. **Enter your desired resolution in the Resolution option box.**

   Check the sidebar, "Yeah, okay, but what resolution should I use?" for some suggestions on acceptable resolution values if you need help.

6. **Check the Pixel Dimensions values.**

   Did either of the values get bigger? If so, you need to either reduce your Print Size width and height values or lower the resolution. Otherwise, Photoshop adds pixels to your image, and you won't be happy with the results.

   If the Pixel Dimensions values got smaller, on the other hand, proceed to Step 7.

7. **Make sure that the Resample Image check box is selected.**

8. **Make sure that the Bicubic option is selected in the Resample Image pop-up menu.**

9. **Click on the OK button.**

   Photoshop resizes — or, if you prefer, resamples — your image in accordance with your perfect settings. If you don't like the results, press ⌘-Z or choose Edit⇨Undo *immediately* to put things back to the way they were.

What Does This Canvas Size Command Do?

There's one more command related to the topic of image sizing that you should know about: Image⇨Canvas Size. Unlike the Image Size command, which stretches or shrinks the photograph, the Canvas Size command changes the size of the page — or canvas — on which the image sits. If you increase the size of the canvas, Photoshop fills the new area outside the image with white (or the background color). If you make the canvas smaller, Photoshop crops the image.

When you choose Image⇨Canvas Size, the dialog box shown in Figure 4-6 pops up out of its virtual hole. You can play with the options found inside the dialog box as follows:

✔ Enter new values into the Width and Height option boxes as desired. You can also change the unit of measurement using the pop-up menus, just as in the Image Size dialog box.

✔ You can't constrain the proportions of the canvas the way you can inside the Image Size dialog box. Therefore, the Width and Height values always operate independently.

✔ The Anchor section shows a graphic representation of how the current image sits inside the new canvas. By default, the image is centered in the canvas. But you can click inside any of the other eight squares to move the image to the upper-right corner, center it along the bottom edge, or place it where you like.

✔ If you reduce either the Width or Height value and press Return, Photoshop asks you whether you really want to crop the image. If you click on the Proceed button (or press Return) and decide you don't like the results, you can always choose Edit⇨Undo or press ⌘-Z to restore the original canvas size.

Figure 4-6:
Use the Canvas Size dialog box to change the size of the page on which the image sits.

R. Pozzi

Chapter 5

Auntie Em versus the Munchkins (Death Match)

*I*n case you're wondering what the title of this chapter means, it's all about color — the same kind of color that Dorothy encountered when she passed over the weather-beaten threshold of her old Kansas porch onto a path of lemon-yellow bricks in that beloved classic, *The Wizard of Oz*. As you might imagine, Auntie Em represents the world of black and white, and the munchkins represent the wonderful world of color.

With that in mind, you might think that Auntie Em is pretty well doomed. I mean, how can one woman cope with an entire Ozfull of rowdy munchkins? And how can drab black and white compete with rich, beautiful color?

Well, I'm rather fond of black and white myself. To me, the absence of color offers its own special attractions. It's the mysterious essence of a torch-lit castle on a stormy night. It's the refreshingly personal vision of a 16mm short-subject film you stumble across one evening on Bravo!. It's the powerful chiaroscuro of an Ansel Adams photograph or a Rembrandt oil. In an age when every screen, page, and billboard screams with color that's more vivid than real life, black and white can beckon the eye like an old friend.

But on the off chance you think all that's a pretentious load of hooey, I can tell you one area in which Auntie Em kicks major munchkin keister, and that's cost. Despite the increasing influence of computers in print houses, color printing remains extremely expensive. Major four-color magazines — including the ones I write for — spend more on ink than they do on their writers. The color medium costs more than the message, and that's a sad fact.

Though by no means free, black-and-white images are substantially less expensive to reproduce. Only one ink is involved — black. Other supplies, such as film and plates for the printing press, are kept to a minimum. Black-and-white printing is also incredibly versatile. You can print black-and-white images with any laser printer, you can photocopy black-and-white images using cheap equipment, and you can fax black-and-white images with relatively little loss in quality. And finally, black-and-white images require one-third of the overhead when you're working in Photoshop, meaning that you can edit black-and-white images that contain three times as many pixels as color images without Photoshop complaining that it's out of memory. This is one match in which Auntie Em can be counted on to hold her own. No surprise, really. Farm women are well-known troupers, while the munchkins — to hear Judy Garland tell it — were a bunch of randy booze hounds.

Whether you choose black and white, color, or — like most folks — vacillate between the two, this chapter tells you how it all works. You find out how to use color, create colors that you can apply with the painting tools, and switch between color modes. Not bad for a chapter based on an old MGM musical, eh?

Looking at Color in a Whole New Light

To understand color in Photoshop, you have to understand a little color theory. To this end, I'd like you to do me a favor and open some random color image that you have sitting around. Chances are that you'll see the telltale initials RGB inside parentheses in the image title bar. (If you don't, try opening a different image.) These initials mean that all colors inside the image are created by blending red, green, and blue light.

Red, green, and blue? That doesn't sound particularly colorful, does it? But in fact, these colors are the primary colors of light. The red is a vivid scarlet, the green is so bright and tinged with yellow that you might be tempted to call it chartreuse, and the blue is a brilliant Egyptian lapis. It just so happens that these colors correspond to the three kinds of cones inside your eyeball. So in theory, your monitor projects color in the same way your eyes see color.

Surfing the color channels

To get a hands-on feel for the inner workings of a color image, follow these steps:

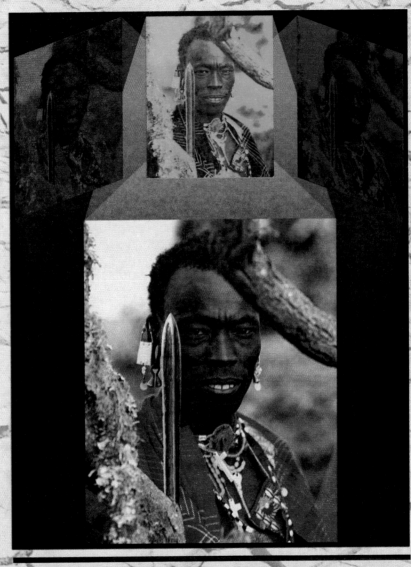

Color Plate 5-1:
The red, green, and blue color channels in Photoshop act like slides in separate projectors pointed at the same spot on a screen. You may find it hard to believe that three primary hues could mix together to produce so many colors, but it's true.

Color Plate 15-1:
To create this composition, I combined eight images and blended them together using various modes and Opacity settings from the Layers palette. I selected all the images using the Color Range command, tinted the astronaut using the Variations command, and erased, scaled, and rotated a few others.

Color Plate 5-1:
The red, green, and blue color channels in Photoshop act like slides in separate projectors pointed at the same spot on a screen. You may find it hard to believe that
three primary hues could mix together to produce so many colors, but it's true.

Color Plate 5-2:
This shows the way light, dark, and medium pixels in the red, green, and blue channels mix to form various sample colors. Altogether, you can create more than 16 million color variations.

Color Plate 5-3:
Pure white light from the sun (or a man-made light source) is made up of red, green, and blue light. When light passes through the cyan, magenta, or yellow printing ink, the ink filters out the red, green, or blue light and lets the other two pass through.

Color Plate 7-1:
The cyan, magenta, and yellow channels as they appear when inked in their proper colors (top row). Each color channel takes on new depth and detail when combined with black (middle row). During the commercial printing process, the cyan image is first combined with magenta (bottom left), and then yellow (bottom center), and then black (bottom right).

When I used the paintbrush tool to paint in the sun with yellow and the sky with blue, the paint obscured the sun's face and rays. When I started over again and lowered the Opacity setting to 40 percent, I just got weaker color (right).

Multiply

Screen

Overlay

Difference

Color Plate 8-2:
The results of applying yellow and blue with the paintbrush using each of four brush modes.

Color Plate 9-1:
Using the smudge tool, I turned a common, household-variety shark into a red-hot shark torpedo. In the Smudge Tool Options palette, I turned on the Finger Painting check box, set the brush mode to Color, and set the Pressure slider bar to 90 percent.

Color Plate 10-1:
By cloning from the top left image onto the bottom left image with the rubber stamp tool, I was able to merge the two images to create the strange but nonetheless believable specimen on the right.

Tolerance: 32

Tolerance: 90

Tolerance: 180

Color Plate 12-1:
By raising the Tolerance value in the Magic Wand Options palette, I instructed
Photoshop to select a wider range of colors around the point at which I clicked (just to
the right of the forward giraffe). In this case, 90 seems to be the best setting.

One base color, Fuzziness: 200

Color Plate 12-2:
The result of clicking just to the right of the monster's nose and applying the Color Range command with a Fuzziness setting of 200. In the right image, I filled the selection with white and then deselected it.

Three base colors, Fuzziness: 60

Color Plate 12-3:
By Shift-clicking in the image while inside the Color Range dialog box and lowering the Fuzziness value, I selected more of the blue sky and made the selection outline less blurry.

Color Plate 14-1:
I filled the area behind the jar with custom gradients created using the Gradient Editor.

Color Plate 15-1:
To create this composition, I combined eight images and blended them together using various modes and Opacity settings from the Layers palette. I selected all the images using the Color Range command, tinted the astronaut using the Variations command, and erased, scaled, and rotated a few others.

1. **Open an RGB image.**

   Oh, you already did that. My mistake.

2. **Choose File⇨Preferences⇨Display & Cursors.**

   The Preferences dialog box shown in Figure 5-1 appears.

   The Preferences dialog box actually contains several panels of options.
   You switch between the panels via the pop-up menu at the top of the
   dialog box. Another way to display the dialog box is to press ⌘-K, which
   brings up the Preferences dialog box with the General preferences panel
   showing. Then press ⌘-3 or choose Display & Cursors from the pop-up
   menu to display the options shown in Figure 5-1. After you close the dialog
   box, you can redisplay the last panel you viewed by pressing ⌘-Option-K.

Figure 5-1:
Select the
Color
Channels in
Color option
to better see
how the
primary
colors work.

3. **Select the Color Channels in Color check box and then press Return.**

   Highlighted in the figure, this option makes the individual layers of red,
   green, and blue color appear in red, green, and blue. These layers of color
   are called *channels*.

4. **Press ⌘-1 to view the red channel.**

   You see a black-and-red image. Notice that the RGB in the title bar changes
   to Red to show that you're viewing the red channel. This image is the one
   being sent to the red cones in your eyes.

5. **Press ⌘-2 to view the green channel and then press ⌘-3 to view the blue
   channel.**

   These images are the ones being sent to your green and blue cones.

6. **Press ⌘-~ (tilde) to return to the full-color RGB view.**

The tilde key, by the way, is found in the upper-left corner of the keyboard, next to the 1 key. To type an actual tilde, you have to press the Shift key, but you don't need to press Shift to invoke the full-color view shortcut. The shortcut really should be ⌘-` (grave) because pressing the key without Shift accesses the grave mark. But Photoshop prefers to label this shortcut ⌘-~ (tilde), so I follow suit.

At any rate, when you press ⌘-~, you can see the red, green, and blue channels all mixed together.

The keyboard shortcut for viewing the channels together has changed in Version 4. The old shortcut, ⌘-0, now switches you to the Fit on Screen view.

Pretty nifty, huh? Here's another way to think about it: If you were to take the images you saw in the red, green, and blue channels, print them to slides, put each of the slides in a different projector, and shine all three projectors at the same spot on a screen so that the images precisely overlapped, you would see the full-color image in all its splendor. Check out Color Plate 5-1 for the pictorial representation.

Now try something different. Choose File⇨Preferences⇨Display & Cursors (or press ⌘-K, ⌘-3) to bring up the Preferences dialog box again. But this time, turn off the Color Channels in Color check box. Now look at the color channels once more by pressing ⌘-1, ⌘-2, and ⌘-3. Each channel looks like a standard black-and-white image. Figure 5-2, for example, shows the contents of the red, green, and blue channels as they appear in black and white.

Figure 5-2: The black-and-white channels that combine to make a full-color image.

Mixing red, green, and blue to create color

Every channel contains light areas and dark areas, just like a black-and-white image. With the Color Channels in Color check box turned off, you can better see these light and dark areas without a bunch of distracting colors getting in your way (which is why the option is off by default). The light and dark pixels from each channel mix together to form other colors.

The following list explains how corresponding pixels from the different channels mix together to form a single full-color pixel.

- A light pixel from the one channel mixed with dark pixels from the other two channels produce the color from the first channel. For example, if the red is light, and green and blue are dark, you get a red pixel.

- Light pixels from the red and green channels plus a dark pixel from the blue channel form yellow. This may sound weird — two colors, red and green, mixing to form a lighter color — but that's exactly how things work in the upside-down world of RGB. Because you're mixing colors projected from a monitor, two colors projected together produce a still lighter color.

- With me? No? Well, say that you had a flashlight with a red bulb and your friend had one with a green bulb. I don't know, maybe it's Christmas or something. At any rate, if you were to point your flashlight at a spot on the ground, the spot would turn red. No surprise there. But if you then said, "Look, Nancy, it's the missing key from the old Smithers place," and your friend pointed her green flashlight at the same spot, the spot wouldn't get darker, it would get lighter. In fact, it would turn bright yellow. "Gee wizikers, Ned, do you suppose this means Mrs. Johnson is innocent after all?" I'm afraid we'll never know.

- Light pixels from the green and blue channels plus a dark pixel from the red channel make a bright turquoise color called cyan. Light red and blue pixels plus a dark green pixel make magenta.

- By a strange coincidence, cyan, magenta, and yellow just happen to be the main ink colors used in the color printing process. Well, actually, it's not coincidence at all. Color printing is the opposite of color screen display, so the two use complementary collections of primary hues to produce full-color images. The difference is, because cyan, magenta, and yellow are pigments, they become darker as you mix them. Yellow plus cyan, for example, make green. This won't affect how you edit RGB images, but I thought you might find it interesting.

- Light pixels from all three channels mix to form white. Dark pixels all around form black. Medium pixels make gray.

Although all this is highly stimulating, I have a feeling that it would make more sense if you could see it. If you're the visual type, take a look at Color Plate 5-2. The left side of the figure shows the RGB combinations I just discussed. The right half shows RGB mixes that result in other colors, including orange, purple, and so on. Give it the once-over and see whether you can't feel your brain grow by leaps and bounds.

Using the Channels palette

Keyboard equivalents such as ⌘-1 and ⌘-2 aren't the only way to access different channels. You can also use the Channels palette. Choose Window⇨ Show Channels to display the Channels palette, shown in Figure 5-3. Here's how to use the palette:

✔ To switch to a different channel in the palette, simply click on its name. Figure 5-3 finds me clicking on the Red channel.

Figure 5-3:
Click on a channel name in the Channels palette to view that channel.

✔ To return to the full-color RGB view, click on the top name in the Channels palette or press ⌘-~ (tilde).

✔ The Channels palette includes little thumbnails of the contents of each channel. You can change the size of these thumbnails by choosing Palette Options from the palette menu — click on that little right-pointing arrowhead just beneath the title bar — and selecting a different Thumbnail Size icon.

Being Your Own L.J. Grand Master Funky Glow

In case you're hip-hop impaired, L.J. stands for Light Jockey, and that's exactly what you have to be to create colors in Photoshop. In other words, to define a color, you have to specify the quantities of red, green, and blue that go into it.

Uh, just so you don't go and make a fool of yourself the next time your kid's friends come over by saying something painfully embarrassing like, "Hey, check me out, I'm L.J. Grand Master Funky Glow!" I admit that L.J. isn't a real hip-hop term. I just made it up. I mean, for all I know, L.J. means lemon juice or lantern jaw in today's imaginative middle-school lingo. "You're what, Dad? A lentil jar?"

Juggling foreground and background colors

In Photoshop, you can work with two colors at a time: a foreground color and a background color. Some tools and commands paint your image with the foreground color; others splash it with the background color.

The two colors are displayed in the lower portion of the toolbox. As shown in Figure 5-4, the foreground color is on top and the background color is on the bottom. To get some idea of how these colors work, read the following list. (Skip the following list if you'd like to remain ignorant.)

- ✔ The foreground color is applied by the painting tools, such as the airbrush, paintbrush, and pencil.

- ✔ When you use the eraser tool, you're actually painting with the background color.

- ✔ When you increase the size of the canvas using Image⇨Canvas Size (as explained in Chapter 4), Photoshop fills the empty portion of the canvas with the background color.

- ✔ The gradient tool creates a rainbow of colors between the foreground and background colors (assuming that you use the default gradient option, Foreground to Background, as explained in Chapter 14).

The toolbox includes a few icons that enable you to change the foreground and background colors, swap them around, and so on.

- ✔ Click on the foreground icon to display the intensely complex Color Picker dialog box, which is filled with about 17,000 options you don't need to know anything about.

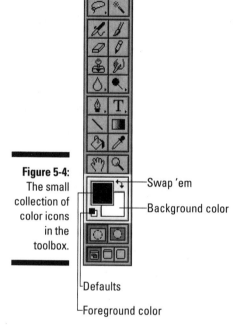

Figure 5-4:
The small
collection of
color icons
in the
toolbox.

Swap 'em

Background color

Defaults

Foreground color

✔ Press ⌘-period to leave that dialog box. Then pick up a Bible or some other holy relic and swear that you'll never go back there again. The next section tells you a better option for defining the foreground and background colors.

✔ Click on the background color to go to that same terrible dialog box. Hey, didn't I specifically instruct you to stay out of there?

✔ Click on the defaults icon (labeled in Figure 5-4) to restore the foreground color to black and the background color to white.

✔ Click on that little two-way arrow icon — childishly labeled *swap 'em* in the figure — to swap the foreground and background colors with each other.

✔ You can also access the default and swap 'em icons from the keyboard. Press D to restore the default colors, black and white. Press X to swap the foreground and background colors.

Defining colors

You can define the foreground and background colors in Photoshop in three ways:

- ✔ You can click on the foreground or background color icon in the toolbox and battle your way through the Color Picker. If you read the preceding section, you know that I think that this option is a real stinkeroo and should be avoided at all costs.

- ✔ You can use the handy-dandy Color palette. The Color palette is pretty much the same thing as the Picker palette found in Version 3 and just one "s" away from the Colors palette found in Version 2.5. You wouldn't think there would be so much controversy about naming this particular palette, would you?

- ✔ You can lift colors from your image using the eyedropper tool.

Using the Color palette

To define colors using the Color palette, shown in Figure 5-5, choose Window⇨Show Color or press the F6 key. You should see three slider bars labeled R, G, and B (for Reginald, Gertie, and Bert). If you don't, choose RGB Sliders from the palette menu. (Click on the right-pointing arrow in the upper-right corner of the palette to display the menu.)

┌Background color

┌Foreground color

Figure 5-5:
The Color palette fully adorned with its cheerful RGB slider bars.

Closest printable color   Color bar

└Alert: Colors won't print

Here's how you go about changing a color using the Color palette:

1. **Decide which color you want to change.**

   The palette offers its own foreground and background color icons, as labeled in Figure 5-5. Click on the icon for the color you want to change. A double outline surrounds the icon to show that it's selected.

2. **Drag the little RGB slider bar triangles to change the color.**

Think of red, green, and blue as ingredients in baking the perfect color. You can add 256 levels of each of the primary hues, 0 being the darkest amount of the hue, 255 being the lightest, and 128 being smack dab in the middle. For example, if you set the R slider to 255, the G slider to 128, and the B slider to 0, you get a vibrant orange, just like the one shown in the upper-right corner of Color Plate 5-2.

If you've never mixed colors using red, green, and blue, it can be a little perplexing at first. For example, folks often have a hard time initially accepting that all yellows and oranges are produced by mixing red and green. I encourage you to experiment. Better yet, I order you to experiment.

3. **Click on the triangular alert icon if desired.**

If a little triangle with an exclamation point appears in the lower-right corner of the palette, Photoshop is pointing out that the color you have mixed will not print exactly as you see it on-screen. The closest printable color appears inside a little square to the right of the alert icon. Click on either the icon or the square if you want to use the printable color instead.

Just a few other things I'd like to pass along about the Color palette:

- ✔ If you can't get the knack of using the RGB slider bars, you can also select a color by clicking inside the color bar at the bottom of the palette. By default, all the colors in the bar are printable. (To make sure that this is true, ⌘-click on the color bar, select CMYK Spectrum from the Style pop-up menu, and press Return.)

- ✔ Option-click in the color bar to change the opposite color. For example, if the foreground color is active, Option-click to select the background color. If the background color is active, Option-click to select the foreground color.

- ✔ If you want to set the foreground or background color to a shade of gray, you can set all sliders to the same value. Or better yet, choose Grayscale Slider from the palette menu and adjust the single K slider. (K stands for black, remember?)

Lifting colors with the eyedropper tool

You can also change the foreground or background colors by lifting them from the image. Just select the eyedropper tool — on the right side of the toolbox just above the zoom tool — and click inside the image on the color you want to use. If you have more than one image open, you can even click inside a different image than the one you're working on.

Why won't my color print?

You may be wondering why you can define a color that won't print. Isn't a color on the screen the same as a color on the page? No, and the reason has to do with the differences between the principles of colored light and colored pigments. (Hold on, this is a long but mighty interesting topic — if I do say so myself.)

As I mentioned earlier, your monitor creates white by mixing the lightest amounts of red, green, and blue. In the Color palette, for example, you set all sliders to 255 to get white. This is just the opposite of how things work on a printed page.

Color printing exploits the fact that sunlight, household light bulbs, fluorescent and halogen lamps, and other so-called "white light" sources contain the entire spectrum of visible light, including all shades of red, green, and blue. The primary printing inks that I alluded to earlier in this chapter — cyan, magenta, and yellow (CMY) — are actually color filters. When white light hits cyan ink printed on a white page, for example, the cyan ink filters out all traces of red and reflects only green and blue, which (as I mentioned earlier) mix to form cyan. Similarly, magenta is a green light filter, and yellow is a blue light filter, as illustrated in supreme detail in Color Plate 5-3.

In a perfect world, RGB and CMY would be exact opposites. Photoshop would simply print the red channel in cyan ink, the green channel in magenta ink, and the blue channel in yellow ink, and everything would come up roses. But on the off chance that you haven't learned this important lesson yet, the world is not perfect. In the case of color, it's half near perfect and half totally whacked.

The culprit is color purity. The basic rule of thumb is that red, green, and blue light represent pure colors, and cyan, magenta, and yellow inks are impure. What does this mean? Well, scientific types have been able to split white light into its precise red, green, and blue components since Isaac Newton discovered the spectral powers of a common prism in 1666. The red you see on-screen may not exactly match the red you see on a neighbor's screen, but it comes awfully darn close.

Unfortunately, the world's technicians have had a harder time coming up with pure inks. Not only do the specific tints of commercial-grade cyan, magenta, and yellow vary widely, but the most accurate of them isn't right on. You can't split a chemical dye into its primary color components. So like economics and child rearing, CMY inks represent an imprecise science.

To balance things out, color printing throws in one additional ink, black. (Black is the *key* color — the ink that materializes out of thin air to help the other inks out — which is why color printing is sometimes called CMYK.) Black ensures deep shadows, neutral grays, and — of course — nice, even blacks.

But even with black, CMYK can't measure up to RGB. There are just too many random elements involved. Is the paper absolutely white? Are the inks as pure as they can be? Are you viewing the page under ideal lighting conditions? Because the answer to all three questions is generally no, CMYK can produce fewer colors than RGB. Techheads say that CMYK has a smaller *gamut*, which is just a fancy word for range. (Can you imagine a bunch of nerdy computer guys out on the lone prairie singing, "Home, home on the gamut"?) Bright reds, oranges, greens, blues, and purples all fall outside the CMYK range. In fact, by comparison to RGB, CMYK is dull.

But all things are relative. It's highly doubtful that the word "dull" comes to mind when viewing a typical glossy magazine ad because it looks very colorful compared to the surrounding magazine color. But if you were to hold it up to the same image on an RGB screen, you'd be surprised at how lackluster it looks.

The upshot of all this? Just one thing. Don't worry that the closest printable color (the little box in the Color palette) looks duller than the RGB color you'd like to use. It very likely won't look dull when you print the image. All the colors in Color Plate 5-3 were printed, after all, and they don't look dull. Just accept the duller color and go on with life.

Here's some stuff to know about this incredibly easy-to-use tool:

- ✔ You can press I (for I-dropper) to select the eyedropper tool instead of clicking on its toolbox icon.

- ✔ The eyedropper affects whatever color is selected in the Color palette. So if the foreground color icon is selected, the eyedropper tool changes the foreground color, and if the background icon is selected — well, you get the idea.

- ✔ To select the opposite color — in other words, to select the background color when the foreground color icon is active or the foreground color when the background color icon is active — Option-click with the eyedropper.

- ✔ You can temporarily access the eyedropper when another tool is selected by pressing the Option key. As long as the key is down, the eyedropper is available. This trick doesn't always work; in fact, it only works when you're using the type, paint bucket, gradient, line, pencil, airbrush, or paintbrush tool. But it can come in handy.

- ✔ If you use the preceding tip, you can only change the active color in the Color palette. You have to select the eyedropper tool for real to change the opposite color because that also involves the use of the Option key. (If your keyboard offers two Option keys, it doesn't help to press both of them.)

Going Grayscale

Now that I've wasted most of the chapter on the colorful munchkins, you may be wondering when I'm ever going to get around to discussing the much lauded Auntie Em. Friends of Kansas, take heart, the heralded hour of black-and-white images has arrived.

The first thing to understand about black-and-white images is that the black-and-white world offers more colors than just black and white. It includes a total of 256 unique shades of gray and is therefore more properly termed *grayscale*. Each one of these shades is a color in its own right, which is why the term "black and white" can inspire fisticuffs among some grayscale devotees.

Secondly, all the stuff I told you about creating colors holds true for grayscale image editing as well. You have a foreground and background color. You can define colors in the Color palette. (Be sure to choose Grayscale Slider from the palette menu so that you just have to use one slider bar.) And you can lift colors from a grayscale image using the eyedropper tool.

But some aspects of grayscale editing are different than full-color editing, which is what led me to write the next two sections.

The road to grayscale

Most images that you'll come across will be in color. Most commercial images and all Photo CD images are in color. Scans from a commercial quick-printer or service bureau may be either in color or in grayscale, but you never know. My point is that working in grayscale generally requires a conversion inside Photoshop.

Unlike a three-channel RGB image, a grayscale image includes only one channel of imagery. That's why the red, green, and blue channels all appear in black and white — each is its own grayscale image. If you plan on printing in black and white, you should jettison all the extraneous color information, for two reasons. First, it's easier for Photoshop to keep track of one channel than three. In fact, given the same image size and resolution, Photoshop performs faster and with fewer problems when editing a grayscale image than when editing in color. Second, you can better see what your printed image will look like. When you're designing an image to be printed in black and white, color just gets in the way.

To convert a color image to grayscale, just choose Image⇨Mode⇨Grayscale. Photoshop asks you whether you want it to discard color information. You can answer OK or chicken out and cancel. That's all there is to it. You now have a single-channel grayscale image. No matter what color you choose in the Color palette, it will look gray in the foreground and background color icons. (If you don't like the results of your conversion to grayscale, you can go back to the full-color original by choosing Edit⇨Undo or pressing ⌘-Z.) But you have to choose the command *immediately* after you apply the Mode⇨Grayscale command — if you choose some other command or apply a painting or editing tool, you won't be able to undo the color conversion. And after that color is gone, it's gone for good; you can't bring it back by choosing one of the other commands on the Mode menu.

Before you change a color image to grayscale, you may want to make a backup copy of the original image, just in case you ever want to have the image available in color some day. For details on saving images, see Chapter 6.

When you choose Image⇨Mode⇨Grayscale, Photoshop merges all three RGB channels together to create the new colorless image. But what if the contents of any one of the RGB channels strikes you as just right and you want to simply dump the other two? The answer is to just go to that channel (press ⌘-1, ⌘-2, or ⌘-3) and choose Image⇨Mode⇨Grayscale. This time Photoshop asks you whether you want it to discard all the other channels. If the channel you see on-screen is the one you want to keep, press Return to give Photoshop the go-ahead. Otherwise, click on Cancel and go back to channel surfing.

Figure 5-6 shows an example of the difference between converting all channels in an image and retaining just one. In the first image, I chose Image⇨Mode⇨ Grayscale in the RGB view to merge all channels. The result is washed out, with little distinction between lights and darks. I didn't like it, so I chose Edit⇨Undo to restore my RGB image. Then I tiptoed through the channels to find something better, and wouldn't you know, the red channel looked just right. So after pressing ⌘-1, I again chose Image⇨Mode⇨Grayscale to toss out the green and blue channels, thus arriving at the second image in Figure 5-6.

Figure 5-6:
The difference between converting a color image to grayscale (left) and throwing away all but the red channel (right).

More grayscale tips from Auntie Em

That's basically all there is to tell about grayscale images. Future chapters explain how to edit color and grayscale images, and Chapter 18 explains how to make automated adjustments, such as changing brightness and contrast. So I'll wrap things up with four last-minute grayscale tidbits:

✔ If you decide to convert a single channel from an RGB image to grayscale, you'll almost always want to use either the red or green channel. The red channel is generally lighter than the other two because skin tones gravitate toward red. The green channel is the detail channel, full of nice edges. Blue is the dark and dank channel. Except for skies and oceans, not much in this world is blue. Also, your eye contains fewer blue cones than red or green ones. So many scanners generate some pretty cruddy detail in the blue channel, knowing that you won't be able to see it.

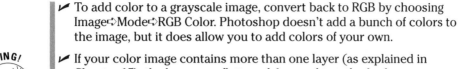

✔ To add color to a grayscale image, convert back to RGB by choosing Image➪Mode➪RGB Color. Photoshop doesn't add a bunch of colors to the image, but it does allow you to add colors of your own.

✔ If your color image contains more than one layer (as explained in Chapter 15), the layers are flattened (merged together) when you convert to grayscale. So before you go ahead with the conversion, do all editing that involves layers and also make a backup copy of the layered image.

✔ If you're using an 8-bit monitor — that is, a monitor that can display only 256 colors — you're better off editing grayscale images. When you edit full-color RGB images, Photoshop only shows 256 of the 16 million possible colors at a time, resulting in *dithering,* an effect in which a random pattern of pixels is used to emulate lots more colors. When you edit a grayscale image, however, you can see every shade just right. Don't worry that Photoshop converts your entire screen to grays, including Finder icons and all other background items. This is a normal effect of editing in grayscale on an inexpensive computer system.

Chapter 6
Save Before You Say Goodnight

● ●

In This Chapter

▶ Saving an image to disk

▶ Updating images and making backups

▶ Understanding file formats

▶ Deciding when to use TIFF, EPS, JPEG, PICT, and other formats

▶ Quitting Photoshop

● ●

*I*f you've used a computer before, you may be wondering why I devote an entire chapter to saving files. After all, you just press ⌘-S and you're done, right? Well, if we were talking about any other program, I'd have to agree with you. If this book were about Microsoft Word, for example, I'd say, "Not to worry, Dear Reader, saving a file is so simple, a newborn lemur could pull it off with the most cursory supervision from a parent or older sibling." If this book were about PageMaker, I'd add, "Saving makes tying your shoes look like a supreme feat of civic engineering," all the while gently smiling and donning a cardigan sweater in a manner not unlike Mr. Rogers.

But this book is about Photoshop. And Photoshop, as you may or may not be aware, allows you to save images in more flavors than Willy Wonka manages to squeeze into an Everlasting Gobstopper. In the software world, these flavors are called *file formats,* and each one has a different purpose.

This chapter offers a thorough explanation of the saving process, including an exhaustive — well, okay, pretty decent — review of the various file formats you can use. With this chapter by your side, ⌘-S can be a pretty easy command, after all.

Save an Image, Save a Life

I don't know you from Adam — or Eve for that matter — but I'm guessing that you're the kind of person who doesn't like to spend hours editing an image only to see your work vanish in a poof of on-screen smoke as the result of some inexplicable and unforeseen computer malfunction. If you are indeed that kind of person, learning to save your image is essential. By saving your image early and often, you improve your chances of weathering any digital storm that may come your way.

Saving for the very first time

After applying the first few edits to your image, save it under a new name and — if necessary — specify where you want to store the edited image on disk. If you do this, the original image remains untouched, allowing you to return to it at a later date for inclusion in a different project. Here's how to save your customized image without harming the original:

1. **Choose File⇨Save As.**

   The dialog box shown in Figure 6-1 appears.

   You can also open the dialog box by pressing ⌘-Shift-S.

Figure 6-1:
Use this dialog box to name your image and decide where you want the image to hang out on disk.

> 🍎 Football ▾   ⊂ DekeMC
>
> 🖼 Crowd.Colts   ┌─────────┐
> 🖼 Drummer   │ Eject │
> 🖼 End.zone.dance   ┌─────────┐
> 🖼 First Down   │ Desktop │
> 🖼 Kickoff   ┌─────────┐
>   │ New 📁 │
> Save this document as: ┌─────────┐
>   │ Cancel │
> Mascot   ┌─────────┐
> Format: │ TIFF   ▾│   │ Save   │

2. **Enter a name into the Save This Document As option box.**

   You can enter any name up to 31 characters long, putting periods and spaces anywhere you want them. Personally, I like to keep my filenames below 20 characters so that I can see them in their entirety at the Finder level. Longer filenames become abbreviated when viewed by name. For example, the name FamilyReunion.UnpleasantBrawl might appear as FamilyReunion.Unpleasan... at the Finder.

3. **Select a format from the Format pop-up menu.**

   This is the point at which you have to deal with the image flavors I touch on in the introduction to this chapter. The pop-up menu provides all kinds of options, such as TIFF, JPEG, PICT, and others. I discuss the ramifications of the important formats later in this chapter.

Some formats are restricted to certain kinds of images. For example, you can only save images that contain layers (as explained in Chapter 15) in the native Photoshop format. If a format is grayed out in the Format pop-up menu, that format isn't available for the kind of image you're trying to save.

4. **Use the Desktop button, folder bar, and any other controls to hunt down the folder in which you want to save the image.**

   These controls are explained in the "Don't Just Sit There, Open Something" section of Chapter 3.

5. **Click on the Save button or press Return.**

   Watch out. If the button with the heavy outline reads Open instead of Save, Photoshop selects a folder in the central list. If you press the Tab key to activate the file name, the button automatically changes back to Save. Then you can press Return.

6. **If another dialog box appears, fill out the options and press Return.**

   Most formats present additional dialog boxes that enable you to modify the way the image is saved. I explain this in more detail later.

Your image is now saved! Come heck or high water, you're protected.

Join the frequent-saver program

After you name your image and save it to disk for the first time, press ⌘-S or choose File⇨Save every time you think of it. In either case, Photoshop updates your image on disk, without any dialog boxes or options popping up and demanding your attention. Then, when something goes wrong — notice that I said *when,* not *if* — you don't lose hours of work. A few minutes, maybe, but that comes with the territory.

Creating a backup copy

If it takes longer than a day to create an image, you should make backup copies. The reasoning is, if you invest lots of time in an image, you're that much worse off if you lose it. By creating backup copies — DogMeat.1, DogMeat.2, DogMeat.3, and so on, one for each day that you work on the project — you're that much less likely to lose mass quantities of edits. If some disk error occurs or you accidentally delete one or two of the files, one of the backups will probably survive the disaster, further protecting you from developing an ulcer or having to seek therapy.

At the end of the day, choose File⇨Save As. The Save dialog box appears, as when you first saved the image. Change the file name slightly and then click on the Save button. Way to be doubly protected!

You can also use the Photoshop Save a Copy command to make a backup copy of an image, but that command offers a few extra options specifically designed for saving images that have multiple layers. Ignore it for now. For more information on working with layers, see Chapter 15.

Photoshopper's Guide to File Formats

Even though the Format pop-up menu appears at the bottom of the Save dialog box — as if it were an afterthought or something — selecting a format is a critical decision. So you need to pay attention to the sections to come, even if the subject is a rather dry one — which it is. Get a Jolt cola if you need one, but don't skip this information.

What is a file format, anyway?

Glad you asked. A *file format* is a way of saving the electronic bits and pieces that make up a computer file. Different formats structure those bits and pieces differently. In Photoshop, you can choose from about a zillion file formats when you save your image to disk, which makes things a tad bit confusing.

Luckily, you can ignore most of the file format options. The Amiga IFF and Raw formats, for example, sacrifice colors and other image information, so avoid them. The Pixar, Targa, and Scitex CT formats are very sophisticated formats used by very sophisticated (and well-funded) creative types, so you can forget about those formats, too. In fact, you probably will have use for only five formats: TIFF, JPEG, EPS, PICT, and the native Photoshop format. (For the technically curious, native formats are explained in the sidebar, "Why are there so many different formats?") If you plan on publishing your image on the World Wide Web, you may also want to use the CompuServe GIF format at times, too.

The following sections explain the most important file formats and when to use them.

Why are there so many different formats?

Why don't we have just one format instead of dozens? Because back in the early days of home and office computing, every program saved its stuff in its own unique way. This unique way was dubbed the program's *native format*.

At first, programs couldn't decipher data that was stored in any format but their own. But over time, that changed. For example, PC Paintbrush was an early painting program in the DOS world, back before the Mac arrived on the scene. The native format for PC Paintbrush was called PCX. (Who knows what the X stands for? Xavier, maybe.) PC Paintbrush became so popular that a groundswell of images emerged in the PCX format. In an effort to attract users, other programs started supporting PCX, making it a de facto standard.

Photoshop supports PCX as well as BMP — the native format for Microsoft's Windows Paint —

and PixelPaint, which is the native format for, oddly enough, the PixelPaint program, the first color painting program on the Mac. However, it's very unlikely that you'll want to save an image in any of these native formats today. Although PCX and BMP are still used in some circles and do a fine job of saving images, they aren't supported by many other programs on the Mac. The PixelPaint format can only accommodate 256 colors, so you'd never want to use it unless someone specifically asked you to do so. Photoshop offers support for this format just in case you have an old PixelPaint image lying around.

Photoshop also offers its own native format, which can be a good option in some scenarios. For the lowdown on this format, see the section, "What about Photoshop's native format?" later in this chapter.

TIFF: The great communicator

One of the best and most useful formats for saving Photoshop images is TIFF (pronounced *tiph*), which stands for *Tagged Image File Format*. TIFF was developed to serve as a platform-independent standard so that both Macintosh and Windows programs could take advantage of it.

When you select the TIFF option from the Format pop-up menu and click on the Save button, Photoshop displays another dialog box, shown in Figure 6-2. In the area labeled Byte Order, you can tell Photoshop whether to save the TIFF image for use on the Mac or with a Windows program. Unless you're going to open your image in a Windows program, select Macintosh. (Why are these options labeled Byte Order? Just to confuse you.)

Figure 6-2:
The options
that appear
when you
save a
TIFF file.

The TIFF Options dialog box also offers a check box labeled LZW Compression. If you check the box, Photoshop compresses your image file so that it takes up less room on disk. Unlike some types of compression, LZW Compression doesn't sacrifice any data to make your file smaller. It's what's known as a *lossless compression scheme.*

Most programs that support TIFF also support LZW. For example, you can import a compressed TIFF image into either PageMaker or QuarkXPress. Only obscure programs don't support LZW, so there's really no reason not to select this option.

JPEG: The space saver

Photoshop also supports the JPEG (pronounced *jay peg*) format. JPEG stands for some Joint Photographers convention, but that doesn't really matter. What matters is that the JPEG format uses *lossy compression.* Lossy is the computer nerd's way of saying that stuff is lost during the compression process — namely, some of the data that makes up your image.

The good news, however, is that you probably won't miss what's not around anymore — sort of like when you were a kid and "lost" your little brother at the park. You may notice a slight difference in your on-screen image after you save the file using JPEG, but when the image is printed, the compression is virtually undetectable.

Like LZW compression, JPEG compression saves you lots of disk space. In fact, a JPEG image takes up less space on disk than a compressed TIFF file — half as much space, maybe a tenth as much, depending on your settings. JPEG isn't supported by as many programs as TIFF, but it's becoming more and more common.

So should you use JPEG or TIFF? My philosophy is this: Save in TIFF when you're editing an image. Then, when you think you're finished editing, save in JPEG at the Maximum setting. You generally won't see the results of JPEG right away. But editing an image can bring out its weaknesses, and JPEG definitely weakens an image. So it's best to go to JPEG after you finish editing. It's not a hard-and-fast rule — I've edited plenty of JPEG images without incident — but it's a good rule of thumb.

Also, if you want to distribute your image on the World Wide Web, you have to save it in either the JPEG or GIF format. TIFF isn't an option for Web publishing.

When you choose the JPEG option in the Save dialog box and press Return, the dialog box shown in Figure 6-3 appears.

Figure 6-3:
When saving a JPEG file, select the Maximum option or, if space is limited, High.

Here's a rundown of the options you need to worry about:

✔ The Quality pop-up menu lets you choose the amount of compression that is applied to your image and therefore the quality of your saved image. The higher the image quality, the less the file is compressed and the more space it takes on disk.

✔ The Quality option box and the slider bar beneath it give you other ways to choose your compression setting. The slider bar and option box give you access to 11 settings (0 through 10), whereas the pop-up menu gives you access to only 4. But unless you're a real control freak like me, you can just select one of the pop-up menu options.

✔ For print images, choose the Maximum or High option from the Quality pop-up menu. The Maximum option is best because it preserves the most image data, but High is okay if you're really short on disk space.

✔ If you will be publishing your image on the World Wide Web, choose the Medium option from the pop-up menu. The Medium option is the standard because it can retain a fair amount of image data while still substantially reducing file size. But before you save your image using this option, make a backup copy using the Maximum or High setting first. Because of how much image data is dumped with the Medium setting, you won't be able to successfully edit the image after you save it using that setting.

✔ Another option for images published on the Web is to save them as *progressive* JPEG files. A progressive image initially appears on the Web surfer's monitor at a very low quality and then improves as more and more image data is downloaded. If you want to save your image in this way, select the Progressive radio button at the bottom of the dialog box. The Scan pop-up menu lets you choose the number of intermediate images the browser displays before the image appears in full. Be aware that not all browsers support progressive images.

✔ If you want to save an image for the Web but you don't want to create a progressive image, choose the Baseline Optimized radio button. For regular print graphics — that is, those that aren't going to be distributed over the Web — use the default setting of Baseline Standard.

GIF: For Webbies only

GIF, which was developed for CompuServe specifically for transferring images via modem, is one of two options you can consider when you want to distribute your image online, whether on CompuServe, America Online, or the World Wide Web. (The other format is JPEG, discussed in the preceding section.)

Computer hacks are divided on how you pronounce GIF. Some folks swear that the proper pronunciation is with a hard *G* — as in one *t* short of a *gift.* Other experts insist that you say it with a soft *g,* so that the word sounds just like that famous brand of peanut butter. Regardless of which camp you decide to join, GIF is best used for high-contrast images, screen shots, and text. The biggest drawback to GIF is that it can only save images with 256 colors or less; its advantage is that it results in crisper image details than JPEG.

If your image contains more than 256 colors, choose Image⇨Mode⇨Indexed Color to reduce the number of colors before you can save in the GIF format. In the Indexed Color dialog box, choose Adaptive from the Palette pop-up menu. For Color Depth, start with the lowest possible setting (the smallest number of bits per pixel) and see what happens to your image. If it turns to muck, choose ⌘-Z to undo things and choose the next highest Color Depth setting. Use the lowest setting that keeps your image reasonably intact.

You need to do similar experimentation with the Dither option. The best choice is None, but if that setting wrecks your image, choose Diffusion. You can ignore the Colors setting entirely; Photoshop handles that one for you automatically.

When you save an image to the GIF format, you're presented with a dialog box containing just two radio buttons, Normal and Interlaced. The Interlaced setting results in an image that appears gradually when it is downloaded, like a progressive JPEG image. If you don't want your image to be downloaded in this way, choose Normal.

Meet GIF89a

Photoshop 4 includes a command on the File⇨Export menu that enables you to create a transparent GIF image for use on the World Wide Web. Using this command — which has the user-friendly name of GIF89a Export — you can make portions of an image transparent so that a background pattern on your Web page can be seen through the image.

After choosing the Indexed Color command to reduce your image to 256 colors, as described in the section "GIF: For Webbies only," choose File⇨Export⇨GIF89a Export. In the dialog box that appears, click on the image preview on each color that you want to make transparent. Or click on the color swatches at the bottom of the dialog box. ⌘-click on a color if you change your mind and want to make the color opaque again.

If you choose the Interlace check box, your image is drawn incrementally when a Web surfer downloads it, just like a progressive JPEG image.

After you press Return to exit the dialog box, Photoshop prompts you to save the image by displaying the familar Save dialog box. Give your image a name, specify where you want to store the image on disk, click on Save, and you're done.

The GIF format also enables you to create images that include transparent areas that allow other parts of your Web page to show through. If you want to give this trick a try, see the sidebar "Meet GIF89a."

EPS: The 1 percent solution

EPS (pronounced *E-P-S*) stands for *Encapsulated PostScript*. PostScript is a page-description language used by LaserWriters, Linotronic imagesetters, and hundreds of other printers. While TIFF and JPEG can save only images, the EPS format accommodates anything that the printer can print. Unfortunately, an EPS image takes up about three times as much disk space as the same image saved in the TIFF format — even more if the TIFF image is compressed.

For the most part, EPS is used by high-end professionals producing high-end projects. EPS is also the format to use if you want to create expert color separations from QuarkXPress. In other words, you can ignore the EPS format 99 percent of the time and use TIFF instead.

PICT: The generic picture format

Apple developed PICT as the primary format for Macintosh graphics. Just as EPS is based on the PostScript printer language, PICT is based on the QuickDraw screen language. Although you might assume that PICT would be the best option for Mac graphics, it can be a rather shaky format. Just about every Macintosh graphics program supports PICT, but support varies. PageMaker, for example, does a terrible job of printing imported PICT images.

I sometimes choose PICT if I am going to be using the image only in Photoshop, however, because it offers JPEG compression. Say that you select the PICT File option from the Format pop-up menu in the Save dialog box and press Return. Assuming that QuickTime is running — Apple's digital video system extension that installs with Photoshop — the dialog box shown in Figure 6-4 appears.

If you're saving a grayscale image, the Resolution options are 2, 4, and 8 bits per pixel instead of the 16 and 32 bit per pixel options shown in the figure. But regardless of which Resolution options you see in your dialog box, don't change them! Doing so deletes colors from your image and prevents you from accessing the JPEG options.

As for the JPEG compression options available to PICT files, they're different than those available to the regular JPEG format. PICT JPEG can cause more damage over time. It's nothing serious, just something to keep in mind. I wouldn't select any option other than JPEG (Maximum Quality) in this dialog box.

Figure 6-4:
The PICT
format
offers JPEG
compression
options.

What about Photoshop's native format?

The Format pop-up menu in the Save dialog box offers two different Photoshop options: Photoshop 2.0 and plain old Photoshop. The Photoshop 2.0 format is the one to use when you want to open your image in Version 2 of the program. The plain old Photoshop format is the format for Version 4. Photoshop 3 can also open images saved in the Photoshop format.

The Photoshop format is the only format that saves the layers in your image; all the others "flatten" (merge) the layers together. The Photoshop format is also the only format that can save grids and guides (explained in Chapter 3).

If you need to open a Photoshop 4 image in Version 2.5 of the program — or in a page layout or illustration format that only supports Version 2.5 Photoshop files, you should still use the Photoshop format. By default, the program saves a version of your image that can be opened by programs that recognize Version 2.5 files. But unless and until you need to take advantage of this feature — which is likely to be never — choose File➪Preferences➪Saving Files and deselect the 2.5 Compatibility check box in the Preferences dialog box. When the option is deselected, your images consume less space on disk.

Like TIFF, the Photoshop formats offer a lossless compression scheme. And Photoshop can open and save images faster in its native format than in any other format. But very few programs other than Photoshop support the native format. So use the native format when you don't plan on importing the image into another program and you don't need JPEG compression.

What format to use when

Ooh, you cheated, didn't you. You skipped right over the sections on how formats work and why they were invented. Instead of reading all that juicy background information I offered up — information that would help you make your own decision about which format to use — you want me to make the decision for you.

Okay, fine. You plunked down good money so that I would make things easy for you, so I suppose that I can give you a break just this once. Think of the following list as your Cliff's Notes to File Formats. Just don't blame me when you're standing around at a cocktail party and the discussion turns to JPEG compression versus TIFF, and you don't have an intelligent word to offer.

✔ If you are just going to use the image in Photoshop, save it in the Photoshop format. You can open images saved in this format in Version 3 as well as in Version 4. You can open images in Version 2.5 as well (if you turn on the 2.5 Compatibility check box in the Preferences dialog box, as discussed in the preceding section) but any layers, grids, and guides won't be available to you in Version 2.5.

✔ If your image contains layers (as explained in Chapter 15) and you want to preserve those layers, choose the Photoshop format.

✔ Use the Photoshop 2.0 format if you need to open an image in Version 2 of the program.

✔ If you are going to use the image in Photoshop only and you're short on disk space, try the PICT format.

✔ If you want to import your image into another program, use TIFF, as long as you have the available disk space.

✔ If you want to import your image into another program and you don't have the available disk space, use JPEG.

✔ If you want to import your image into a program that doesn't support either TIFF or JPEG, resort to EPS.

✔ If you're creating a photograph for online distribution, use JPEG. For high-contrast graphics or partially transparent images, use GIF.

Goodnight, Image, Don't Let the Programming Bugs Bite

To put Photoshop to bed for the night, choose File⇨Quit or press ⌘-Q. Photoshop may display a message asking you whether you want it to save the changes you made to your image. Unless you have some reason for doing otherwise, press Return to select the Save button. The program quits, leaving you back at the Finder.

If you don't want to save your changes, press the D key, which is the same as clicking on the Don't Save button. If you didn't mean to press ⌘-Q or you suddenly remember one last-minute thing you want to change, press ⌘-period or click on the Cancel button. This not only cancels any saving that might have occurred, but the quitting as well. Photoshop continues to run as if ⌘-Q were nothing more than a bad dream.

Chapter 7

Going to Hard Copy

● ●

In This Chapter

▶ Making sure that your printer is ready to go

▶ Selecting a printer on a network

▶ Previewing the image on the page

▶ Using the Page Setup command

▶ Printing multiple copies

▶ Making CMYK color separations

● ●

*I*n case you didn't already know this, *hard copy* is a term for the printed page. The on-screen image is just a figment of your computer's imagination. The final printed piece is something tangible that you can really sink your teeth into (assuming that you're extremely hungry).

In this chapter, I explain how to go from on-screen, imaginary image to hard copy. But I have to confess, there's a lot that I don't know. For example, I don't know what kind of printer you're using, I don't know what kind of cabling is installed, I don't even know where the printer is located in your home or office. In other words, I'm suffering from a terrific deficit of knowledge. With this in mind, I ask for your sympathy and understanding as I explain — very briefly — how to print from Photoshop using an everyday, generic printer.

For starters, I'll be totally rash and assume the following:

✔ You have a printer. If I've said it once, I've said it, I don't know, two or three times: You have to have a printer to print.

✔ Your printer is plugged in, it's turned on, and it doesn't have a 16-ton weight sitting on top of it. In other words, it works.

✔ The printer is properly connected to your computer. A cable running out of your computer and into your printer is a good sign.

✔ The proper printer software is installed on your computer.

✔ Your printer is stocked with ribbon, ink, toner, paper, film, chew toys, little bits of felt, springlike gizmos that go "bazoing," or whatever else is re-quired in the way of raw materials.

If you've used your printer before, everything is probably ready to go. But if something goes wrong, I advise that you call your local printer wizard and ask for assistance. Or you might walk into the boardroom and start wringing your hands and weeping in a cloying but professional way. This strategy has been known to produce the desired effects.

This May Be All You Need to Know

When things are in working order, printing is not a difficult process. Though it involves slightly more than picking up your mouse and saying "print" into it, it does not require a whole lot of preparation. In fact, a quick perusal of the following steps may be all you need to get up to speed:

1. **Turn on your printer.**

   And don't forget to remove that printer cozy your uncle knit for you.

2. **Select the printer you want to use with the Chooser.**

   If your Mac is on a network, you may have access to more than one printer. If not, skip this step. (By the way, the following sections in this chapter explain this step and others in more detail, should you need more information.)

3. **Check that the image fits on the page.**

   Press and hold on the page preview box in the lower-left corner of the image window to see a little preview of the printed page. The page preview box is just to the right of the magnification box. (If you can't remember where the preview box is located, flip back to Figure 3-3 for a refresher.)

   If the image doesn't fit on the page, or if you want to change its size or orientation, move on to Step 4. Otherwise, skip ahead to Step 5.

4. **Choose File⇨Page Setup or choose ⌘-Shift-P.**

   This command lets you change the size and orientation of the printed image. You can also change the printed size and resolution using Image⇨Image Size, as discussed in Chapter 4, but this command affects the image permanently, while the Page Setup command just affects how the image prints.

5. **Choose File⇨Save or press ⌘-S.**

   Although this step is only a precaution, it's always a good idea to save your image immediately before you print it because the print process is one of those ideal opportunities for your computer to crash. Your computer derives a unique kind of satisfaction by delivering works of art from the printer and then locking up at the last minute, all the while knowing that the image on disk is several hours behind the times. If you weren't the brunt of the joke, you'd probably think that it was amusing, too.

6. Choose File⇨Print or press ⌘-P.

The Print dialog box lets you request multiple copies of an image or print colors on separate sheets of paper.

7. Press Return.

Experts say that this is the easiest step. Well, one guy got a blister on the end of his finger, but otherwise the vote was unanimous.

Congratulations, you now have what is commonly known as a brand new, one gram, baby piece of output. But on the off chance that you're unclear on how a couple of the preceding steps work or you're simply interested in excavating every possible nugget of information from this book, I encourage you to probe the depths of the rest of this chapter.

Choosing a Printer

If you use the same printer day in and day out to produce pages of text and numbers, you probably don't need to worry about the Chooser. Provided with every Mac, this little program is designed to let you confirm the connection to your printer and select a different printer over a network. So unless you just want to make sure that everything's A-OK or you want to specify the exact printer you intend to use, skip to the next section.

To access the Chooser dialog box shown in Figure 7-1, choose the Chooser command from the Apple menu. The left side of the dialog box contains a bunch of icons that represents the kinds of printer drivers that are available to your system. Not to be confused with the drivers that allow you to knock golf balls into uncooperative printers, these drivers serve as a liaison between your computer and your printer.

- If you use a PostScript device — meaning a printer that supports the PostScript printer language — select the LaserWriter driver icon. Nearly every printer over $2,000 supports PostScript, which is without a doubt the professional printing standard.

- If you see a driver icon that matches your specific model of printer, select it. For example, I recently bought a portable HP DeskWriter 320 for use with my PowerBook. Figure 7-1 shows an icon labeled DW 300 Series 5.11, which happens to look just like my little printer. I'd be plum crazy not to select it.

- Some fax/modems allow you to print to remote fax machines over the phone lines. If you own a fax/modem and it's cabled up correctly, you may be able to select a driver icon for the modem, such as the GlobalFax icon in Figure 7-1.

Printer drivers   Networked printers

Figure 7-1:
You can
select the
kind of
printer you
want to use
from the
Chooser.

After you select a driver from the left-hand list, some additional options appear
on the right side of the dialog box.

- If you're on a network, you see a list of networked printers, as in Figure 7-1.
  Select the printer you want to use by clicking on it.

- If you're not on a network, you are more likely to see two icons labeled
  Select a Printer Port. The first icon represents the printer port; the second
  represents the modem port. Select the port into which the printer cable is
  plugged. More likely, your printer is hooked up to the printer port, but
  some people do use the modem port.

After you finish doing all that stuff, click on the close box on the left side of the
Chooser title bar. A message may appear telling you to confirm your settings
using the Page Setup command. Don't worry, the next section explains how to
do exactly that.

If any other message appears — one announcing that the printer is not available or has taken leave of its senses, for example — you very likely have a
cabling problem or your printer is not turned on. Otherwise, you're in business.

Getting Image and Paper in Sync

In addition to making sure that your computer and printer are on speaking terms, as discussed in the preceding section, you need to make sure that the image you want to print will actually fit on a piece of paper. To see whether all is well in this regard, click and hold on the page preview box in the lower-left corner of the image window. As shown in Figure 7-2, Photoshop displays a preview of how your image fits on your chosen paper size.

The white area in the page preview represents the size of the page; the rectangle with an X through it represents the image. (All right, so the image preview isn't particularly accurate when it comes to showing actual images, but it's good enough for showing the dimensions.) If the rectangle with an X fits entirely inside the white area, as in Figure 7-2, your image fits on the page. If the X exceeds the boundaries of the white area, the image is too big for the page and needs to be reduced. After you know whether the image fits or not, you can release your mouse button.

Figure 7-2: You can preview how the image fits on the page by clicking and holding on the page preview box (hidden by the preview in the figure).

Page preview — Image representation

If the image doesn't fit, you need to reduce it. The easiest way to accomplish this is to either reduce it or rotate it on the page. For example, if the image is wider than it is tall, you might want to print it out horizontally by rotating the page 90 degrees. Following are some of the options available to you:

✔ To rotate the image on the page, choose File⇨Page Setup or press ⌘-Shift-P to display the Page Setup dialog box. Though your dialog box may not look exactly like the one shown in Figure 7-3, you should find two Orientation icons, one with a guy standing up and another with a guy on his side like a felled tree. Select the guy on his side to rotate the image on the page.

Figure 7-3:
Not all Page Setup dialog boxes look the same, but most let you rotate and scale an image for printing purposes.

✔ The specific options found inside the Page Setup dialog box vary depending on the kind of printer you're using, but you can generally find a Reduce or Enlarge option box. Enter any percentage below 100 percent to reduce the dimensions of the printed image. The printer still prints all pixels in the image; the pixels are just smaller.

✔ If you can't find a Reduce or Enlarge option, you have to abandon the Page Setup dialog box and choose Image⇨Image Size instead. Be sure to deselect the Resample Image check box so that you don't affect the number of pixels in the image. Then increase the Resolution value or decrease the values in the Print Size Width and Height option boxes. (You can find a complete explanation of the Image Size dialog box in Chapter 4.)

After trying one of these options, you may want to click and hold on the page preview box again to see if you're making any progress. If the image still doesn't fit, move on to the second option and give it a try.

Keep in mind that any changes made inside the Page Setup dialog box have absolutely no effect on anything about your image except how it prints. You can't do any permanent damage via this particular dialog box, so feel free to change settings recklessly and without regard to personal safety.

Changes made inside the Image Size dialog box are another story. As I explain in Chapter 4, you can easily do permanent damage if you forget to deselect the Resample Image check box.

Sending the Image to the Printer

After you confirm that the image fits inside the page, choose File⇨Print or press ⌘-P. If the image is still too large for the page, an error message appears, asking whether you want to proceed. If the image fits, the Print dialog box appears, much like the one shown in Figure 7-4.

Figure 7-4: The mostly irrelevant Print dialog box.

```
Printer: "LaserWriter II NTX"                          8.1.1      [ Print ]

Copies: [1]      Pages: ◉ All    ○ From: [    ]  To: [    ]     [ Cancel ]

┌Paper Source─────────────────────┐  ┌Destination────┐
│ ◉ All  ○ First from: [Cassette ▼]│  │ ◉ Printer     │   [ Options ]
│ Remaining from: [Cassette ▼]     │  │ ○ File        │   [  Help   ]
└──────────────────────────────────┘  └───────────────┘

☐ Print Selected Area          Encoding: ○ ASCII ◉ Binary ○ JPEG
Print in: ○ Gray ◉ RGB ○ CMYK
```

What I love about the Print dialog box is that you can ignore almost all of it. Only a couple of options are the least bit useful:

- If you want to print more than one copy of the image, enter how many you want into the Copies option box.

- If you selected a portion of your image using one of the tools I don't get around to discussing until Chapter 12, you can print the selected area only by turning on the Print Selected Area check box. If you just want to take a quick look at an isolated area, this option can save time.

✔ When you're printing a full-color image, the Print In radio buttons — Gray, RGB, and CMYK — appear. If you have a color printer, leave this option set to RGB. If you're printing to a black-and-white device, you can speed things up by selecting Gray. Don't ever select CMYK.

✔ The CMYK option doesn't create color separations, incidentally. To accomplish that feat, read the next section.

That's it. Don't worry about the Pages options or the Encoding radio buttons or the Options button. Just click on the Print button or press Return, and you're off. Depending on the size of the image, it should print in a matter of a few minutes.

Printing CMYK Color Separations

So far, I've explained how to print *composite* images, in which all colors are combined together on a single page. Unfortunately, composite images are a poor solution if you intend to make more than, say, 50 copies of an image. Oh, sure, you can print multiple pages directly from your color printer or you can reproduce them with one of those mondo-expensive photocopiers, but the colors don't always fare very well, and the cost per page is exceedingly high. Using either solution, a print run of 1,000 copies could cost you $500 or more, and you wouldn't get professional quality for your money.

The more accepted solution is to print color separations. You print four pages, one each for the primary printing colors cyan, magenta, yellow, and black. Then you let your commercial printer — the person, not the machine — combine the color separations to create mass quantities of colorful pages. This process is the same one used to create magazines, newspapers, and other professional color publications.

To print color separations of a full-color image from Photoshop, you have to go through these steps:

1. **Save your image to disk.**

   Before diving into CMYK, you want to make sure that your RGB image is backed up and safe from harm. Chapter 6 provides assistance with the saving process if you need help.

2. **Choose Image⇨Mode⇨CMYK Color.**

   Photoshop converts the image from the world of RGB to the world of CMYK. After the conversion, you have a four-channel image with one channel each for cyan, magenta, yellow, and black. You can even view the channels if you want by pressing ⌘-1, ⌘-2, ⌘-3, and ⌘-4. (This channel thing is explained in Chapter 5.)

3. **Choose File⇨Page Setup, select the check boxes shown selected in Figure 7-5, and press Return.**

   For the record, select Calibration Bars, Registration Marks, Corner Crop Marks, Center Crop Marks, and Labels. These five options print a series of alignment markings that will prove very useful to your commercial printer. (If you're printing to a non-Postscript printer, some of these options may not be available; select the ones that are.)

   Be sure to select *all* these check boxes. If you miss any of them, your commercial printer may have problems lining up the images on the press, and your pages may come out like a page from the Sunday comics.

4. **Press ⌘-P, select the Print Separations check box, and press Return.**

   The Print Separations check box takes the place of the Print In radio buttons when you print a CMYK image. Selecting this check box (as shown in background dialog box in Figure 7-5) tells Photoshop to print each channel from the image to a separate page.

Figure 7-5:
Check these
check boxes
to print
color
separations
from
Photoshop.

When printed, each page looks like a standard black-and-white printout, but don't let that worry you. When you take the pages to your commercial printer, a technician will photographically transfer your printouts to sheets of metal called *plates*. Each plate is inked with cyan, magenta, yellow, or black ink. The technician prints all the pages with the cyan plate first; then runs the pages by the magenta plate; then the yellow plate; and finally, the black plate. The inks mix together to form a rainbow of greens, violets, oranges, and other colors.

For example, Figure 7-6 shows four color separations for the full-color photograph that appears in Color Plate 5-1. (Compare these separations to the red, green, and blue channels I included back in Figure 5-2 to get a feel for the dramatic changes that occur when you convert from RGB to CMYK.) Color Plate 7-1 shows the separations as they appear when inked with cyan, magenta, yellow, and black. I also show a few examples of how the inks look when combined.

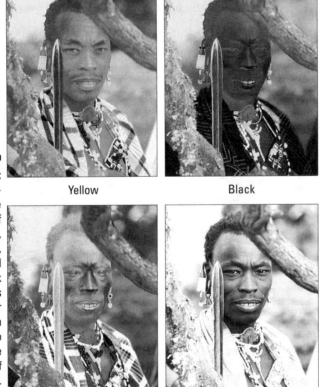

Cyan   Magenta

Yellow   Black

Figure 7-6: The black-and-white contents of the cyan, magenta, yellow, and black channels as they appear when printed to separate sheets of paper.

Part III
Tiptoe through the Toolbox

The 5th Wave By Rich Tennant

NATIONAL ENQUIRER PHOTO IMAGING WORKSHOP

"Remember, your Elvis should appear bald and slightly hunched -- nice Big Foot, Brad -- keep your two-headed animals in the shadows and your alien spacecrafts crisp and defined."

In this part . . .

In real life, a paintbrush is a fairly static tool. You dip it in
paint and drag it across the canvas; in return, it paints a
line. The line varies depending on how much paint you
dabbed onto the brush and how hard you press, but your
options are limited. In Photoshop, on the other hand, a
single tool is capable of literally hundreds of variations. You
can change the size of the brush tip, the angle of the brush,
the translucency of the paint, and the way colors mix, all at
the drop of a hat. You can even paint straight lines and
change the brush strokes from hard-edged to soft.

If painting isn't your primary interest, Photoshop provides
an assortment of editing tools for smearing colors, changing
their focus, lightening or darkening pixels, and adjusting the
intensity of colors. You'll also find a rubber stamp tool for
cleaning up dust and hairs on an image and an eraser for
eliminating mistakes. All these tools go beyond anything
that's available in real life, providing a degree of flexibility
and forgiveness that natural media simply do not offer.

But my favorite thing about Photoshop is the convenience.
No wiping up spills, no soaking brushes, and no opening
windows to clear the fumes. You just paint what you want
and erase what you don't want. Everything you do on-screen
is imaginary — until you print the image, you haven't
changed one scrap of real-life material — so spills, stains,
and fumes are a thing of the past. And when it comes time to
clean up for the day, you just press ⌘-Q and you're finished.
Who says things aren't better now than they used to be?

Chapter 8

Paint Me Young, Beautiful, and Twisted

· ·

· ·

*O*kay, here's a big assumption: As a novice or casual Photoshop user, you fall into one of two camps: artist or nonartist. Some people are so comfortable with a pencil or paintbrush that they feel like they were born with the device. But a much larger group of Photoshop users falls into a camp that modern sociologists call "artistically challenged."

Take this quick test to determine where you fall:

> ✔ After doodling in the phone book, are you so horrified by the results that you rip out the page, pour ketchup on it, and feed it to your dog?

> ✔ When you're asked to draw a map to your house, do you try to lie your way out of the situation by asserting that you have no idea where your house is located and you doubt very seriously that you live anywhere?

> ✔ Do you have recurring dreams in which you suddenly remember that today is the day your final project is due in the art class you've forgotten to attend all year? And as you attempt to quickly paint a lounging model, you notice that the model is fully clothed and you're the one who's naked?

If you answered "Yes" to any of the above questions, you can safely assume that you belong to the nonartist camp. If you answered "Yes" to any two of the questions, you are so firmly entrenched in the nonartistic tradition that completing a dot-to-dot picture seems like an immense and terrifying project. And if you answered "Yes" to two of the questions and "Oh, wow, I had that exact dream just last night!" to the third, I am obliged by the code of computer ethics to ask you one more question: Are you sure that your analyst isn't overcharging you?

Whatever your level of artistic skill, though, there will probably come a time when you'll want to rub a couple of the Photoshop painting tools against an image. Sure, it'll be scary. But you'll be prepared, thanks to this chapter.

Doodling with the Pencil, Paintbrush, and Airbrush

Photoshop offers just three painting tools, the bare minimum for artists and nonartists alike. Shown in Figure 8-1, they work like so:

- ✔ The pencil tool draws hard-edged lines of any thickness.
- ✔ The paintbrush draws soft lines with slightly blurry edges to create more natural transitions.
- ✔ The airbrush paints soft lines like the paintbrush. The only difference is that the airbrush pumps out color continuously even when you hold it in place — as long as the mouse button is down. By contrast, the pencil and paintbrush tools only paint as you drag.

You can select each of the painting tools from the keyboard. Press A to select the airbrush, B to select the paintbrush, and Y to select the pencil. In Photoshop 3, the P key selected the pencil tool. But that keyboard shortcut is now assigned to the pen tool, which earned a spot in the toolbox in Version 4.

The pen tool, by the way, doesn't draw beautiful, flowing lines that look as if they're emanating from a kazillion-dollar status pen. In Photoshop, you use the pen tool to create *paths*. Paths enable you to select a portion of your image by creating a sort of connect-the-dots outline. Because paths are an advanced and, frankly, frustrating topic — geared only for hard-core users — I don't cover them in this book.

By default, Photoshop displays a little paintbrush, airbrush, or pencil cursor when you select the painting tools. If you press the Caps Lock key, however, the cursor changes to a crosshair cursor that makes it easier to see what you're doing. Use the crosshair when the standard cursor gets in your way. Press Caps Lock again to return to the standard cursor.

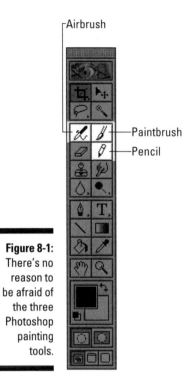

Airbrush

Paintbrush

Pencil

Figure 8-1:
There's no
reason to
be afraid of
the three
Photoshop
painting
tools.

If you prefer, you can make your cursor match the brush size exactly. (The upcoming section "Switching the brush size" explains how to change brush sizes.) To make the cursor reflect the brush size, press ⌘-K to display the Preferences dialog box. Then choose Display & Cursors from the top pop-up menu or press ⌘-3 to get to the cursor options. Select Brush Size from the Painting Cursors radio buttons and press Return.

The painting tools are small, nonpoisonous, and good with children. So why not take them for a walk and see how you like them? The following steps show you how to use the paintbrush, pencil, and airbrush to create the friendly Mr. Sun image shown in Figure 8-4 (go ahead, flip forward to take a look).

1. **Choose File⇨New (⌘-N) to create a new canvas.**

   Photoshop displays a dialog box that asks what size to make the new canvas. The dialog box offers Width, Height, and Resolution options, just like the Image Size dialog box discussed in Chapter 4.

2. **Make the canvas about 400 pixels wide by 400 pixels tall.**

That's about 5 $\frac{1}{2}$ by 5 $\frac{1}{2}$ inches with a Resolution value of 72 ppi or 4 by 4 inches with a Resolution of 100 ppi. Alternatively, you can select Pixels from the Width and Height pop-up menus, enter 400 into each, and forget about the Resolution value. Also, choose the RGB Color option from the Mode pop-up menu.

3. Press Return.

The new empty canvas appears in a new window.

4. Select the paintbrush tool.

Click on its icon in the toolbox or press the B key. That's B for buff, as in, "Boy howdy, Biff, this brush is beaucoup buff!" That's what the programmers told me, anyway.

5. Draw a circle in the middle of your new canvas.

A rude approximation of a circle is fine. Experts agree that a lumpy circle has more personality.

6. Now paint some rays coming off the circle.

Figure 8-2 shows more or less how your image should look so far.

Figure 8-2:
The beginnings of a sun, drawn exclusively with the paintbrush tool.

7. Now select the pencil tool.

To access the pencil from the keyboard, press Y, as in "Yellow number 2."

8. Draw a little face inside the sun.

Using the pencil, you get hard-edged lines, as in Figure 8-3.

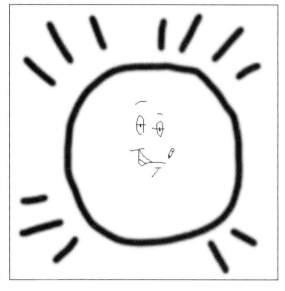

Figure 8-3:
A face
drawn with
the pencil
tool.

9. **Select the airbrush tool.**

   Press A for . . . hey! Here's a shortcut that actually makes sense.

10. **Change the foreground color to orange.**

    Use the RGB slider bars in the Color palette (press F6 to display the palette). Max out the R slider to 255, set the G slider to 150, and leave the B slider at 0.

11. **Click and hold — without moving your mouse — inside the sun.**

    Notice that the airbrush continuously pumps out paint. Neither the paintbrush nor the pencil do this.

12. **Paint some shading in the lower-right region of the sun.**

    Figure 8-4 shows what I mean. The airbrush is useful for shading images. Of course, the real sun can't possibly have a shadow, but it doesn't have a face either, so I think that we can allow room for some personal expression.

That's good enough for now. You may want to save this image because I come back to it later in this chapter. Then again, if something goes wrong and you don't save the sun, no biggie. You can always re-create it or experiment with a different image.

Remember that at any stage in the previous exercise — or during any other painting mission you may embark on — you can eliminate the last brush stroke by choosing Edit⇨Undo or pressing ⌘-Z. Everyone makes mistakes, and the Undo command is there to correct them.

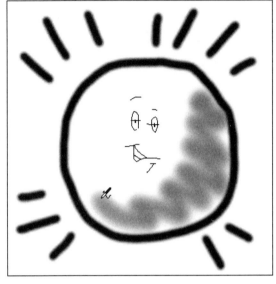

Figure 8-4:
Use the airbrush to paint a highly unrealistic shadow on the sun.

Performing Special Painting-Tool Tricks

Dragging with a tool inside the image window is obviously the most common way to paint in Photoshop. But it's not the only way, as the following list makes clear:

✔ To create a perfectly straight line, click at one point in the image with any of the three painting tools and Shift-click at another. Photoshop automatically creates a straight line between the two points.

✔ Continue Shift-clicking at various points in the image to create a straight-sided polygon. This method is great for creating triangles, five-pointed stars, and all sorts of other geometric shapes.

✔ To create a straight line that is exactly vertical or horizontal, click and hold with one of the painting tools, press and hold the Shift key, and then drag with the tool while the Shift key remains down. In other words, press Shift immediately after you begin to drag and hold Shift throughout the length of the drag. If you release the Shift key while dragging, the line returns to its naturally free-form and wiggly ways.

✔ You can also use the line tool to draw straight lines. But using the Shift key in combination with the painting tools is usually a better option, because the painting tools give you more flexibility. You can vary the softness of your lines if you use the painting tools, but you can't if you use the line tool. The only time I use the line tool is to create lines with arrowheads at the end. To create this kind of line, double-click on the line tool in the toolbox to display the Line Tool Options palette, which contains options that enable you to specify the placement of the arrowhead, the shape of the arrowhead, and the width of your line. Then drag with the tool to create the line.

✔ Option-click to lift a color from the image. Then drag to start painting with that color. (As you may recall from Chapter 5, pressing Option when you're using a painting tool accesses the eyedropper.)

Choosing Your Brush

If the preceding two sections covered everything there is to know about the painting tools, Photoshop would be a royal dud. But as we all know, Photoshop is not a dud — far from it — so there must be more to the painting tools than I've shown you so far. (This is classic Sherlock Holmes-style deductive reasoning at work here.)

You can modify all three tools to a degree that no mechanical pencil or conventional paintbrush can match. For starters, you can change the size and shape of the tip of the tool, as explained in the next few sections. You can draw thick strokes one moment and then turn around and draw thin strokes the next, all with the same tool.

Switching the brush size

To change a tool tip — called a brush size, or just plain brush — for a different one, choose Window⇨Show Brushes or press the F5 key. Photoshop displays the Brushes palette, shown in Figure 8-5. Here you can find a total of 16 brush sizes (assuming default settings), all free for the taking.

Most brush size icons are shown at actual size, but the last four are too large to fit inside their little boxes. The numbers below the icons represent the diameters of the brushes. (In case that year of high-school geometry has altogether removed itself from your brain, diameter is merely the width of a circle measured from side to opposite side.)

To change the brush size associated with the pencil, paintbrush, or airbrush tool, select the desired tool and then click on an option in the Brushes palette. The left column of Figure 8-6 shows how each of the predefined brushes affects the performance of the paintbrush tool. (In each case, an icon from the Brushes palette is shown directly to the left of a stroke created with that brush.) Notice that the first six brushes have soft edges, while the remaining ten have downright blurry edges.

Figure 8-5:
The Brushes
palette lets
you switch
out one size
brush for
another.

In Photoshop, soft edges are said to be *antialiased* (pronounced *an-tie-ay-lee-ast*), while blurry edges are *feathered*. Both terms are proof positive that computer professionals actually don't want to be understood by the greater public. They prefer to speak in their own private code.

Figure 8-6 also shows the effect of some of the brushes on the pencil and airbrush tools. As you can see, the pencil tool draws a harsh, jagged line no matter which brush you select. Even the feathered brushes produce jagged lines when used with the pencil. The airbrush generally produces softer lines than the paintbrush.

Making your own brush

You might think that 16 brushes would be enough to keep you happy well into your declining years. But I assure you, one day you'll want a brush size that's a little thicker than Option A and a little thinner than Option B. You'll have to modify one or the other to come up with a custom brush of your own.

To edit a brush, you can select one of the options in the Brushes palette and then choose the Brush Options command from the palette menu. But I recommend that you just double-click on a brush icon and be done with it. In response to your double-click, Photoshop displays the Brush Options dialog box, shown in Figure 8-7. Here's how you modify the brush:

- ✔ Drag the Diameter slider to make the brush bigger or smaller. If you know the exact width value, enter it into the option box on the right side of the slider. This value is measured in pixels.

- ✔ The Hardness value represents the blurriness of the brush size. A value of 100 percent is soft, like the first six options in the Brushes palette. Anything else is progressively fuzzier. The ten feathered options in the Brushes palette have Hardness values of 0 percent.

- ✔ Don't change the Spacing value. And don't even think about turning off the Spacing check box. The Spacing option determines how many dollops of paint are applied to your canvas and is better left unmolested.

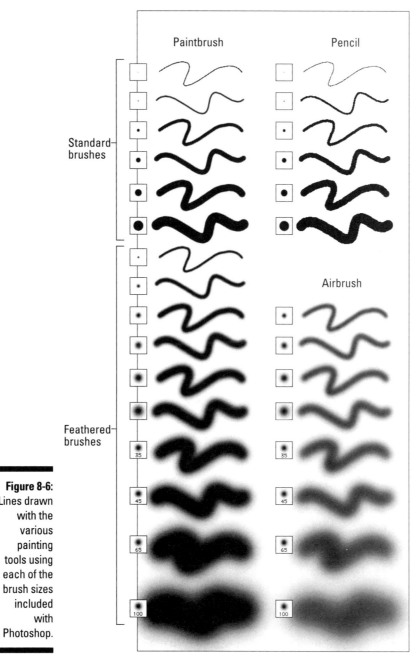

Figure 8-6:
Lines drawn with the various painting tools using each of the brush sizes included with Photoshop.

Figure 8-7:
The inner
workings of
a brush size.

Drag to rotate   Drag to change roundness

✔ Before I tell you about the Angle option, which comes next, I need to explain how Roundness works. (You see, the Angle value doesn't have any effect unless you first change the Roundness value.) The Roundness option lets you make the brush oval instead of round. A value of 100 percent is absolutely circular, as are all the predefined brushes; anything less results in a shape that is shorter than it is wide.

✔ If you want an oval brush to be taller than it is wide or some other variation on its present state, you can rotate it by changing the Angle value. Keep in mind that 360 degrees represents one complete counterclockwise turn, so 90 degrees is a quarter-turn, 180 degrees is a half-turn, –90 degrees is a clockwise quarter-turn, and so on.

✔ I never use the Angle and Roundness option boxes to change the values. Instead, I use that diagram in the lower-left corner of the dialog box. Drag one of the two circular handles on either side of the circle to make the brush oval. To rotate the brush, either drag the gray arrowhead or just click at the position where you want the arrow to point. The labels in Figure 8-7 tell the story.

As you change the settings, the preview box in the lower-right corner of the dialog box shows what the brush will look like. If the diameter of the brush is too large for the preview to fit in its box — 74 pixels or larger — Photoshop automatically reduces the preview and displays a zoom ratio above the box. A zoom ratio of 1:2, for example, means that you're seeing the preview at half size.

When you finish editing the brush, press Return to accept your changes.

Going nuts with the Brushes palette

Whenever I explain some feature or other associated with Photoshop, I'm tempted to say, "But wait, there's more!" like some daft Ginsu Knife salesman. But that's because there always is more. Photoshop is never satisfied to supply you with anything short of everything. You have to admire that in a program.

Here's what I mean:

- ✔ You don't need to manually click on a brush icon in the Brushes palette to select it. You can change the brush size from the keyboard, even when the Brushes palette is hidden. Press the right bracket key ( ]) to select the next brush in the Brushes palette. Press the left bracket key ([ ) to select the previous brush.

- ✔ To select the very first brush size option — something that comes in especially handy when using the pencil tool — press Shift-[To select the last option, press Shift-].

- ✔ To delete a brush size option from the palette, ⌘-click on it. (When you press the ⌘ key, you get a miniature pair of scissors. That's the way Photoshop tells you that you're ready to clip a brush into oblivion.)

- ✔ To add a new brush icon, click in the empty area in the lower-right corner of the Brushes palette. The dialog box from Figure 8-7 appears, though it's titled New Brush instead of Brush Options. Change the settings as desired and press Return.

- ✔ You can load additional custom brushes from disk by choosing the Load Brushes command from the palette menu. Go inside the Photoshop folder; then inside the Goodies folder and then inside the Brushes & Patterns folder, and you find a file called Assorted Brushes. That's a fun one. Click on Open to add the custom brushes to the Brushes palette.

- ✔ To get rid of any changes made to the brush size options in the Brushes palette, choose Reset Brushes from the palette menu. After the message appears, click on the OK button or press Return.

Exploring More Painting Options

The Options palette represents the heart and soul of the Photoshop tool modification options. While the Brushes palette controls only one aspect of a painting tool, the Options palette lets you modify tools in a whole bunch of ways. You can modify nearly every tool in the toolbox to some extent using the Options palette.

Ogling the Options palette

To get to the Options palette, you can choose Window⇨Show Options. Or you can press F8 and then click on the Options tab in the Info palette. Both of those methods are the sucker's routes for displaying the Options palette. Here are two better ways:

- ✔ Double-click on the toolbox icon for the tool you want to modify.
- ✔ If the tool you want to modify is already selected, just press the Return key. Photoshop not only displays the Options palette, it highlights the first option box in the palette so that you can enter a new value without selecting the option box.

Figure 8-8 shows the Paintbrush Options palette that appears when the paintbrush is active. With a few exceptions, these options are the same ones that appear when the pencil and airbrush tools are selected. Here's how they work:

- ✔ The pop-up menu in the upper-left corner of the palette provides access to a bunch of different brush modes, which control how the foreground color applied by the tool mixes with the existing colors in the image. The modes have confusing and seemingly meaningless names such as Multiply, Hard Light, and Difference, so beginners tend to avoid them like the plague. I show you some fun tricks you can perform with some of the modes in the next section.

Figure 8-8:
The Options panel is headquarters for modifying the painting tools.

Navigator	Inf	**Paintbrush Options**	▶
Exclusion ▼	Opacity:	100%
☐ Fade: 0	steps to	Transparent ▼
Stylus Pressure: ☐ Size ☐ Color ☐ Opacity
☐ Wet Edges

- ✔ Available when you use the pencil or paintbrush, the Opacity slider bar controls the translucency of the foreground color. A setting of 100 percent ensures that the paint is opaque, so that you can't see the colors underneath. (When you use a feathered brush, the edges are translucent even at 100 percent, but the center is opaque.) Any Opacity setting lower than 100 percent makes the brush translucent.

✔ If you're still a little fuzzy on how the Opacity slider works, it may be because you're a visual learner. Figure 8-9 shows four lines drawn with the paintbrush, two using a standard soft brush and two using a feathered brush. In each case, one line is set to 100 percent Opacity and the other is set to 40 percent.

Standard brush, 100%

40%

Feathered brush, 100%

40%

Figure 8-9: Here's what it looks like when you paint over sea anemone at different Opacity settings.

✔ When the airbrush is selected, the Opacity slider bar changes to the Pressure slider bar. Rather than producing translucent lines at lower settings, the airbrush applies less paint. It's as if you tightened the nozzle on a real airbrush.

✔ You can change the Opacity or Pressure value in 10-percent increments by pressing a number key. As long as one of the painting tools is selected, pressing 9 changes the Opacity to 90 percent, 8 changes it to 80 percent, and so on. Press the 0 key to change the Opacity back to 100 percent. If you want a more precise setting — say, 75 percent — just type the value quickly.

✔ Fade does not rank among the most useful Photoshop options. It fades out the line over the course of several "steps," which are those dollops of paint I discuss a few pages back, in the context of the Spacing option in the Brush Options dialog box. Skip it.

✔ The Stylus Pressure check boxes affect how pressure-sensitive tablets work in Photoshop. But if you've never even seen a pressure-sensitive tablet, let alone have one hooked up to your computer, don't give these options another thought.

✔ The Wet Edges check box appears only when the paintbrush tool is selected. When selected, this option makes your lines translucent with dark edges, as if they were drawn with a magic marker. Give it a try. For a variation on the effect, choose the Multiply mode from the brush mode pop-up menu.

✔ When the pencil is selected, the check box changes to Auto Erase. This option draws in the background color whenever you click or drag on a pixel painted in the foreground color (the accepted practice in other painting programs). It's very useful for making touch-ups with the single-pixel brush — click to add the foreground color, click again to change it to the background color. I almost always leave this option on because it lets you add and erase color with a single tool.

Experimenting with brush modes

Of all the controls in the Options panel, the brush modes in the pop-up menu make the least sense. Don't worry, I'm not going to list every one of them and explain how it works. That would just fry your brain, and you need your brain for other chapters. Instead, I demonstrate a few specific effects you can achieve using brush modes and let you experiment with the others at your own pace.

For example, consider the sun image shown back in Figure 8-4. Suppose that you want to color in the sun with yellow and the sky with blue.

The problem is, if you try to color in the sun and sky with one of the painting tools — even the airbrush — you end up covering the face inside the sun and the rays outside the sun. You can't fix the problem by lowering the Opacity value because it just results in washed out colors, and you still obscure some of the sun's detail.

The two images in Color Plate 8-1 show what I'm talking about. In the left image, I've painted in the sun and sky with the paintbrush tool at 100 percent Opacity. Obviously a bad move. In the right image, I changed the Opacity to 40 percent and tried again. It looks like I smeared chalk all over the image. Yuk.

The solution is to select a brush mode. Change the Opacity back to 100 percent by pressing the 0 (zero) key. Then select Multiply from the brush modes pop-up menu in the Options palette. Miraculously, you can now paint both sky and sun without covering up the rays and the face. This is because the Multiply option darkens colors as if you had painted with water color. It mixes the colors together to create darker colors. The top left example in Color Plate 8-2 shows the result.

Here are some other brush modes that you may find interesting:

- ✔ The Screen mode is the exact opposite of Multiply. Rather than mixing colors together to create darker colors, you mix them together to create lighter colors. In the upper-right example of Color Plate 8-2, I was able to apply color exclusively inside the black outlines and orange shadow. When I painted over white areas, nothing happened, because any color mixed with white just makes more white.

- ✔ Does that make sense? Let me take another stab at it. Multiply mixes colors as if they were pigments, which is why the colors get darker. (Remember my discussion of CMYK colors from Chapter 5? Well, it's just like that.) By contrast, Screen mixes colors as if they were lights — just like RGB colors — which is why they get lighter.

- ✔ The Overlay mode darkens dark colors and lightens light colors, resulting in a heightening of contrast. In the case of our sun, Overlay creates halos around the black lines because it darkens the inside of the lines and lightens the feathered edges. The bottom-left example in Color Plate 8-2 shows what I'm talking about.

- ✔ The Difference brush mode is the loopiest mode of them all and the most likely to surprise you. It creates a photo-negative effect by mixing colors and finding their opposites. Check out the final example in Color Plate 8-2 to see the resulting plum sun against a tomato sky. Way cool.

- ✔ You can also have some fun experiementing with Difference's cousin, Exclusion. It sends all blacks to white, all whites to black, and all medium colors to gray.

- ✔ Use the Color brush mode to colorize grayscale images or change the color of portions of RGB images. Suppose that you want to change the color of the sky in the upper-left example of Color Plate 8-2 from blue to green. You can't use the Normal mode because that would wipe out the rays and the other lines. And you can't use Multiply again because that would further darken the sky. The answer is the Color mode, which replaces a color with the foreground color without harming underlying detail.

- ✔ The Color Dodge and Color Burn brush modes offer an interesting new twist on the dodge and burn tools discussed in Chapter 9. In case you haven't discovered the dodge and burn tools yet, you drag with the dodge tool to lighten a portion of your image and drag with the burn tool to darken a portion of your image. If you use one of the painting tools and the Color Dodge mode, you can both lighten your image and infuse it with color. Using Color Burn, you can darken and infuse with color. For example, to darken your image and give it a greenish tint, you would paint with green using the Color Burn brush mode.

- ✔ To paint normally again, just select the Normal brush mode.

I'd rate six of the brush modes discussed above — Multiply, Screen, Overlay, Difference, Color, and Normal — as super-useful, the kinds of modes you want to get to know on a first-name basis. Exclusion, Color Dodge, and Color Burn are also worth some attention. The others aren't nearly so useful. In fact, they're mostly boring and obscure. With that in mind, I encourage you to freely experiment with the ones discussed here to the exclusion of all the others.

If brush modes seem a little daunting at first, don't give up. Just keep on plugging away. Remember, everything's daunting at some time. Heck, walking upright on two legs once seemed impossible, and yet look how well you do that today. Sure, not as well as some folks, but you're still learning. Keep your chin up.

Chapter 9
Making a Mockery of Reality

*B*ack in the old days, retouching a photograph was a formidable task. If you wanted to remove the reflection from someone's glasses, sharpen the focus of a detail, or tidy up a wrinkle or two, you had to actually take paint or airbrush to the photo and hope for the best. Anyone short of a trained professional would more often than not make a complete mess of the project and wish to heck it had never been started. Even the pros found it difficult to match flat colors on a palette to the ever-changing landscape of a photograph.

The beauty of Photoshop is that you can paint not only with specific colors — as explained in the previous chapter — but also with colors and details already found in the image. Using the editing tools — smudge, blur, sharpen, dodge, burn, and sponge — you can subtly adjust the appearance of pixels by shifting them around, boosting contrast between them, or lightening and darkening them. The results are edits that blend in with their surroundings.

With the Photoshop crop tool and Image⇨Crop command, you can also snip away unwanted portions of your image. Never before has it been so easy to cut relatives you hate out of your family photos.

Photoshop not only enables you to retouch images in ways that traditional photographic techniques simply don't allow, but Photoshop also offers a built-in safety net. You can undo any change you make or simply revert back to your original image if you don't like how your retouched image turns out. In other words, Photoshop is a real pleasure for modern retouching enthusiasts. After you finish this chapter, you'll be so inspired to enhance and modify photographic details that you'll welcome problem images with open arms.

Trimming Excess Gunk off the Edges

In Chapter 4, I explain how to change the size of your image without changing the elements therein — in other words, how to turn that 8-x-10 wedding photograph into a nifty wallet-size snapshot without trimming off anyone's vital body parts. But suppose that your spouse up and runs off to Lagos with your next-door neighbor? What do you do then? Why, you use the crop tool to cut the cretin out of the picture, that's what.

The sharp edges of the crop tool

Novice photographers have a habit of worrying about getting too much imagery into their pictures. This can be a dangerous concern. In your effort to cut out background flack, you may overcompensate and cut off Grandma's head or the right half of little Joey's body. The fact is, it's better to have too much stuff in your photos than too little, for the simple reason that excess stuff can be cut away, but missing stuff has to be reshot. Since photography was invented, production artists have been taking knives and scissors to just about every image that passes over their light tables in an effort to clip away the extraneous gook around the edges and home in on the real goods. Called *cropping,* this technique is so pervasive that professional photographers purposely shoot subjects from too far away knowing that someone, somewhere, is going to slice the image and make it right.

Inside Photoshop, you can cut away the unpalatable parts of an image using the crop tool. The crop tool used to have its own single-family home in the toolbox but now is forced to share a cramped apartment with the marquee tools in the top-left corner of the toolbox. To select the crop tool without messing with the toolbox, press C.

The crop tool has changed a lot since the last version of Photoshop. Here's how to use the new, improved crop tool:

1. Drag with the tool around the portion of the image you want to retain.

In Figure 9-1, I dragged around the floating spaceman. A dotted rectangle called a *marquee* follows your drag to clearly show the crop boundaries. Don't worry if you don't surround your image elements just right; you get the chance to edit the boundary in the next step.

"Photo-Retouching menace spreads wave of panic"

A certain line of popular logic argues that because of computer programs such as Photoshop, we as viewers have no idea which portions of a photograph to believe and which not to believe. But the truth is, photo manipulation is anything but new. Folks have been retouching photographs throughout the latter half of the previous century and all of this one. Old magazines, for example, are rampant with flagrantly augmented advertisements and subtly adjusted editorial photographs. These sorts of changes have generally been accepted as an ethical synthesis of photography and art.

That's fine, goes the argument, but now the edits are incredibly believable and sometimes even impossible to detect. Well, I hate to burst a bubble, but today's startling fiction is tomorrow's obvious fakery. In other words, viewer sophistication improves over time. Can you imagine being frightened half to death by a radio broadcast of "War of the Worlds" or shocked and amazed by the realism of *The Creature from the Black Lagoon*? And yet, these were exactly the reactions of previous generations. Even relatively recent films such as *Star Wars* and *Jaws* are beginning to show their age. Darth Vader wears a cheesy plastic mask with fingerprints all over it, and the mechanical great white shark appears limited to two movements — bite and blink.

Just as special-effects engineers are constantly raising the bar and making their predecessors look bad, future image-editing techniques will put current solutions to shame. So despite what you may hear about the terrifying miracles of computer technology, don't be surprised if the masterpiece of seamless image editing that you create today gets mixed reactions several years from now. "Gips, Gramps," your granddaughter may react (employing a bit of kiddy vocabulary that should hit full stride around 2025), "That's so fakey!"

If you press the Spacebar during your drag, Photoshop stops resizing the crop boundary and starts moving the entire boundary. This technique can be helpful when you're trying to position the boundary precisely. (You can also move the boundary after you create it, though.)

2. **Drag the crop boundaries as desired.**

   After you release your mouse button, Photoshop displays square handles around the edges of the marquee, as shown in Figure 9-1. If the marquee is not the right size, drag a handle to change the crop boundary. Your cursor changes to a double-headed arrow when you place it over a handle, indicating that you have the go-ahead to drag the handle. You can drag as many handles as you please — one at a time, of course — before cropping the image.

   If you move the cursor outside the crop boundary, the cursor changes to a curved, double-headed arrow. Dragging then rotates the crop boundary.

Handle   Resize cursor   Crop boundary

Figure 9-1:
Drag the
square
handles to
change the
crop
boundary.

3. **After you get the crop boundary the way you want it, double-click inside the boundary to crop the image.**

   Or just press Return. Photoshop throws away all pixels outside the crop boundary, as shown in Figure 9-2. If you rotated the crop boundary in Step 2, Photoshop rights the rectangular area and thus rotates the image, as illustrated in Figure 9-3.

When you rotate an image in this way, Photoshop *resamples* your image — that is, it rearranges the pixels to come up with the rotated image. As I discuss back in Chapter 4, resampling can do some damage to your image. For best results, don't rotate your image more than once. Also, make sure that the Interpolation option in the General panel of the Preferences dialog box is set to Bicubic. (Press ⌘-K to display the dialog box.)

More good news about cropping

Cropping is easy and fun for the whole family. You can do it at home or at work, with friends or by yourself, in the car or while performing household chores. Learn how you can make cropping an everyday part of your new life. Here's how to order:

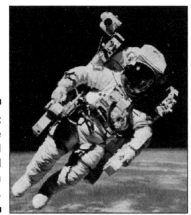

Figure 9-2:
Up close
and
personal
with a
spaceman.

Figure 9-3:
If the
photograph
isn't
straight, you
can rotate
the crop
boundary to
match (top)
while telling
Photoshop
to crop and
straighten
the image at
the same
time
(bottom).

Rotate cursor

✔ Sorry, I misplaced the real intro to this section and nobody seems to be able to find it. But while I hunt around, I'll just mention briefly that the next few items explain more cropping techniques that you might find useful.

✔ If you change your mind about wanting to crop your image, press Esc to get rid of the cropping boundary.

✔ If you try to drag with the crop tool when a portion of the image is selected (as discussed in Chapter 12), Photoshop deselects the image but doesn't respond to your drag. You have to drag a second time to get the full attention of Photoshop.

✔ To move the cropping boundary in its entirety, just drag inside the boundary.

✔ In addition to using the crop tool, you can crop an area selected with the rectangular marquee tool (discussed in Chapter 12) by choosing Image⇨Crop. I take advantage of this alternative quite often because Photoshop can slow down and react lethargically when you edit the crop marquee.

The only trick is that the selected area has to be exactly rectangular. If one side is even slightly crooked — which might happen if you modify the selection outline slightly — the Crop command doesn't work. Also, the Feather option in the Marquee Options palette must be set to 0. (To display the palette, double-click on the tool icon in the toolbox.)

✔ The Fixed Target Size option in the Crop Tool Options palette is useful for cropping one image so that it's the exact same size as another image. Suppose that you want to make Image A the same size as Image B. First, open Image B, turn on the Fixed Target Size option, and then click on the Front Image button. Next, open Image A and use the crop tool as you normally would. When you press Return to execute the crop, Photoshop automatically resizes the image to match Image B.

✔ You can also crop an image by using the Canvas Size command, as discussed at the end of Chapter 4. You may want to consider this method if you need to trim your image on one or more sides by a precise number of pixels to get the image to a certain size. The Canvas Size command can also come in handy if you want to crop a very small area — say 3 pixels worth — along one or more edges of the image and you have trouble selecting the area with the crop marquee. You can reduce the size of the canvas using Image⇨Canvas Size to eliminate the offensive pixels.

Touching Base with Retouching Tools

When push comes to shove, the editing tools are more like the painting tools than unlike them. You use an editing tool by dragging with it, just as you do with a painting tool. You change the size of the tool tip by selecting an option from the Brushes palette. You modify the performance of an editing tool from the

Options palette. You can even apply brush modes and Opacity settings. (Brush modes, the Brushes palette, and the Options palette are all introduced in Chapter 8, in case your response to these last few sentences was, "Huh?")

But the editing tools are sufficiently different than their painting cousins to confuse and perplex the unsuspecting neophyte. Moreover, unlike the pencil, paintbrush, and airbrush, the editing tools don't have any common real-world counterparts. I can't say, "The Photoshop smudge tool works just like the conventional smudge tool that's hanging out in your garage right next to the leaf rake," because almost no one has a smudge tool hanging in the garage or anywhere else.

What do the editing tools do, exactly?

Editing tools would be extremely useful in real life, if only someone would get around to inventing them. Take the task of touching up the walls in your rec room. (Come on, everyone has a rec room!) Using paintbrushes and rollers alone, this job can be a nightmare. The paint on the walls and the paint in the can may no longer exactly match. If you have to scrape away any dry paint, you'll have a heck of a time matching the texture. And knowing you, you might very well trip over something and spill paint all over the carpet.

But scan the walls of the rec room into Photoshop, and your problems are solved. Even if you have to retouch both paint and wallpaper, the editing tools, labeled in Figure 9-4, can handle the job without incident:

- Use the smudge tool to smear colors from a pristine area of the wall over the bare spots and the stains. You can smear the paint as far as you want, just as if it were still wet and in infinite supply. This is the editing tool you'll use most. It's discussed further in the section "Smudging Away Imperfections," in this chapter.

- If the transitions between elements in the wallpaper are a little ragged — for example, if the pixels in the little polka-dot mushrooms don't seem to blend naturally with those in the cute little frogs sitting beneath them — you can smooth them out with the blur tool, which looks like a water drop. This tool blurs the edges between colors so that the colors blend together.

- To rebuild textures, drag with the sharpen tool — which looks like a pointy cone of some sort. The sharpen tool increases the amount of contrast between colors and builds up edges.

- Together, the blur and sharpen tools are known as *focus tools*. The former downplays focus; the latter enhances it. Both tools are eloquently explained later in this chapter in the section "Focusing from the hip."

- To lighten a dark area in the wallpaper, drag with the dodge tool, which looks like a circle on the end of a stick. This tool lightens up the area evenly.

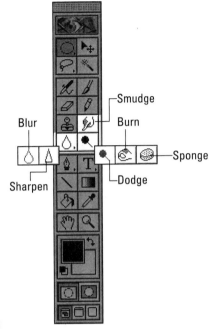

Figure 9-4:
Alas, the editing tools are not yet available at your local hardware store.

- ✔ If an area on the wall has become faded over the years, you can darken it using the burn tool, which looks like a hand in the shape of an O.

- ✔ Are the colors just too darn garish? Or has the color been drained right out? I admit, these aren't common rec room problems, but if they do occur, you can take up the sponge tool to remedy them.

- ✔ The dodge, burn, and sponge tools are called *toning tools,* meaning that they change the colors in an image. The last two sections in this chapter are devoted to the toning tools.

See, don't you wish you had a crack at using these tools in real life? Seems to me that Bob Vila or that *Home Improvement* guy should get to work on them.

Uncovering hidden editing tools

When you first saw Figure 9-4, you may have noticed that the toolbox in my figure doesn't look anything like the one on your screen. In order to show you all the tool icons, I enhanced the screen shot (using Photoshop, of course).

By default, the smudge, blur, and dodge tools appear in the toolbox. As discussed in Chapter 2, the little arrow in the bottom-right corner of the blur and dodge tools means that additional tools lurk behind the icons, on a flyout menu.

To get to the hidden tools on the flyout menu, press and hold on the icon and then drag across to the tool you want to use. Or just Option-click on the icon to cycle through the tools on the menu.

You can also cycle through the tools by using their shortcuts: Press R to select the tool that's currently showing in the blur/sharpen compartment of the toolbox; press R again to switch to the tool that's hidden. Likewise, you can press O (that's the letter O, not zero) to cycle through the dodge, burn, and sponge tools. To select the smudge tool from the keyboard, press U (as in smUdge).

Keep tapping the R key to make the blur and sharpen icons do a little hula dance. This trick keeps me amused for hours.

Smudging Away Imperfections

To demonstrate the powers of the proudest Photoshop editing tool, the smudge tool, I'd like to start with the image of the shark shown in Figure 9-5. Like so many rough-and-tumble sharks that occupy the inner cities of our oceans, this guy is no stranger to the occasional toothy brawl. Frankly, his face is a mess. If he were old enough to shave, I'd say that he had problems operating a razor. But because he's at that violent age where his friends think it's fun to rip an innocent tuna to shreds, I'm guessing that these marks are war wounds.

Figure 9-5:
This shark is on the road to ruin.

But whatever caused his scars, I can fix them with the help of the smudge tool. As you may recall from my earlier rec room analogy, the smudge tool pushes color from one portion of your image into another. When you drag with this tool, Photoshop "grabs" the color that's underneath your cursor at the start of your drag and smears it in the direction of your drag.

The smudge tool is a great contraption for smearing away scars, wrinkles, overly large noses, droopy ears, and all the other things that plastic surgeons keep their eyes out for. Figure 9-6 shows a magnified view of me using the smudge tool on the shark. The various sharkish defects are smoothed away to the point that the guy looks like he's made out of porcelain.

Figure 9-6:
As these before (top) and after (bottom) photos prove, the smudge tool can take years off a shark's face.

Smudge cursor

Smearing with style

Notice that in Figure 9-6 I rubbed with the grain of the detail. I traced along the shark's gills, rubbed along the length of its fins, and dragged up its snout, all in short, discreet strokes. I'd say something about how you don't want to rub a shark the wrong way, but my editor told me to lay off the puns. So I'll just point out that you get more naturalistic results if you carefully trace along the details of your subject and don't simply drag haphazardly all over the place.

Retouching with the smudge tool requires a certain amount of discretion. If you really go nuts and drag over every single surface, you get an oil-painting effect, like the one shown in Figure 9-7. Don't get me wrong — you can create some cool stuff this way, but smudging is not the same as retouching.

Smudge-specific controls

You can modify the performance of the smudge tool as follows:

✔ Click and Shift-click to smudge in a straight line. Or Shift-drag to smudge horizontally or vertically. These techniques work for all the edit tools, by the way.

Figure 9-7:
You can convert a photo into an oil painting by dragging all over the place with the smudge tool.

✔ Select another option in the Brushes palette to enlarge or reduce the size of the smudge brush. This likewise goes for all the edit tools. To display the palette, press F5. (For more on changing brushes, see Chapter 8.)

✔ Double-click on the smudge tool icon in the toolbox to display the Smudge Tool Options palette, shown in Figure 9-8. Or, if the smudge tool is selected, just press Return to display the palette.

Figure 9-8:
The options
that affect
the smudge
tool.

✔ Adjust the Pressure slider below the default setting of 50 percent to create more subtle retouching effects. Increase the Pressure setting to make the effect more pronounced.

✔ Remember that you can change the brush size from the keyboard by pressing the bracket keys and change the Pressure setting by pressing the number keys, as I explain in the preceding chapter.

✔ The brush modes pop-up menu (in the upper-left corner of the Smudge Tool Options palette) doesn't offer the Multiply, Screen, Overlay, or Difference options I discuss at the end of Chapter 8. Instead, you get two options, Darken and Lighten, which let you smear only those colors that are darker or lighter than the original colors in the image.

✔ You also have the Color brush mode, which lets you smear the colors in an RGB image without harming the detail. Pretty nifty.

✔ The other brush modes — Hue, Saturation, and Luminosity — range from nearly useless to completely useless. Don't worry about them.

✔ Change the brush mode back to Normal to make the smudge tool function, er, normally.

✔ Depending on your computer system, Photoshop may slow down dramatically when you increase the Pressure setting above 80 or 90 percent, select a large brush size, or change the brush mode. And if you do all three at once, the program may run so lethargically that you may think you've crashed. Just go get a cup of coffee for a few minutes, and Photoshop should be finished when you get back.

✔ Select the Finger Painting check box to dip your brush into the foreground color before smudging. You get a little dab of color at the beginning of your drag and eventually smear into the existing colors in the image as usual.

To temporarily turn on Finger Painting when the check box is deselected, press Option as you drag with the smudge tool. If the Finger Painting check box is selected, Option-drag to smudge in the normal fashion.

✔ The Sample Merged check box doesn't make any difference unless you're editing an image with layers, and even then it doesn't make much difference. Ignore it.

Color Plate 9-1 shows before and after shots of a few effects mixed together. I created the second image by selecting the Finger Painting check box, setting the Pressure slider to 90 percent, and changing the brush mode to Color. I dragged several times with the smudge tool, about half the time with the foreground color set to red and the other half with it set to yellow.

All Them Other Edit Tools

The remaining edit tools fall into a group that experts call "the other guys." Whereas you may pick up the smudge tool every third day or so, you'll be lucky if you select one of the other guys once a week. Even so, they can prove fantastically helpful — well, moderately helpful, anyway — if used properly. The upcoming sections contain my choice bits of wisdom for using the other guys.

Focusing from the hip

It's true that the smudge tool is a wonderful little device. But it's not always the right tool for the job. For example, let's say that you have a harsh transition between two colors. Maybe one of the shark's teeth looks a little jagged, or you want to soften the edge of a fin. Which of the following methods would you use to fix this problem?

✔ Smear the colors a bit with the smudge tool.

✔ Soften the transition between the colors using the blur tool.

I prepared you for that question by saying that the smudge tool isn't always the right tool and using words like "soften," so naturally you chose the second answer. (You did choose the second answer, didn't you?) But believe me, there will come a time when you run into this exact situation and your first reflex will be to reach for the smudge tool.

So let me try to drive the point home a bit with the aid of Figure 9-9. The figure starts off with the harshest of all possible color transitions, that between white and its archenemy, black. You want to smear the colors together so they blend a little more harmoniously, so naturally you reach for the smudge tool. The problem with this method — as illustrated in the second example in the figure — is that you can't get a nice, smooth transition between the two colors no matter how hard you try. Even if you Shift-drag with the smudge tool, you get some inconsistent smudging. You also run the risk of smearing surrounding detail. All this happens because the smudge tool is designed as a free-form smearing device, not as an edge softener.

Meanwhile, an edge softener is sitting nearby waiting for you to snatch it up. If you drag the blur tool between the white and black shapes — whether you drag perfectly straight or wobble the cursor back and forth a bit — the result is a softened edge like the one shown in the final example of Figure 9-9.

Harsh transition

Smeared with smudge tool

Softened with blur tool

Figure 9-9:
The parable of the harsh transition, the smudge tool, and the blur tool.

While I've got your attention, let me jot down a few other items about the focus tools:

- Just as the blur tool softens transitions, the sharpen tool firms the transitions back up.

- At least, that's what the sharpen tool is supposed to do. In practice, it tends to make an image overly grainy. Use this tool sparingly, and be sure to save your image before you experiment.

- You can adjust the impact of the blur and sharpen tools by changing the Pressure setting in the Focus Tools Options palette — which you get to by pressing Return when the tool is selected or double-clicking on the tool icon in the toolbox. I like to set the Pressure to about 60 percent for the blur tool and 30 percent for sharpen.

- When you work with the focus tools, you have access to the same brush modes as you do when using the smudge tool. The important ones are Darken, Lighten, and Color. Any of the three can help downplay the effects of the sharpen tool and make it more usable.

- If you want to adjust the focus of large areas of an image — or an entire image — use the commands under the Filter menu as described in Chapter 17. These commands work much more uniformly than the focus tools.

Dodge? Burn? Those are opposites?

Wondering why the dodge and burn tool icons look they way they do? It's because the dodge and burn tools have their roots in traditional stat camera techniques in which you shoot a photograph of another photograph to correct exposure problems. The dodge tool is supposed to look like a little paddle that you wave around to block off light, and the burn tool is a hand focusing the light. It may seem, therefore, that dodging would make the image darker and burning would make it lighter. But Photoshop is thinking in terms of negative film, where black is white, up is down, right is left, and Tweedle Dee is a Cornish game hen.

I must confess that, although I've been using Photoshop since I was in diapers, I still can't remember which tool lightens and which darkens without looking it up. To help both you and me remember, I offer the following:

- The dodge tool lightens images, just as a dodge ball lightens your body by about ten pounds when it tears off your head.

- The burn tool darkens images, just as a sunburn darkens your body and eventually turns it a kind of charbroiled color from melanoma.

If those little insights don't help you, remember how the dodge and burn tools work, nothing will.

Generally, you adjust the performance of the dodge and burn tools just like the other edit tools and the paint tools — by changing the brush size, alternating the brush mode, and so on. (You can read more about brush sizes and brush modes in Chapter 8.) To get to the Brush size options, press F5 to display the Brushes palette. To get to the other tool options, double-click on the dodge or burn tool icon in the toolbox, or — if you like to do things the easy way — just press Return.

A few of the options in the Toning Tools Options palette require some explanation:

✔ The Exposure slider bar indicates how much an area will be lightened or darkened. As always, lower the value to lessen the impact of the tool and raise the value to increase the impact.

✔ The pop-up menu in the upper-left corner of the palette contains just three options: Highlights, Midtones, and Shadows. The default setting is Midtones, which lightens or darkens medium colors in an image and leaves the very light and dark colors alone. Figure 9-10 shows the result of dragging all over the shark with the dodge tool while Midtones was the active brush mode.

Figure 9-10:
By setting the brush mode to Midtones and dragging indiscriminately with the dodge tool, I lightened the shark without eliminating contrast.

✔ The Shadows brush mode ensures that the darkest colors are affected, while Highlights impacts the lightest colors. In Figure 9-11, I set the brush mode to Shadows and scribbled with the dodge tool. The payoff is a shark that looks like it ate the world's supply of glowworms. Even the darkest shadows radiate, making the image uniformly light.

✔ To darken an image with similar uniformity, select the burn tool and set the brush mode to Highlights.

Figure 9-11:
Using the dodge tool in combination with the Shadows brush mode makes the shark's darkest shadows tingle with light.

Version 4 offers a variation of the dodge and burn tools in the form of the Color Dodge and Color Burn brush modes, as explained in Chapter 8. When you use the regular dodge and burn tools, you simply lighten or darken your image. But when you use one of the painting tools with the Color Dodge or Color Burn brush modes, you can both lighten or darken and infuse the image with color. For example, if you wanted to lighten an image and give it a yellowish glow, paint with yellow and the Color Dodge brush mode.

Playing with the Color knob

The sponge tool is designed to be used on full-color images. Don't try using it on grayscale images because it won't do you any good. It's not that it won't work — it will — it just won't work correctly. On a grayscale image, the sponge tool either lightens or darkens pixels like a shoddy version of the dodge or burn tool.

When you work on a color image, the sponge tool increases or decreases saturation. Ever used the Color knob on your television? Turn the knob up, and the color leaps off the screen; turn it down, and the colors look gray. What you are doing is adjusting the TV's saturation. Increasing saturation makes the colors more vibrant; decreasing saturation makes the colors more drab. The sponge tool works in much the same way.

Here's how you use the sponge tool:

1. **Select the tool.**

   Press the O key until the sponge icon appears in the toolbox.

2. **Press Return.**

   Photoshop displays the Toning Tools Options palette.

3. **Select the desired option from the pop-up menu in the upper-left corner of the palette.**

   Select Saturate to make color vibrant; select Desaturate to make the colors drab.

4. **Press a number key to change the Pressure value.**

   Or drag the slider bar in the palette. Either way, the setting affects the impact of the sponge tool.

5. **Drag with the tool inside a color image.**

   Watch those colors change.

The primary reason that the programmers provide the sponge tool is to desaturate colors that may get lost when you convert from RGB to CMYK. As I mention in Chapter 5, red, green, and blue can mix to form some very bright colors that cyan, magenta, yellow, and black can't express. So you can dab at the colors with the sponge tool to bring them more in line with the CMYK spectrum.

But I like to use the sponge tool for the exact opposite purpose — to make colors more saturated. Oh, sure, maybe you won't be able to print the colors correctly, but at least they'll be as bright as they can be. If dragging with the sponge tool set to Saturate doesn't have any effect on the colors in an image, it's because the colors are already as bright as they can be.

Chapter 10

Cleaning Up Goobers

● ●

In This Chapter

▶ Using the Dust & Scratches command

▶ Previewing automated effects

▶ Setting the Radius and Threshold values

▶ Cleaning up an image with the rubber stamp

▶ Specifying a clone source

▶ Adjusting settings in the Rubber Stamp Options palette

● ●

*1*f you've ever had an image scanned to disk or CD, you know the story. You send out a lovely photograph that you've cherished all your life, and the scan comes back looking like someone stuck it inside the lint trap of a dryer. Big, gnarly hairs wiggle across the image. Little dust flecks seem to have reproduced like rabbits. And if you really hit the jackpot, you may even spy a few fingerprints on your image. It's enough to make you call up the service bureau and ask them whether they recently employed a shedding malamute that hasn't bathed in six weeks and has a penchant for jelly sandwiches.

Unfortunately, sarcasm won't get you anywhere. But the dust-busting tools of Photoshop will. With a keen eye and a little bit of elbow grease, you can scrub away those imperfections and make your image appear absolutely spotless.

Photoshop offers two different methods for dusting away the specks:

✔ The Dust & Scratches command automates the removal of image imperfections, but it can do more harm than good by getting rid of important detail as well.

✔ The rubber stamp tool lets you clone (copy) portions of an image to cover up blotches. The rubber stamp takes more time to use than the Dust & Scratches command and requires a considerable amount of clicking and dragging, but it also results in a better looking picture.

This chapter explains the pros and cons of each method and throws in a few other ideas for spit-shining your images as well.

Using the Dust & Scratches Command

Ever own a really nice sports car, like a Porsche or a Jaguar? Me neither, but I've known folks who have, and they can be amazingly protective of their automobiles. Most Porsche/Jaguar owners would sooner vote for a Socialist than take their cars through one of those drive-through wash joints where big floppy pieces of blue plastic flog your car and take little bits of your paint job along with them. Automobile aficionados know that the only way to clean a car is to tenderly rub its surface with specially treated pieces of felt dipped in no-tears baby shampoo.

Although I might think that those car buffers are off their rockers, I wholeheartedly endorse this policy when it comes to cleaning images. That's why I'm not so fond of the Dust & Scratches filter — it's akin to sending your image through a car wash.

I should mention that the Dust & Scratches command is a *filter,* meaning that it automatically corrects an image by mixing up the pixels in some predefined manner. It works much like filters that change the focus of an image, discussed in Chapter 17.

But just because I may not approve of the Dust & Scratches command, that's no reason not to give you a crack at it. You're an adult. I'm not your keeper. Who knows, maybe the command will even come in useful. Maybe you need to clean up an image in a hurry for that last-minute space in the company newsletter, and the car wash solution is the only one you have time to try.

With that enthusiastic endorsement out of the way, it's high time I show you how to use the Dust & Scratches filter. The lab rat for today's outing is Figure 10-1. This figure demonstrates another variety of splatter that can plague images — old photo gunk. The lines, scratches, and dots in this image weren't introduced in the scanning process; they were a part of the original photo. Shot near the beginning of this century, this picture of Halley's comet has held up amazingly well over the years. I hope to look half as good when I'm its age.

Incidentally, if you're a fellow lover of things extraterrestrial, you can't go wrong with Digital Stock's "Space & Spaceflight" CD, which includes about as many views of the sun, moon, planets, and outlying nebula as a person could hope for.

To tidy up an image that presents similar symptoms, choose Filter⇨Noise⇨Dust & Scratches. Photoshop displays the strange and mysterious Dust & Scratches dialog box, which is pictured in all its glory in Figure 10-2 and explained in the next two sections.

Figure 10-1:
Halley's comet as it appeared in 1910, replete with old photo gunk.

Preview cursor   Preview box   Zoom buttons

Figure 10-2:
The Dust & Scratches dialog box provides a hefty supply of previewing options.

Previewing the filter effects

The makers of the Dust & Scratches dialog box know that it doesn't make a lick of sense, so they thoughtfully provide some preview options (all labeled in Figure 10-2) to enable you to see what happens when you make some otherwise meaningless adjustment. Here's how these preview options work:

✔ The preview box shows how your modifications look when applied to a tiny portion of the image.

- ✔ If you move the cursor outside the dialog box, it changes to a hollow square. Click on an area in the image to capture it inside the preview box.

- ✔ You can also scroll the contents of the preview box by dragging inside the box. Your cursor changes to a little hand.

- ✔ To magnify or reduce the contents of the preview box, click on the plus or minus zoom button.

- ✔ You can also access the standard magnifying glass cursor inside the preview box by pressing the ⌘ key (to zoom in) or the Option key (to zoom out).

- ✔ As long as the Preview check box is selected, Photoshop previews your settings in the image window as well as in the preview box.

- ✔ You can even use the standard hand and zoom cursors inside the image window while the Dust & Scratches dialog box is open. Just press the spacebar to get the hand cursor or ⌘-spacebar and Option-spacebar to get the zoom cursors. This technique is a great way to preview an effect at two different zoom ratios, one inside the dialog box and one outside.

- ✔ If Photoshop seems to be slowing down too much as it tries to preview an effect in the image window, just click on the Preview check box to turn the function off.

I know, I know, you didn't want to know quite that much about previewing, but it will serve you well in the future. These same options are found in a few dialog boxes that I describe in Chapter 17 as well as a couple of others that you may decide to discover on your own (you Vasco da Gama, you).

Specifying the size of the speck

The Dust & Scratches dialog box (Filter⇨Noise⇨Dust & Scratches) offers just two options that affect the performance of the filter: the Radius and Threshold slider bars. The slider bars work as follows:

- ✔ Change the Radius value to indicate the size of the dust specks and the thickness of the hairs that you want to eliminate. In geometry, radius means half the width of a circle, so the Radius value is half the width of a dust speck. The minimum value is 1, meaning that the filter wipes out all specks and hairs up to 2 pixels thick.

- ✔ "Ah ha," you might think, "If I just crank up the Radius value as far as it goes (16 pixels), that should be enough to eliminate entire colonies of dust bunnies." Well, no. See, the Dust & Scratches filter doesn't really know a speck from a tiny bit of detail. So if you have it rub out 16-pixel radius dust globs, it also rubs out 16-pixel details such as Uncle Ralph's head. Figure 10-3 shows the effects of setting the Radius value to 1 on the left and 3 on the right. Notice how fuzzy the image became when I applied a 3-pixel Radius? If you value my advice — I guess you value it to the tune of $19.99, anyway — you'll never set the Radius value higher than 2.

Figure 10-3:
The results of applying the Dust & Scratches filter with the Radius slider set to 1 pixel (left) and 3 (right).

✔ The Threshold value tells Photoshop how different the color of a dust speck has to be from the color of the surrounding image to be considered a bad seed. The Threshold slider works just like the RGB sliders in the Color palette (discussed in Chapter 5) — that is, it varies from 0 to 255.

✔ The default Threshold value of 0 tells Photoshop that dust and image need only be 0 color levels different from each other. Because all colors are at least 0 levels different, Photoshop ignores the Threshold value and considers only the Radius value. Both images in Figure 10-3 were filtered with a Threshold value of 0.

✔ By raising the Threshold value, you tell Photoshop to be more selective. If you set the value to 10, speck and image colors must vary by at least 10 levels before Photoshop covers up the speck, as in the first example of Figure 10-4. If you raise the Threshold to 20 — as in the second example — Photoshop disregards still more potential impurities. Notice that the two horizontal streaks in the second image remain intact, having been ruled out by the Threshold setting. (By the way, I set the Radius value to 3 in Figure 10-4 — something I earlier warned you against doing — in order to make the effects of the Threshold setting more noticeable.)

✔ If you set the Threshold value any higher than 100, the dust specks have to be white and the image black — or vice versa — to receive any attention. I don't recommend using values over 15.

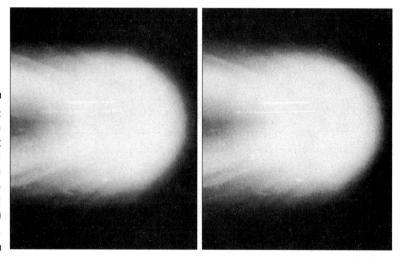

Figure 10-4:
With the Radius set to 3 pixels, I set the Threshold to 10 (left) and then to 20 (right).

In my long ramblings about the Radius and Threshold values, I neglected to mention one disconcerting fact. Even though the Dust & Scratches filter variously obliterated the detail in Figures 10-3 and 10-4, none of the images is completely free of spots and streaks. Admittedly, this old, moldy picture is a lot worse off than most of your images will be, but the fact remains that the Dust & Scratches filter is an imperfect solution. Just like a cheap car wash, it gets rid of most of the dirt — but not all of it — and it takes away some of the paint and detailing along with it.

Spot Cleaning Your Image with TLC

If you're willing to expend a little extra energy and you can stand up to your friends when they call you compulsive, the tool of choice for cleaning up images is the rubber stamp. The fifth tool from the top on the left side of the toolbox, the rubber stamp lets you take a good portion of an image and paint it onto the bad portion. This miraculous process is called *cloning*.

You can also clone part of your image by copying and pasting it, as described in the section "Moving and Cloning Selections" at the end of Chapter 13. You should get familiar with both methods of cloning because both have their place in the retouching world.

Stamping out splatters

Want to see how the rubber stamp tool works? Try out these steps:

1. **Select the rubber stamp tool and press the Return key.**

   To select the rubber stamp from the keyboard, press the S key. Pressing the Return key — or double-clicking on the rubber stamp tool icon in the toolbox — displays the Rubber Stamp Options palette, shown on the right side of Figure 10-5.

┌Rubber stamp tool

Figure 10-5:
The rubber
stamp and
its trusty
Options
palette,
partners in
cloning.

2. **Make sure that Clone (Aligned) is chosen in the Option pop-up menu.**

   This option lets you clone from relative points in your image. You'll see what I mean in a sec.

3. **Start dragging randomly inside your image.**

   Whoops, I bet you got an error message, didn't you? If I'm right, the message says something about — I can almost see it; it's becoming clearer — Option-clicking to define a source! How do I know these things? Because I am psychic, that's how. Even from here in Boulder, Colorado, months before you'll read this, I can foresee the error messages in your future. Ah, really, it's nothing. Been able to do it since I was a kid.

Okay, I'm lying, I just got that message myself and I reckoned that you might get it, too. See, to use the rubber stamp, you have to tell Photoshop which portion of your image you want to clone before you begin cloning it. Photoshop isn't a mind reader, you know. I might be a mind reader, but Photoshop most certainly is not.

Now that you've learned this valuable lesson, grab a pen and put a big *X* through Step 3 so that you never make the same mistake again.

4. Option-click on the portion of the image that you want to clone.

For example, to fix that big goober near the beginning of the lower tail of Halley's comet, I Option-clicked at a location that appeared to contain similar gray values to the comet stuff that surrounds the goober, as demonstrated in Figure 10-6. The point is to pick a portion of your image that will blend in with areas around the blemish you want to eliminate.

When you Option-click, the little upside-down triangle at the bottom of the rubber stamp cursor becomes white. Fascinating, huh?

According to Webster's, the word *goober* is derived from the Kongo word *gnuba,* which means peanut. And peanut (wink) is exactly what I mean (nudge, nudge).

5. Now click or drag on the offending blemish.

Actually, that mark on my comet looks more like a pimple than a peanut, doesn't it? To apply the digital zit cream, I clicked directly on the critter and purged it good. No muss, no fuss, the glitch is gone.

The dreaded cosmic goober

Option-click with rubber stamp

Figure 10-6:
Option-click on a good portion of an image to establish the cloning source.

When you click or drag with the rubber stamp, Photoshop displays a cross cursor along with the stamp cursor, as shown in Figure 10-7. This cross represents the clone source, or the area that you're cloning from. As you move the mouse, the cross cursor also moves, providing a continual reference to the portion of your image that you're cloning. (Things work differently when you have an option other than Clone (Aligned) selected in the Rubber Stamp Options palette, however, as explained in the next section.)

Clone source   Rubber stamp cursor

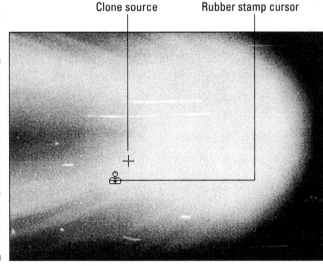

Figure 10-7: When you use the rubber stamp, a small cross follows you to show you what part of the image you're cloning.

If the cloned area doesn't blend in well, just choose Edit⇨Undo (⌘-Z), Option-click in the image with the rubber stamp to specify a better source for your cloning, and click or drag with the tool to test out a different clone. You may have to do this several times to get it just right.

Just for the sheer heck of it, Figure 10-8 shows the comet after I finished using the rubber stamp. Now isn't that way better than anything from Figures 10-3 and 10-4? And it took about 15 minutes. We can all afford 15 minutes, can't we?

Figure 10-8:
Halley's comet, all dressed up and nowhere to go for 76 years.

Performing more magic with the rubber stamp

If you never learned another thing about the rubber stamp tool, you'd be able to clean images quite easily after reading the preceding section. But the rubber stamp is an amazing tool with more facets and capabilities than any other Photoshop tool:

- ✔ To change the size or shape of the area that's cloned, change the brush size in the Brushes palette, just as you would for other painting or editing tools. (Press F5 to display the Brushes palette.) For more information about the Brushes palette, see Chapter 8.

- ✔ To make the clone more translucent or less translucent, use the Opacity slider in the Rubber Stamp Options palette. A setting of 100 makes your clone opaque. (To display the palette, press Return or double-click on the rubber stamp tool in the toolbox.)

- ✔ To clean up a straight hair or scratch, Option-click with the tool to specify the source for the cloning as you normally would. Then click at one end of the scratch and Shift-click at the other.

- ✔ If the first clone doesn't look exactly right but it's pretty close, you may want to modify the clone slightly rather than redo it. Lower the Opacity setting in the Rubber Stamp Options palette by pressing a number key and then clone from a different position by again Option-clicking and dragging. This allows you to mix multiple portions of an image together to get a more seamless blend.

- ✔ The blocky rubber stamp cursor that apppears by default makes predicting the outcome of your clone difficult. To get a better idea of the size of your clone before you click, press ⌘-K, ⌘-3 to open up the Display & Cursors panel of the Preferences dialog box. (Or choose File➪Preferences➪Display & Cursors.) Select the Brush Size radio button from the Painting Cursors area of the dialog box. Now your cursor reflects the size of your brush.

- ✔ Normally, the rubber stamp tool clones from a relative location. If you move your cursor to a different location, the clone source moves with you. But what if you want to clone multiple times from a single location? In this case, choose Clone (Non-Aligned) from the Option pop-up menu in the Rubber Stamp Options palette. Now you can Option-click once to set the source and click and drag multiple times to duplicate that source.

- ✔ The other options in the Option pop-up menu let you paint with a pattern (the two Pattern options), revert the image (From Snapshot and From Saved), or paint a goofy effect (Impressionist). The From Snapshot and From Saved options are discussed in the next chapter. The other three options are too stupid to merit your attention.

- ✔ You can clone between images. What am I talking about? If you have two images open, you can Option-click inside one image to specify the source and drag in the other image to clone. It's like painting one image onto another.

- ✔ Color Plate 10-1 shows an example of cloning between images. Starting with the two images on the left side of the figure (which I scaled to the same file size using Image➪Image Size, as discussed in Chapter 4), I Option-clicked inside the top image and then dragged with the rubber stamp inside the bottom image. I cloned the woman's face and blouse using a large fuzzy brush and then switched to a smaller brush for the touch-ups. To match the skin tones in the forehead and the base of the nose, I cloned from the woman's cheeks at an Opacity setting of 50 percent. Gruesome, huh?

- ✔ If your image contains layers, as discussed in Chapter 15, remember that the rubber stamp tool normally clones from the active layer only. If you select the Sample Merged check box in the Rubber Stamp Options palette, the rubber stamp reads the pixels in all visible layers to create the clone. When you then click or drag with the rubber stamp, Photoshop paints the clone onto the active layer.

- ✔ All the brush modes that apply to the painting tools apply to the rubber stamp as well. This means that you can achieve interesting special effects by selecting the Multiply, Screen, Overlay, Difference, or Color option from the pop-up menu in the upper-left corner of the Rubber Stamp Options palette. For more on brush modes, see the end of Chapter 8.

- ✔ Try cloning between two different images with a special brush mode in effect. For example, if you clone with the Multiply brush mode, you emblazon the first image onto the second. If you have half an hour to waste, play with the different modes and see what you can do.

Chapter 11

Turning Back the Digital Clock

. . . .

In This Chapter

▶ Undoing operations

▶ Using the eraser tool

▶ Erasing to the image saved to disk

▶ Selecting different kinds of erasers

▶ Choosing the Revert command

▶ Taking a snapshot

▶ Erasing with the rubber stamp

. . . .

*H*ere's how you know that you're a consummate computer nerd: When you snag your favorite sweater, say something highly objectionable to your spouse, or spill a well-known staining agent on your newly installed carpeting, your first reaction is not one of panic or regret. You merely think, "Undo."

Unfortunately, the real world provides no Undo command. After a horrible deed is done, it takes an obscenely disproportionate amount of fussing, explaining, or scrubbing to fix the transgression.

Not so in the magical world of personal computing. Edit⇨Undo is standard equipment with just about every Macintosh (and Windows) program out there. With one press of ⌘-Z — the Undo command's keyboard equivalent — your previous operation disappears for good, leaving you one step backward in time.

But Photoshop doesn't stop there. You can revert specific portions of an image back to the way they looked when you last saved the image to disk. You can also take a picture of an image and later revert to that. This chapter explains all the Photoshop methods for regaining the past so that you can edit worry-free, safe in the knowledge that nearly everything you do can be undone.

Nuking the Last Operation

The more you work with Photoshop, the more reflexive your actions become. Certainly, this means that you can do work more quickly, but it also means that you are likely to make more mistakes. Reflexive, after all, is a close cousin to thoughtless. And when you don't think, you can wander into some pretty nasty situations.

Doing the Undo

The Undo command ensures that you aren't punished for working reflexively. To get a sense of just how wonderful this command can be, try out these steps:

1. **Open an image.**

   If you already have an image open, good for you.

2. **Select the paintbrush tool and drag across the image.**

   Draw a mustache or something. Just make sure to draw a single brush stroke and no more.

3. **Take a break.**

   You've worked hard, you deserve it. Watch TV for your daily allowance of six hours. Take up macramé. Enlist in the armed forces. The point is, no matter how long you're away, Photoshop will remember that last operation (as long as you don't have a power outage or some similar computing disaster).

4. **Choose Edit⇨Undo.**

   Actually, the name of the command should be Undo Paintbrush. The name of the Undo command changes to tell you what action you're about to undo.

   You can also choose the Undo command by pressing ⌘-Z. Either way, your brush stroke is gone.

After you choose the Undo command, the command changes to the Redo command. For example, if you choose Undo after taking Step 4, the command name is Redo Paintbrush. If you choose the Redo Paintbrush command, your brush stroke comes back and the Redo Paintbrush command becomes the Undo Paintbrush command again. In other words, you can undo an action, and then redo it, and then undo it, and then redo it, and so on, until you make up your mind or collapse from exhaustion, whichever comes first.

The Undo command works even after you choose File➪Print. This means that you can adjust an image, print it to see how it looks, and undo the adjustment if you don't like it. Choosing File➪Page Setup — or any other command except Print — wipes out your chance to undo that adjustment, though.

Undo limitations

Although the Undo command is certainly a powerful tool, bear in mind that it does have some limitations. I'd hate to see you go hog-wild on an image and then discover that your changes are set in stone. So here are a few guidelines to stash away in the back of your brain:

✔ You can't undo the Print command. Print involves marking up real pieces of paper, and the Undo command is powerless in the real world. Instead, Undo just ignores Print, as you saw in the preceding steps.

✔ File➪Save and File➪Save As are beyond the reach of the Undo command. If you initiate the Save command and suddenly think better of it, you can press ⌘-period to cancel it, but you have to think quickly and respond while the command is in progress. After the Save command finishes, the image is saved, and the previous version of the image is gone. (The Save As command leaves the previous version of the image intact, so you need never worry when choosing it.)

✔ Not only can you not undo Save or Save As, these commands render the Undo command null and void. After the Save operation completes, the first command in the Edit menu is Can't Undo, which appears dimmed. This means that the operation you performed before choosing Save is now permanent (doubly so because the changes are saved to disk).

✔ You can't undo the Quit command. There's a surprise. Also, when you relaunch Photoshop, it has no idea what you did during the previous session, so you can't undo the last changes you made before quitting.

✔ You also can't undo changing a foreground or background color, adjusting a setting using one of the commands under the File➪Preferences submenu, hiding or displaying palettes, changing a palette setting, or selecting a tool. Like the Print command, these operations are ignored by Undo, thus allowing you to undo the previous "significant" operation.

✔ You'd think that Photoshop would treat File➪Page Setup like one of the File➪Preferences commands because you're just adjusting printing preferences. But Photoshop remembers your changes inside the Page Setup dialog box and lets you undo them. So don't choose Page Setup before Print if you want to undo a brush stroke or other operation after printing the image.

The Amazing Powers of the Eraser

If you want to undo the cumulative effects of several operations, the eraser is your tool. Immediately to the left of the pencil in the toolbox, the eraser lets you erase in a couple of ways:

- ✔ If you drag with the eraser in an image that contains only one layer, the tool paints in the background color, which is typically white. I suppose that you could call this process erasing, but it's really just painting in a different color. Who needs it?

- ✔ If your image contains more than one layer (layers are discussed in Chapter 15), the eraser works a little differently and becomes a lot more useful. If you drag the eraser on the background layer, the eraser paints in the background color, as usual. But on any other layer, the pixels you scrub with the eraser become transparent, revealing pixels on underlying layers. This assumes that the Preserve Transparency check box is turned off in the Layers palette. If it's turned on, the eraser paints in the background color.

- ✔ If you Option-drag with the tool, you reveal the image as it appeared when you last saved it to disk. If your image has layers, your drag affects the active layer only. Here's another useful function (and one which is explained in the very next section).

Erasing to the last-saved version

On the off chance that you're not clear on what it means to reveal an image to its saved appearance, the following steps give you an opportunity to try it out for yourself. In these steps, you paint a halo around the central subject of an image without harming the subject itself. First, you color outside the lines and then you clean it up with the eraser.

1. **Open an image.**

   For these steps, open something with a strong central subject, like a person or an animal. You can't go wrong with a fish like the one in Figure 11-1.

2. **Set the foreground color to white.**

   Just press D to get the default colors — black for the foreground and white for the background — and then press X to switch them.

3. **Trace the central subject with the airbrush tool.**

   Don't worry about getting white all over the central subject. In Figure 11-2, for example, I've made a complete mess of things. There's no way to be careful with the airbrush — it sprays all over the place.

Figure 11-1:
This lingcod
stands out
proudly
from his
surroundings.

Figure 11-2:
I traced
sloppily
around the
lingcod with
the airbrush.

4. **Select the eraser tool.**

To select the tool from the keyboard, press the E key.

5. Option-click anywhere inside the image.

This may sound like a weird step, but Photoshop has to reload the original image from disk before it can erase to it. By Option-clicking, you tell Photoshop to get its act in gear.

You don't absolutely have to Option-click, but if you just start Option-dragging, you are most likely to wait out a lengthy delay. Photoshop may even ignore your drag entirely.

6. Option-drag to erase inside the central subject.

After Photoshop finishes loading the image — your hard disk stops making noises and/or the little hard drive light stops flashing — Option-drag inside the central subject (in my case, the lingcod).

Getting to the image shown in Figure 11-3 required that I perform Step 6 with some care and effort. I wanted to erase inside the subject only and leave the white airbrush paint intact in the background. Creating similar effects may take many strokes and many undos to get it just right, but it's good for you. Teaches you patience and all that. Just don't forget to press that Option key every time you erase.

Figure 11-3:
The lingcod glows eagerly as he emerges from his nuclear chamber.

Here are some more things to know about erasing to the last saved version of your image:

✔ If you're erasing a multiple-layer image, the eraser tool erases changes to the active layer only.

✔ You can also select a portion of your image, as explained in Chapter 12, and then revert just that portion to the last saved version using the Edit⇨Fill command. For details, see the section "Select your stuffing" in Chapter 14.

✔ Your first thought on finishing the preceding steps might be, "If Option-dragging is so useful, why don't those bozo programmers make it the default setting?" I can't answer that question — and, really, don't call them bozos, they're sensitive — but I can tell you how to change things so that the eraser tool erases to the last saved version of the image by default.

First, display the Eraser Options palette, shown in Figure 11-4. (Either double-click on the eraser tool icon in the toolbox or, if the eraser tool is selected, press Return.) Then select the Erase to Saved check box in the lower right corner of the palette. Dragging with the eraser now reveals the saved image and Option-dragging paints in the background color. This means that in Step 5, you'd simply click inside the image to load it from disk, and in Step 6 you'd drag without ever once pressing the Option key. Much more acceptable, yes?

Figure 11-4:
Select the
Erase to
Saved
check box
to make
using the
eraser
easier.

Adjusting your eraser

Though there is only one eraser tool in the toolbox, Photoshop actually provides four kinds of erasers. To switch erasers, select an option from the pop-up menu in the upper-left corner of the Eraser Options palette.

You can also switch from one kind of eraser to the next from the keyboard by pressing the E key. The first press of E just selects whichever eraser you last used. Press E again to switch to the next eraser in the list. Press E a third time to get the next eraser, and so on.

Three erasers are named after painting tools — Paintbrush, Airbrush, and Pencil — and work exactly like these tools, down to the inclusion of the Wet Edges check box for the paintbrush option. This means that you can change the brush size in the Brushes panel and adjust the Opacity setting to partially reveal the saved image or, in a layered image, make pixels only partially transparent. (For a refresher on changing the brush size and opacity, review Chapter 8.)

The fourth option, Block, changes the eraser to the square, hard-edged, fixed-size eraser featured in Photoshop 2.5. The options in the Brush Size palette don't affect the block eraser, nor do the Opacity slider bar or any of the other settings in the Eraser Options palette except Erase to Saved. The block eraser can be useful when you want to completely erase general areas, but you probably won't take it up very often.

Why won't the eraser work?

Just as the Save command messes up the undo process, a few operations prevent the eraser tool from revealing the saved image. The feature only works if the image on-screen and the one saved on disk share the same file size — that is, they each contain exactly the same number of pixels. Any operation that changes the size of the on-screen image throws a monkey wrench into the works.

The following operations prevent you from revealing with the eraser:

- Trimming the image with the crop tool.

- Applying the Image Size command with the Resample Image check box selected. (As long as Resample Image is unchecked, you can change the dimension or resolution without causing problems.)

- Using the Canvas Size command.

- Applying any of the commands under the Image⇨Rotate Canvas submenu (except 180°) to the entire image.

To avoid problems, be sure that you like what you've done to an image before you initiate any of the above operations. Then save the image immediately after the operation completes. This way, you can erase back to the saved image without any complications.

Abandoning Edits En Masse

Sometimes you make small mistakes, and sometimes you make big ones. If, after several minutes of messing about, you decide that you hate all your edits and want to return the entire image to its original saved appearance so that you can just start over again, choose File⇨Revert. Photoshop displays an alert box to make sure that you didn't choose the wrong command; after all, you've been all thumbs today. If you click on the Revert button or press Return, the program reloads the image from disk and throws away all your changes.

Don't feel bad. I use the Revert command once a day at least. It's a great way to test out changes and then throw them away if they're no good.

You can't undo File⇨Revert, so make sure that you really want to do it before you click on the Revert button.

Capturing the Moment

Most of the time, the Undo command and eraser provide you with all the flexibility and forgiveness you need. But what if you need just a little more? Suppose that you like the way an image looks now, but you may still need access to the saved version, so you don't want to save over it. How do you make it possible to revert to the current on-screen image without saving over the version on disk?

The Take Snapshot command is the answer. Choosing Edit⇨Take Snapshot saves a copy of the image as it currently appears to memory. You can then restore portions of the snapshot later in the game using the rubber stamp tool.

To set the rubber stamp to erase to the snapshot, double-click on the rubber stamp icon in the toolbox. Select the From Snapshot option from the Option pop-up menu in the Rubber Stamp Options palette, as in Figure 11-5. Then click or drag with the rubber stamp on the portions of your image that you want to restore to the snapshot version.

And now for a few other tidbits on this subject:

✔ If your image has layers, Take Snapshot stores only the contents of the active layer. That means that you can use the rubber stamp to revert to the saved version of that layer only. If you choose Edit⇨Take Merged Snapshot instead, you can use the rubber stamp on any layer to erase to the visible image. In other words, the rubber stamp "sees" all the layers that are visible. (For more on layers, see Chapter 15.)

166 Part III: Tiptoe through the Toolbox

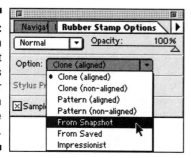

Figure 11-5:
The From
Snapshot
option gives
you another
way to turn
back the
clock.

✔ The Option pop-up menu in the Rubber Stamp Options palette also provides a From Saved option that lets you revert to the saved image, a duplication of the eraser tool's capability. This option doesn't serve much of a function because the eraser tool is equally capable.

✔ If you select a portion of your image, as explained in Chapter 12, you can revert only the selection to the snapshot version by using the Edit⇨Fill command. For more on that juicy topic, see the section "Select your stuffing" in Chapter 14.

Don't confuse the Take Snapshot command with the Save A Copy command. Both commands save a copy of your image. But when you use the Save A Copy command, you can't use the eraser or rubber stamp to revert to the saved version. If you want to be able to bring back portions of your saved image using the eraser or rubber stamp, you have to use Edit⇨Take Snapshot or Edit⇨Take Merged Snapshot.

Also, snapshot copies are only temporary. Photoshop is capable of storing only one snapshot for each image. The next time you choose the Take Snapshot or Take Merged Snapshot command, the current snapshot of that image is re-placed by the new one.

Part IV

Select Before You Correct

The 5th Wave By Rich Tennant

"I'VE GOT SOME IMAGE EDITING SOFTWARE, SO I TOOK THE LIBERTY OF ERASING SOME OF THE SMUDGES THAT KEPT SHOWING UP AROUND THE CLOUDS. NO NEED TO THANK ME."

In this part . . .

The first time children arm themselves with crayons and coloring books, they all do the same thing: They scribble. Few children have sufficient coordination to color tidily and, frankly, I doubt that they see much point in it. But there's always one adult who says, "Darling, try to color inside the lines."

It's tough to unlearn a lesson that's ingrained into every one of us at such a trusting age, but the truth is, carefully coloring inside the lines is and always has been a counter-intuitive and nonartistic operation. It defeats expressionism and prevents you from seeing the larger picture.

"This may be so," you might argue, "But what if I'm trying to perform a delicate adjustment to a complex image? I can't just start scribbling all over the place." Ah, but there's where you're wrong. That's exactly what you can do. See, any time you want to constrain an effect to a small area of your image, you should first select it. After you've done that, Photoshop automatically ensures that the larger image remains intact, no matter how sloppy your motor skills.

As you might expect, selecting is the topic of Chapters 12 through 14. Here you find out how to select an element in your image, how to modify the selection if you don't get it exactly right the first time, and how to color selections.

So the next time you see some kids coloring inside the lines, you'll know what to tell them. "Hey you kids, don't you know that tidy people never prosper? Break off the tips of those crayons and start scribbling!"

Chapter 12

The Great Pixel Roundup (Yee Ha)

. . . .

In This Chapter

▶ Picking the right selection tool

▶ Roping pixels with the lasso tools

▶ Drawing straight-sided selections

▶ Selecting rectangular and oval areas

▶ Using the magic wand

▶ Selecting with the Color Range command

. . . .

*I*f you're an old ranch hand, you may find it helpful to think of the pixels in your image as a bunch of cows. A pixel may not have any horns and it rarely moos, but it's a cow all the same. Consider these amazing similarities:

✔ Both pixels and cows travel in herds. Come on, when's the last time you saw one pixel out on its own?

✔ They're both dumb as dirt. And obstinate to boot.

✔ They both eat alfalfa. (Okay, that's a lie. I was just trying to see if you were paying attention.)

✔ Neither of them lays eggs.

✔ And — here's the absolute clincher — you round up them both by using a lasso.

The only difference between pixels and cows, in fact, is in the vernacular. When you lasso a cow or two on the lone prairie, it's called ropin'. When you lasso a mess of pixels, it's called selectin', as in, "'N case you're lookin' for us, Ma, me 'n' Tex'll be out back selectin' pixels."

I'm allowed ta make fun of Westerners 'cause I am one. My great-grandpappy owned a farm in Kansas, my grandpappy worked on a ranch in New Mexikee, my pappy once took us campin' in Wyomin', 'n I've even been on a horse once or twice. Don't know nothin' 'bout you sissy Easterners and Southerners, but I kin make fun of Westerners till the pixels come home.

Dang, how about that dialect? Anyway, after you select the desired pixels, you can do things to them. You can move them, duplicate them, and apply all kinds of alterations that I describe in future chapters. Selecting lets you grab hold of some detail or other and edit it independently of other portions of your image. It's a way of isolating pixels with the intent to manipulate them, just as you might isolate a few cows and milk them, brand them, or just tip them over.

This chapter and Chapter 13 discuss methods for selecting portions of an image. With a little practice, you can rustle pixels better than most hands rope dogies, and that's no bull.

Learning the Ropes

Photoshop 4 provides several selection tools, all labeled in Figure 12-1. These tools include the lasso, the new polygon lasso, four so-called marquee tools, and an automatic color selector known as the magic wand. Here's how they work:

✔ Drag inside the image with the lasso to select free-form areas. The shape of the selection conforms to the shape of your drag.

✔ Use the polygon lasso tool, which shares a flyout menu with the regular lasso, to draw polygon selections — that is, selections made up of straight sides. In Photoshop 3, you Option-clicked with the regular lasso tool to draw polygons. You can still use that technique in Photoshop 4, but you also have the option of using the dedicated polygon lasso tool.

✔ The rectangular marquee tool lets you select a rectangular area. Just drag from one corner of the area you want to select to the other. The outline drawn with the tool looks like a border of moving dots — which is how *marquee* managed its way into the tool name.

✔ This use of the term *marquee* has been around for several years now. I suppose somebody thought that the moving dots looked like a movie marquee, but whatever the reason, the term stuck. Computer folks even use it as a verb, as in "Marquee that area over there, won't you Brenda?" "No, I will not, Sam. You can darn well marquee your own areas." These computer discussions can get pretty heated.

✔ The elliptical marquee draws oval selections. The word *ellipse,* incidentally, is what mathematicians say when they're talking about ovals. In fact, I'd just call it the *ovoid marquee tool,* but I'm afraid that you'd think I was talking about a home pregnancy test.

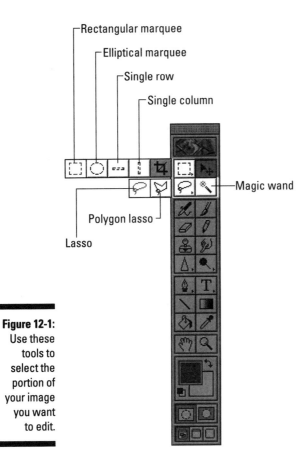

Rectangular marquee
Elliptical marquee
Single row
Single column

Magic wand

Polygon lasso
Lasso

Figure 12-1:
Use these
tools to
select the
portion of
your image
you want
to edit.

✔ The single-column and single-row marquee tools select one solitary column or row of pixels in your image. Both these tools fall under the limited-use category. In Photoshop 3, the single-row and single-column marquee options resided in the Marquee Tools Options palette. They still have a summer home there, but now you can also reach them at their toolbox address.

✔ The magic wand selects areas of continuous color. For example, if you want to select the sky without selecting the clouds, you just click in the sky. At least, that's the way it's supposed to work, but you never know. The magic wand isn't always as magic as you might think.

Getting to the Tools

As explained in Chapter 2, the arrow in the lower-right corner of the marquee and lasso tool icons in the toolbox indicates that a flyout menu of hidden tools lurks beneath each icon.

To switch between the tools on the flyout menus, you can Option-click on whichever tool icon happens to be visible in the toolbox at the time.

You can also select tools using these keyboard shortcuts:

- ✔ Press the M key to access the rectangular and elliptical marquee tools. If the rectangular marquee tool is active, pressing M changes it to the elliptical marquee tool, and vice versa.

- ✔ Press L to get the lasso tools. As with the marquee tools, the same short-cut also switches you between the two lasso tools: If the regular lasso is active, pressing L brings up the polygon lasso.

- ✔ Press W to get the magic wand. The tool is more unpredictable than magic, making W — for Wacky Wand — a logical keyboard equivalent.

- ✔ In Photoshop 3, you could temporarily access the wand by Control-clicking when one of the other selection tools was active. In Photoshop 4, Control-clicking brings up a context-sensitive menu, as discussed in Chapter 2. If you were into bad puns, you could say that Adobe took away Control of your magic.

Throwing Lassos

Both of the lasso tools are so easy to use, your newborn could master them. If you don't have a newborn, I guess that you are going to have to muddle through on your own.

Using the regular lasso

I have only one instruction for using the lasso: Trace around the portion of the image that you want to select with the tool. That's it. In Figure 12-2, for example, I dragged around the mushroom to select it independently of its surroundings. As the figure shows, Photoshop displays a dotted outline around the selected area after you release the mouse button. This outline represents the exact path of your drag. (If you release before completing the shape — that is, before meeting up with the point at which you began dragging — Photoshop simply connects the beginning and ending points with a straight line. So you won't hurt anything if you release too early.)

I was careful to draw the outline just right in Figure 12-2. There's no trick to it; I've just had plenty of practice. If your outlines aren't quite so accurate, however, don't sweat it. There are plenty of ways to modify the outline after you draw it, as I explain in Chapter 13.

Drawing straight-sided selections

Consider the image shown in Figure 12-3. Suppose you wanted to select that cube-with-a-ball thing in the center of the image. You could drag around it with the lasso tool, but a better option is to use the polygon lasso, which makes it easy to create selections with straight sides.

Lasso cursor ⌐   ⌐Selection outline

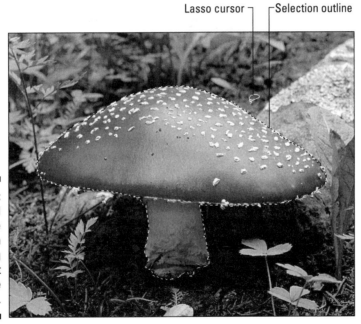

Figure 12-2: I selected the mushroom by dragging around it with the lasso.

The figure shows a close-up view of one of the many cool and unusual images in the Digital Stock "Cyberstock" image collection, by the way.

To select an object like this, click with the polygon lasso to set the beginning of the first line in the selection. Then move the mouse to the point where you want the line to end, and click again. Keep clicking to create new line segments. To complete the selection, you have two options. If you double-click, Photoshop draws a segment between the spot you double-click and the first point in your selection. You can also move the cursor over the first point in your selection until you see a little circle next to the polygon lasso cursor. Then simply click to close the selection.

Marquee   Polygon lasso cursor

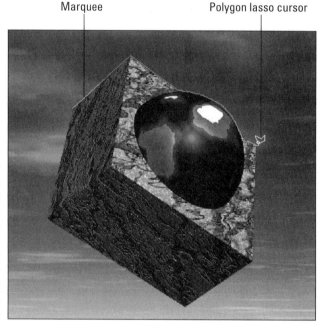

Figure 12-3:
The new
polygon
lasso tool is
helpful for
creating
straight-
sided
selections.

Now, if you paid particular attention to the image in Figure 12-3, you may have noticed that part of the selection is curved. "Hey," you ask, "what up with that? I thought the polygon lasso created straight-sided selections." Well, the answer is that you can switch to the regular lasso in midselection to create a curved segment. Just press and hold down the Option key and drag to draw your curved line. When you release the Option key, the tool reverts back to the polygon lasso.

You can also press Option while drawing a selection with the regular lasso to access the polygon lasso. Just press Option and click to set the endpoints of your straight-sided segments, as you normally do with the polygon lasso. To start another curved segment, just drag. You can keep the Option key down or not — it doesn't matter. But be sure that the mouse button is down any time you press or release the Option key, or Photoshop will complete the selection outline.

The very clever in the audience will realize that because of this Option-key thing, you really only need to make friends with one or the other of the lasso tools. The one time when you might really need to switch back and forth between tools is when modifying an existing selection outline, as explained in Chapter 13. When you have an existing selection outline, the Option key subtracts from the selection in Version 4. So you can't use Option to switch between lassos in that instance.

Exploring your lasso options

Whether you use the regular lasso or the polygon lasso, you can modify the performance of the tool via the two check boxes in the Lasso Options palette. (The palette's called the Polygon Lasso Options palette if you're using the polygon lasso.) To display the palette, double-click on the tool icon in the toolbox or press Return while the tool is selected.

Though small in number, the options for the lasso tools are some tough little hombres:

- First off, both options — Feather and Anti-aliased — affect future selection outlines drawn with the lasso tool. If you want to modify an outline that you've already drawn, you have to choose a command under the Select menu. Because these commands affect outlines drawn with any tool, I describe them in the next chapter, "More Fun with Selections."

- Normally, selections drawn with the lasso tools have soft, natural-looking edges. As I mention in Chapter 8, this softening is called *antialiasing*. To turn the softening off, click on the Anti-aliased check box in the palette to get rid of the check mark. From now on, outlines drawn with the tool will have jagged edges.

- Figure 12-4 shows two lassoed selections moved to reveal the white background in the image. In the left example, the Anti-aliased check box was turned off; in the right example, the option was turned on. The edges of the left example are jagged; those of the right example are soft. (The next chapter explains all the ways to move selections. But if you want to try moving a selection now, just drag it with the move tool, which is the top right tool in the toolbox. Or ⌘-drag with any other tool but the pen or hand tool.)

- Most of the time, you want to leave the Anti-aliased check box turned on. Just turn it off when you want to select precise, hard-edged areas. (Which may be never. Who knows?)

- Enter a value into the Feather option box to make the outline fuzzy. The value determines the radius of the fuzziness in pixels. If you enter a value of 3, for example, Photoshop extends the fuzzy region 3 pixels up, 3 pixels to the left, 3 pixels down, and 3 pixels to the right. As demonstrated in the first example of Figure 12-5, that's a lot of fuzz. A higher value results in a more fuzzy selection outline, as witnessed in the right example, which sports a Feather value of 10.

- Anytime one of the lasso tools is active, you can highlight the Feather value by pressing the Return key. Then just enter a new value and press Return again to apply it. You don't even have to move your mouse. That's what I call slick shootin'.

Antialiasing off   Antialiasing on

Figure 12-4:
The
difference
between
dragging a
jagged (left)
and anti-
aliased
(right)
selection.

Jagged edges   Soft edges

Feather 3 pixels   Feather 10 pixels

Figure 12-5:
A bigger
Feather
value means
more fuzzy
fungus.

Selecting Rectangles, Squares, Ellipses, and Circles

If you want to create a selection that's rectangular or elliptical, you use — guess what — the rectangular and elliptical marquee tools.

The rectangular and elliptical marquee tools are so easy to use that they make the lasso look complicated. You just drag from one corner to the opposite corner and release the mouse button. (Okay, ovals don't have corners, so you have to use your imagination a little bit.) The dotted marquee follows the movements of your cursor on-screen, keeping you apprised of the selection outline in progress.

But Photoshop has never been one to provide you with only one way to use a tool — or, in this case, two tools. For example, you can also use these tools to select perfect squares or circles. The program's cup of flexibility forever runneth over, and the marquee tools are no exception.

Grabbing a square or circle

Every so often, you may feel the urge to apply some puritanical constraints to your selection outlines. Enough of this random width and height business — you want perfect squares and circles. Lucky for you, Photoshop obliges these fussbudget impulses by letting you constrain shapes drawn with the marquee tool:

- ✔ To draw a perfect square, press the Shift key after you begin dragging with the rectangular marquee tool. To draw a perfect circle, press Shift after you begin dragging with the elliptical marquee tool.

- ✔ Drawing squares and circles is a little trickier than you might expect. For the best results, you should first begin dragging; then press and hold Shift, drag to the desired location and release the mouse button, and finally release Shift. In other words, press Shift after you start the drag and hold it until after you complete the drag.

- ✔ If you press Shift before dragging, you run the risk of adding to the previously selected area, as I describe in lucky Chapter 13. Here's the deal: If a portion of your image was selected before you started Shift-dragging, Photoshop sees to it that that area remains selected and selects the marqueed area as well. Meanwhile, the shape of the marquee is not constrained to a square or a circle. Befuddling, huh? If this happens to you, press ⌘-Z to undo the selection and try again, this time taking care to press Shift during — not before — your drag.

The marquee tools can come in handy not only for selecting part of your image, but for creating geometric shapes as well. For example, if you want to draw a rectangle, create a marquee with the rectangular marquee tool. Then choose Edit➪Stroke to *stroke* the marquee with the foreground color — in other words, to paint a line along the marquee. For more on the Stroke command, see the section "Your Image Needs Strokes, Too," in Chapter 14.

Getting even more control over selections

Are you crazed for control? Do your tyrannical desires know no bounds? If so, you probably won't be appeased by drawing a square or a circle. What you want is to apply even more stringent constraints.

For example, say that you're the sort of pixel-oppressor who wants to select a rectangular or oval area that is exactly twice as wide as it is tall. With your marquee tool selected, press Return to display the Marquee Options palette. Then choose Constrained Aspect Ratio from the Style pop-up menu, as shown in Figure 12-6. The Width and Height options boxes then come to life, letting you specify an aspect ratio, which is a precise proportion between the wideness and tallness of a marquee. To make the marquee twice as wide as it is tall, enter **2** as the Width value. Then press Tab to highlight the Height value and enter **1**. The deed is done.

Figure 12-6:
Select Constrained Aspect Ratio (top) and enter Width and Height values (bottom) to make future marquees conform to rigid proportions.

But that's not all. You can also set up the marquee to select a row or column of pixels that is a single pixel tall or wide. To do this, select the Single Row or Single Column icon from the marquee flyout menu in the toolbox or just select the tool option from the Shape pop-up menu in the upper-left corner of the Marquee Options palette. Then click to create the marquee. If you select Single

Row, the marquee is one pixel tall and extends across the entire width of your image; if you select Single Column, the marquee is one pixel wide and as tall as your image. After you click to create the marquee, you can drag it to reposition it if necessary.

Finally, to constrain the marquee to an exact size, select Fixed Size from the Style pop-up menu. Then enter the exact dimensions of your desired marquee into the Width and Height option boxes. The values are always measured in pixels. It's very unlikely that you may ever want to do this — even if you live to be 103 — but I didn't want you to think that I neglected to explain one of these silly options for no good reason.

One last item submitted for your approval: Like the Lasso Options palette discussed earlier in this chapter, the Marquee Options palette sports Anti-aliased and Feather options, which respectively soften the selection outline and make it blurry. However, the Anti-aliased check box is dimmed when you use the rectangular single column, or single row marquee tools. Perpendicular edges never need softening because perpendicular edges can't be jagged. Antialiasing, therefore, would be a waste of time.

Drawing from the center out

As I mentioned earlier, you draw a rectangle or oval from corner to opposite corner. But you can also draw a marquee from the center outward. To do this, begin dragging with either marquee tool and then press Option.

If you decide midway into your drag that you don't want to draw the shape from the center outward, just release the Option key and continue dragging. What was once the center of the marquee now becomes a corner.

To draw a square or circle from the center outward, press both Shift and Option after you begin dragging with the appropriate marquee tool. (If you press Shift and Option before you begin dragging, you select the intersection of two selections, as explained in Chapter 13.)

Wielding the Wand

The magic wand is even easier to use than the marquee tools. (Pretty soon, things will get so easy that you won't need me at all.) But it's also the most difficult selection tool to understand and predict. To use the tool, you just click inside an image. Photoshop then selects the area of continuous color that surrounds the cursor.

'Scuze me while I click the sky

Figure 12-7 provides an example of how the magic wand works. In the first image, I clicked with the magic wand tool in the sky above the fake dinosaur. Photoshop automatically selected the entire continuous area of sky. In the second example, I made the selection more apparent by pressing the Delete key to remove the color, which filled the selection with the background color, white. I also got rid of the selection outline by deselecting the area. (Don't worry, I explain deleting and deselecting in full, rich detail in future chapters.)

Figure 12-7:
Look what
happens
when I click
in the sky
above T-Rex
with the
magic wand
(top) and
press the
Delete key
(bottom).

Notice that the wand selects only uninterrupted areas of color. The patch of sky below the creature's tail, for example, remains intact. Also, the selection bit slightly into the edges of the dinosaur. Very small pieces along the top of the plastic behemoth were removed when I pressed Delete.

The next section explains how to modify the magic wand's performance to select more or fewer pixels. The section after that offers an alternative to try when you can't get the magic wand to select the stuff you want to select.

Teaching the wand tolerance

You can modify the performance of the magic wand by double-clicking on the wand icon in the toolbox or pressing Return with the tool selected. Either way, the Magic Wand Options palette appears, offering three options — Anti-aliased, Sample Merged, and Tolerance.

I covered Anti-aliased earlier, in the section "Exploring your lasso options," so I won't beat that poor horse anymore. Sample Merged only comes into play when your image contains more than one layer, as discussed in Chapter 15. When Sample Merged is turned off, the magic wand selects colors on the active layer only. If you want the magic wand to select colors from all visible layers, turn the option on.

That leaves the Tolerance value, which has the most sway over the performance of the magic wand. It tells Photoshop which colors to select and which not to select. A lower Tolerance value instructs the wand to select fewer colors; a higher value instructs it to select more colors.

Color Plate 12-1 shows what I mean. Each row of images demonstrates the effect of a different Tolerance value, starting with the default value of 32 at the top and working up to 180 at the bottom. In each case, I clicked at the same location, just to the right of the big giraffe's schnoz. The left image in each row shows the selection outline created when I clicked; the right image shows what happened when I deleted and deselected the selection.

In the color plate, a Tolerance value of 32 selected too little sky; a value of 180 selected all the sky but also got some huge chunks of giraffe face and rolling foothill. A value of 90 appears to be just right.

The problem is, finding the best Tolerance setting is a completely random exercise in the futile art of trial and error. Like changes to any tool setting, changes to the Tolerance value have no effect on the current selection. You have to click with the magic wand to try out each and every new value. In fact, here's the typical approach:

1. **Click with the magic wand tool.**

   The point at which you click marks the base color — the one Photoshop uses to judge which other colors it should select.

2. **Express displeasure with the results.**

   Gnash your teeth for good measure.

3. **Press the Return key.**

   Pressing Return while the magic wand is active displays the Magic Wand Options palette — if it's not already visible — and highlights the Tolerance value.

4. **Enter a new Tolerance value and press Return.**

   Enter a higher value to select more colors next time around; enter a lower value to select fewer colors.

5. **Choose Select⇨None or press ⌘-D.**

   Photoshop deselects the previous selection.

6. **Repeat Steps 1 through 5 until you get it right.**

Believe me, even longtime Photoshop hacks like me who've been using the software since Copernicus discovered that the Earth orbits the sun go through this ritual every time they use the magic wand tool. What can I say? It's a useful little tool, but it requires some experimenting.

Selecting with the Better Magic Wand

Photoshop provides an even better magic wand in the form of the Color Range command, which is found under the Select menu. This command lets you select multiple areas of color at a time, even if they aren't continuous. Also, you can adjust the equivalent of the Tolerance setting and see its effect on the selection before you apply the command. The Color Range command is a little complex, but it makes the magic wand look like dog meat.

If you were to investigate the Color Range command and its accompanying dialog box on your own, you might mistake it for one of the most complicated Photoshop functions. But deep down inside, it's a pussycat. You just have to know which options to use and which to ignore.

Strolling through the Color Range

Because we're venturing into some pretty unfriendly territory, I'm going to step you through the Color Range command. Just look where I tell you to look and avert your eyes from the scary stuff, and you won't go wrong.

1. Select the eyedropper tool.

You select the eyedropper by pressing the I key.

2. Click on a spot inside the area you want to select.

Use the eyedropper as if it were the magic wand tool. Nothing becomes selected, of course, but you change the foreground color. The Color Range command uses the foreground color as the base color, just as the magic wand uses the color on which you click as the base color.

3. Choose Select⇨Color Range.

The Color Range dialog box shown in Figure 12-8 appears. I've taken the liberty of dimming all the options that aren't important.

The selection preview box shows your selection in black and white. The white areas are selected, the black areas are not selected, and the gray areas are blurred selection edges (just as if you had feathered them).

In case you're wondering what that big black blob is in the middle of Figure 12-8, it represents the giraffe image shown in Color Plate 12-2. Before choosing the Color Range command, I clicked to the right of the big giraffe's snout.

4. Change the Fuzziness value from 1 to 200 to adjust the tolerance.

As with the magic wand's Tolerance setting, higher Fuzziness values select more colors, lower values select fewer colors. As you change the value, the selection preview box shows you how the new Fuzziness setting affects the selection. In Figure 12-9, you can see how the selected area — in white — grows as I increase the Fuzziness value.

Selection preview

Figure 12-8:
The slider bar, the selection preview, and the OK and Cancel buttons are the only important elements of this dialog box.

Color Range

Select: ✎ Sampled Colors ▼

Fuzziness: 40

OK

Cancel

Load...

Save...

☐ Invert

● Selection ○ Image

Selection Preview: None ▼

Figure 12-9:
Increasing
the
Fuzziness
spreads the
selection,
shown in
white.

5. Click on the OK button when you finish.

Or press Return. Photoshop selects the area displayed as white in the selection preview.

The left example in Color Plate 12-2 shows the result of applying the Color Range command with a maximum Fuzziness value of 200 to the giraffe image. I then pressed Delete to fill the selection with white and deselected the image to arrive at the right example. The Color Range command selected colors on both sides of the giraffe, even though I lifted the base color from the right half of the sky.

The Color Range dialog box in Version 4 offers an Invert check box, which does the same thing as the Select⇨Inverse command: It selects everything that's currently not selected and deselects everything that's selected. In other words, it selects the exact opposite of what's currently selected. For more on the Select⇨Inverse command, see the section "Swapping what's selected for what's not," in Chapter 13.

If you choose the Color Range command when a portion of your image is selected, the command selects colors only if they fall inside the current selection. Colors outside the selection are ignored. Therefore, you generally want to press ⌘-D to deselect the image before choosing Select⇨Color Range. Doing so makes the entire image accessible to the command.

Broadening your color base

Despite the Color Range command's prowess, I wouldn't call Color Plate 12-2 an unqualified success. A lot of blue remains in the second example that the magic wand managed to pick up in Color Plate 12-1.

The fact is, the magic wand and Color Range commands evaluate colors differently (which is why their color-sensing options — Tolerance and Fuzziness — have different names). The wand uses the Tolerance value to decide whether colors are similar to the base color and then selects them. The Color Range command selects all occurrences of the base color in an image and then feathers the selection according to the Fuzziness value. So the magic wand creates definite selection outlines with antialiased edges; the Color Range command creates more nebulous ones with blurry edges.

But there's more to the Color Range command, Horatio, than is dreamt of in your philosophy. Unlike the magic wand, the Color Range command lets you specify more than one base color. After choosing Select⇨Color Range, move the cursor outside the Color Range dialog box and over the image. The cursor changes to the eyedropper, allowing you to change the base color if you like. Press and hold the Shift key, and you see a small plus sign appear next to the eyedropper. Click with this cursor to add a second base color. Continue Shift-clicking to add a third base color, fourth, fifth, and so on. Add as many as you like.

In Color Plate 12-3, I specified three base colors. I set the first one before choosing Select⇨Color Range by clicking to the right of the giraffe nose with the eyedropper tool, just as in Color Plate 12-2. I set the other two by Shift-clicking in the image while inside the Color Range dialog box, once above the giraffe's ear and once below its neck (as the cursors in the color plate indicate).

Adding base colors increased the size of the selected area. To make the selection outline less blurry, I lowered the Fuzziness value to 60. The first image in Color Plate 12-3 shows the resulting selection outline; the second image shows what happened when I deleted and deselected. Even though the background is now completely white, the giraffes still blend in naturally, an effect that you can't easily achieve with the magic wand.

It is possible to add too many base colors. As a result, you may select portions of your image that you don't want to select. If this happens, you can delete base colors from inside the Color Range dialog box by Option-clicking on the image. When the Option key is pressed, a little minus sign appears next to the eyedropper cursor.

If adding and deleting base colors start to get confusing, you can reset the selection in the Color Range dialog box by clicking on the image without pressing Shift or Option. This returns you to a single base color.

Chapter 13
More Fun with Selections

*I*n the old days, image-editing programs expected perfection from their users. If you didn't get a selection outline right the first time, too bad. You had to start over and try again.

Photoshop broke this heartless trend by expanding its range of selection options. In other words, it got smarter so that you and I can be dumber. Like all the world's best computer programs, Photoshop knows that human beings are a pretty fallible lot and need all the help they can get.

So Photoshop lets you modify a selection outline after you draw it. You can select additional pixels or trim the selection down to a smaller area. You can even smooth out sharp corners, expand a selection to include all similar colors, or swap the selected and deselected portions of the image. All things considered, Photoshop is about the most flexible selector there ever was.

This chapter explains how to modify an existing selection and also touches on more techniques that you can use with the selection tools discussed in Chapter 12. It also tells you how to move and clone selections and explores a wealth of commands under the Select menu that you probably haven't even looked at yet. By the end of this chapter, you'll have a clearer understanding of selection outlines than any other kid on the playground (unless he or she read this chapter, too).

The Wonders of Deselection

Before I plow into all that whiz-bang, awesome stuff that Photoshop lets you do to a selection outline, I need to touch on selection's exact opposite, deselection. Though this may seem on the face of it like a ridiculously boneheaded topic — one that hardly merits space in a scholarly tome like *Photoshop 4 For Macs For Dummies* — deselecting is actually an integral step in the selection process.

Suppose, for example, that you select one part of your image. Then you change your mind and decide to select a different portion instead. Before you can select that new area, you have to deselect the old one. You can deselect an existing selection outline in several ways:

- ✔ Click anywhere in the image with one of the lasso or marquee tools.

- ✔ To get rid of an existing selection and create a new one at the same time, just drag or click to create the new selection as you normally would. Photoshop automatically deselects the old selection when you create a new one.

- ✔ Click inside the selection with the magic wand. (If you click outside the selection, you not only deselect the selection, you create a new selection.)

- ✔ Choose Select⇨None or press ⌘-D (for Deselect).

You can regain a selection outline right after deselecting it by pressing ⌘-Z. That's right, the Undo command even keeps track of selections.

Selecting Everything

When no part of an image is selected, the entire image is up for grabs. You can edit any part of it using the paint or edit tools or any of about a billion commands. But you can also make the entire image available for edits by choosing Select⇨All (⌘-A) to select everything.

Beginning to see the mystery here? If you can edit any part of the image by deselecting it, why choose Select⇨All, which also lets you edit everything?

Because some operations require a selection, that's why. In fact, if you want to apply any of the following operations to your image in its entirety, you must first press ⌘-A:

- ✔ Clone an image by Option-dragging it with the move tool, as discussed later in this chapter

✔ Cut, copy, or paste an image using any of the commands under the Edit menu (discussed in Chapter 15)

✔ Apply Edit⇨Stroke (explored in Chapter 14) on the Background layer of an image (as explained in Chapter 15)

✔ Apply the Layer⇨Free Transform command or any of the commands under the Layer⇨Transform submenu on the Background layer of an image. (The Transform commands are sniffed out in Chapter 20.)

Unless you're doing one of these things, you need never worry about Select⇨All. A deselected image usually serves just as well.

Selective Arithmetic

I almost never like the first selection outline I create. Whether I draw it with a lasso or marquee tool, the magic wand, or the Color Range command, I usually have some problem with the selection. I didn't quite get the hair selected right, or that finger is still clipped off. Whatever the problem, I can remedy it by adding to the selection outline or subtracting from it. And so can you.

The last section of Chapter 12 ("Broadening your color base") explains how you can Shift-click on an image while inside the Color Range dialog box to add base colors and Option-click to delete base colors. These two keys — Shift and Option — are the universal add and subtract selection modifiers throughout Photoshop.

For those readers who upgraded to Version 4 from an earlier version of Photoshop, I repeat: The keyboard shortcut for subtracting from a selection is now the Option key, not the ⌘ key as in previous versions. The ⌘ key now accesses the move tool temporarily when another tool is selected.

Adding and subtracting from a selection

To add an area to the current selection, Shift-drag with a lasso or marquee tool. Or Shift-click with the magic wand. It doesn't matter which tool you used to select the image previously, nor does it matter whether you Shift-click inside the selection or outside of it.

For example, in the obligatory person-holding-up-the-Tower-of-Pisa photo in Figure 13-1, I first selected the tower by dragging around it with the lasso tool, as shown in the left example. To add the woman to the selection, I Shift-dragged around her, creating the selection outline shown in the right example.

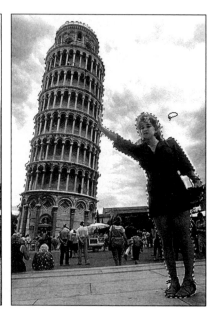

Figure 13-1:
First, I
selected the
tower (left)
and then I
Shift-
dragged
around the
woman to
select her,
too (right).

To remove an area from a selection, Option-drag with a lasso or marquee tool or Option-click with the magic wand. To deselect the gap between the woman's legs in Figure 13-1, for example, I might Option-drag with the lasso tool. To deselect the area under the right arm (her left arm), I could Option-click with the magic wand.

Here are a few more addition and subtraction items to keep in mind:

✔ When you're adding to a selection, a little plus sign appears next to your cursor. When you're subtracting from the selection, a little minus sign appears. And when you're selecting the intersection of two existing selections (as explained next), a little multiply sign appears. See, your math teacher was right — knowing arithmetic comes in handy in all kinds of situations.

✔ You can also use the Shift and Option keys in conjunction with the Color Range command. Shift-choose Select➪Color Range to add to the selected area; Option-choose the command to subtract from the selection.

The intersection of Selection and Selection

If you press the Shift and Option keys together while clicking with the magic wand or dragging with a lasso or marquee tool, you select the intersection of the previous selection and the newest one. (Like that made any sense, right?) Take a look at Figure 13-2. I first dragged around the black rectangle. Then I Shift-Option-dragged around the gray rectangle. Photoshop then selected all portions of the second marquee that fell inside the first marquee and deselected everything else, leaving me with the selection shown in the right half of the figure. That's an intersection.

Figure 13-2:
I marqueed the black rectangle and Shift-Option-marqueed the second rectangle (left). Photoshop then selected the intersection of the two marquees (right).

Try selecting an area with the lasso or one of the marquee tools and then Shift-Option–clicking inside it with the magic wand. Or click with the magic wand and then Shift-Option drag with one of the other selection tools. Either technique lets you limit the area of colors selected with the magic wand tool.

As I discussed earlier in this chapter, if a portion of your image was selected using the Color Range command, you can Shift-choose or Option-choose the command again to add to or subtract from the selection. If you don't press any key when choosing Select⇨Color Range, Photoshop selects an area inside the current selection. In other words, it already creates an intersection, so you don't gain anything by pressing both Option and Shift when choosing this command.

Avoiding keyboard collisions

In Chapter 12, I discuss a variety of ways to use the lasso and marquee tools while pressing keys. Pressing Option while using one of the lasso tools, you may recall, temporarily accesses the other lasso tool. Pressing Shift while using a marquee tool results in perfect squares and circles.

But what happens when you start combining all these add, subtract, and intersect shortcut keys with the ones discussed in the previous chapter? The following list answers your most burning questions:

✔ To add a square or circular area to an existing selection, start by Shift-dragging with the appropriate marquee tool. You get an unconstrained rectangle or oval, just as if the Shift key weren't down. Then midway into the drag — here's the catch — release the Shift key and then press it again, all the while keeping the mouse button down. The shape snaps to a square or circle with the second press of Shift. Keep the Shift key down until after you release the mouse button. Bet you didn't see that one coming.

✔ Pressing Option to temporarily access the polygon lasso when the regular lasso is active causes trouble when you have an existing selection, because pressing Option in that scenario sets you up to subtract from the selection. So if you want to add or subtract a straight-sided selection, use the polygon lasso — don't try to Option-click with the regular lasso.

✔ The same advice goes if you want to find the intersection of a selection and a straight-sided shape.

Automatic Selection Discombobulators

Shift-dragging, Option-dragging, and all those other wondrous techniques that I just finished describing — and, possibly, you just finished reading about — are wildly helpful when it comes to selecting complex details. But they aren't the only selection modifications you can make. Photoshop offers a handful of automatic functions that reshape selection outlines, blur them, and otherwise mess them up.

All the commands discussed in the next few sections — Grow, Similar, Inverse, Feather, and so on — reside under the Select menu. I don't discuss every command under the Select menu, just the ones you need to know. But you can take it from me, the commands I don't mention are just so much wasted space.

Extending the magic wand

Two commands, Grow and Similar, are extensions of the magic wand tool. The Grow command expands the size of the selection to include still more continuous colors. For example, if clicking with the magic wand doesn't select all the colors you want it to, you can either increase the Tolerance value inside the Magic Wand Options palette and reclick with the tool or just choose Select⇨ Grow to incorporate even more colors. It's kind of a clunky method, especially now that the Grow command doesn't have a keyboard shortcut, as it did in earlier versions of Photoshop. (⌘-G now groups layers.) I prefer Shift-clicking with the wand tool, but every once in a while the Grow command works like you'd expect. (You can use the Grow command with selections made with tools other than the magic wand, by the way.)

The Similar command selects all colors that are similar to the selected colors regardless of whether they're interrupted by other colors or not. In other words, Similar selects all the continuous colors that Grow selects, as well as all similarly colored pixels throughout the image.

Both Grow and Similar judge color similarity exactly like the magic wand tool does — that is, according to the Tolerance value in the Magic Wand Options palette. So if you increase the Tolerance value, the commands select more colors; if you decrease the value, the commands select fewer colors. For example, if you want to select all colors throughout the image that are exactly identical to the ones you've selected so far, enter 0 into the Tolerance option box and choose Select⇨Similar.

Swapping what's selected for what's not

Sometimes it's easier to select the stuff you don't want to select and then tell Photoshop to select the deselected stuff and deselect what's selected. This technique is called *inversing a selection,* and you do it by choosing Select⇨ Inverse or pressing ⌘-Shift-I.

For example, suppose that you want to select the clock tower shown on the left side of Figure 13-3. A typical work of baroque madness, this building has more spikes and little twisty bits than a porcupine. Therefore, selecting it would prove a nightmare.

Selecting the sky, on the other hand, is quite easy. By clicking and Shift-clicking a couple of times with the magic wand tool (set to the default Tolerance of 32), I was able to select the entire sky in a matter of 2 or 3 seconds. When I then chose Select⇨Inverse, I inversed the selection so that the building became selected and the sky became deselected. To better show off the selection, I pressed the Delete key to fill it with white, as shown in the right example in the figure.

Figure 13-3:
This building (left) is too darn ornate to select easily, but it's a snap to select the sky and then inverse the selection. Pressing Delete shows how accurate the selection is (right).

Making the selection fuzzy around the edges

Chapter 12 explains how you can blur the edges of a selection created with the lasso or marquee tools by increasing the Feather value in the corresponding Options palette. But more often than not, you want to leave the Feather value set to 0 and apply your feathering after you finish drawing the outline.

To feather an existing selection, choose Select⇨Feather or press ⌘-Shift-D. A dinky dialog box with a single option box appears on-screen. Enter the amount of fuzziness, in pixels, that you want to apply to the selection and press Return. The selection outline probably won't change very much, but you'll see a distinct blurring effect when you edit the selection.

You can use feathering to make an image appear to fade into view. For example, take a look at the kid-in-a-basket image shown on the left side of Figure 13-4. I selected the elliptical marquee tool and encircled the little duffer. Then I chose Select➪Inverse to select the background instead. Next I chose Select➪Feather, entered a value of 8 pixels, and pressed Return. Finally, I pressed the Delete key to fill the selection with white. The result is the locket with fuzzy edges shown on the right side of Figure 13-4. Isn't he just adorable?

Figure 13-4:
A tiny tot trapped in a basket (left) receives a classic feathering treatment (right).

Border, Smooth, and the rest

The remaining selection outline modifiers, all found in the Select➪Modify submenu, aren't quite as useful, but they come in handy every now and then:

✔ The Border command selects an area around the edge of the selection. You tell Photoshop the width, in pixels, of the border you want to select. This command is probably the least useful command of the bunch. If you want to color the outline of a selection, it's easier to use Edit➪Stroke, as described in Chapter 14.

✔ Select➪Modify➪Smooth rounds off the corners of a selection outline. If the selection is very irregular and you want to straighten out the twists and turns, use this command. Photoshop asks you to enter a value from 1 to 16 to tell it how far it can move any point in the outline. Enter 2 or 3 to be safe.

✔ If you want to increase the size of a selection a few pixels outward, choose Select⇨Modify⇨Expand and then enter the number of pixels. The maximum value is 16 pixels; if you want to expand the outline farther, you have to choose Expand a second time.

✔ Select⇨Modify⇨Contract is the opposite of the Expand command. This command shrinks the selected area by 1 to 16 pixels all the way around.

Moving and Cloning Selections

Before bidding a fond farewell to Chapter 13, I want to quickly touch on the two most common things you can do with a selection: move it and clone it.

Moving and cloning work differently in Version 4 — very differently — thanks to the addition of the new move tool, which is the one in the upper-right corner of the toolbox. Here's the lowdown:

✔ To move a selection, grab the move tool (press V to select the tool from the keyboard) and drag the selection. A little pair of scissors appears by your cursor to show that you're about to move the selection from its current home. When you move the selection, the area where the selection used to be is filled with the background color, as illustrated in Figure 13-5.

✔ You can temporarily access the move tool by pressing ⌘ when any tool but the hand or pen tool is selected.

✔ To nudge a selection one pixel, press one of the arrow keys while the move tool is selected. Or press ⌘ and an arrow key when any tool but the pen or hand tool is selected. The up arrow nudges the selection one pixel up; the right pixel nudges it to the right, and so on, just like you'd think. To nudge a selection 10 pixels, press Shift along with an arrow key while the move tool is selected.

✔ To clone and move a selection, Option-drag with the move tool or ⌘-Option-drag with any other tool but the hand or pen tool. Your cursor changes into two arrowheads — your reminder that you're creating a clone of your selection.

✔ To clone and nudge, select the move tool and then press Option and one of the arrow keys. Or, when any other tool but the hand or pen tool is selected, press ⌘ and Option as you press the arrow keys. Press Shift and Option with an arrow key to clone the selection and move it 10 pixels.

Figure 13-5:
After selecting the Washington Monument (top), I dragged it to a more convenient location, leaving a gaping hole in the Capitol skyline (bottom).

✔ To move a selection outline without moving the image inside it, select a lasso or marquee tool. Then just drag the selection outline or nudge it with the arrow keys. This is a great way to reposition a selection outline without disturbing so much as a single pixel in the image.

✔ You can move and clone selections and selection outlines between images just as you would within a single image. Just drag the selection or selection outline from its current window into the other image window.

✔ Yet another way to move a selection is to use the Layer⇨Free Transform command, discussed in Chapter 20, in the section "Stretching the Face This Way and That." Free Transform enables you to move, resize, rotate, and distort your image by manipulating a special selection marquee. To move the selection, just drag inside the marquee. To discover how to perform other Free Transform tricks, see the aforementioned section in Chapter 20.

✔ When you're moving or cloning a selection, those animated dots that parade around the outline — called marching ants in some quarters — can be downright distracting. Sure, the ants permit you to see the boundaries of your selection, but sometimes you need to see how the edges of the selection blend in with their new surroundings. To do this, choose View⇨Hide Edges or press ⌘-H.

✔ To bring back the marching ants, press ⌘-H again.

✔ If you'd like to see more than an outline of your selection as you move it about, press and hold inside the selection for a full second and then start dragging. This slight pause tells Photoshop to display the selection in full detail as you move it. Your movements may appear a little jerkier because Photoshop has to work a lot harder to display the image in motion, but if you need to see exactly what's going on, this is the only way to go.

Chapter 14

Coloring Inside the Lines

. . . .

In This Chapter

▶ Painting and editing inside a selection outline

▶ Using the paint bucket tool

▶ Filling from the keyboard

▶ Using the Fill command

▶ Reverting a selection

▶ Creating gradients

▶ Applying different types of gradients

▶ Stroking a selection

. . . .

*E*ver spray-painted with a stencil? In case you've never engaged in this riveting pastime, let me explain how it works:

1. Hold the stencil up to the surface you want to paint.

2. Spray recklessly.

When you take the stencil away, you discover a painted image that matches the shape of the stencil. It's the epitome of a no-brainer.

In Photoshop, a selection outline works the same way. Just as a stencil isolates the area affected by the spray paint, a selection outline isolates the area affected by a paint or edit tool. You can also fill a selection outline with color or trace an outline around it.

Sounds easy, doesn't it? Like an unremarkable bit of information that virtually flings itself at the attention of the most casual observer. Like something you could have figured out on your own, for example, and saved $19.99. Well, whatever it sounds like, I intend to walk you through every nuance of painting, filling, and tracing selections. I reckon that after spending two chapters creating and manipulating selection outlines, it's high time you found out what to do with them. (The selection outlines, that is, not the chapters. You already know what to do with the chapters — tear them out and use them to line the parrot cage.)

Put Down Newspaper Before You Paint

If some portion of an image is selected, Photoshop treats all deselected areas as protected. You can use any paint or edit tool inside the selection without worrying about harming areas outside the selection.

Fix your gaze upon Figure 14-1. This jar-in-a-nook has a certain austere beauty about it — it's just the sort of prop that would feel right at home in a hoity-toity kitchen of the idle rich. But imagine that you are consumed with a desire to muck it up. Specifically, you want to paint inside the jar without harming the background. To this end, you would do the following:

1. **Select the jar.**

   This is the only step that takes any work. You might start out by selecting the body of the jar with the elliptical marquee tool. If you have problems getting the marquee exactly on the jar — it's hard to know where to start dragging so that it comes out right — just make sure that the marquee is approximately the right size, select one of the marquee or lasso tools and then use the arrow keys to nudge the outline into position. After you select the body to your satisfaction, you might Shift-drag with the lasso tool to incorporate the neck of the jar into the selection as well.

2. **Make any modifications you deem necessary.**

   In this case, you might want to blur the selection outline a tad using Select⇨Feather, as explained in Chapter 13. If your selection outline isn't dead on, the Feather command helps to fudge the difference a little.

3. **Choose View⇨Hide Edges or press ⌘-H.**

   This step is extremely important. By hiding the selection outline, you can see how your edits affect the image without those distracting marching ants getting in your way.

4. **Paint and edit away.**

   Feel free to use any tool you want. You can paint with the paintbrush, airbrush, or pencil; edit with the smudge, focus, or toning tools; clone with the rubber stamp; or reveal the saved image with the eraser — all with the assurance that the area outside the selection will remain as safeguarded from your changes as the driven snow (or whatever the saying is).

While editing away, be sure not to press ⌘-D or click with one of the selection tools. Because the selection outline is hidden, you won't notice any difference when you deselect the image. If you do inadvertently deselect, press ⌘-Z right away. If you wait until after you apply a brush stroke, ⌘-Z undoes the stroke but not the selection outline.

Figure 14-1:
A jar-in-a-
nook is a
terrible
thing to
leave
unmolested.

In Figure 14-2, I painted inside my selected jar using a single tool — the airbrush — with a single brush size and only two colors, black and white. As a result, I was able to transform the jar into a kind of marble. Looks mighty keen, and there's not so much as a drop of paint outside the lines.

Figure 14-2:
I painted
inside the
selected jar
with the
airbrush.
(You can't
see the
selection
outline
because it's
hidden.)

This stenciling feature is so all-fired handy that I almost always select an area before applying a paint or edit tool. The fact is, the selection tools are easier to control than the painting or editing tools, so you may as well take advantage of them.

Dribbling Paint from a Bucket

Photoshop lets you fill a selection with the foreground color, the background color, or a gradual blend of colors called a *gradient.* You can even fill a selection with the saved version of the image or a snapshot.

But before I explain any of these eye-popping options, I want to cover the paint bucket tool, which is part selection tool and part fill tool. The second tool from the bottom on the right side of the toolbox — it looks like a tilted bucket of paint — the paint bucket tool lets you fill an area of continuous color by clicking on it.

In Figure 14-3, for example, I set the foreground to white and clicked with the paint bucket tool on the row of broccoli in the jar. Photoshop fills the broccoli with white, turning it into the rough facsimile of cauliflower.

Paint bucket tool

Figure 14-3:
The paint bucket fills a continuous area of color with a different color.

To adjust the performance of the paint bucket, press Return to open the Paint Bucket Options palette, also shown in Figure 14-3. As with the magic wand, the Tolerance value determines how many pixels in your image are affected by the paint bucket. The only difference is that the paint bucket applies color instead of selecting pixels. You can also select the Anti-aliased check box to soften the edges of the filled area. (In Figure 14-3, the Tolerance value was 32 and Anti-aliased was turned on, as it is by default.)

The problem with the paint bucket tool is that it's hard to get the Tolerance value just right. You usually end up choosing Undo several times and resetting the Tolerance value until you find the value that colors the pixels you want to color and no more. Overall, I consider the paint bucket a poor tool for filling areas in Photoshop. If you select an area in your image using the magic wand, discussed in Chapter 12, and then fill the area with color — as described in the next sections — you not only produce the same effect as with the paint bucket, you have more alternatives at your disposal.

If you decide to ignore my advice and take up the paint bucket at your earliest opportunity, you can select quickly by pressing the K key. You know, for bucKet.

Applying Color to Selection Innards

Now that I've expressed my opinion regarding the paint bucket — ick, yuk, stay away — it's time to move on to the essential methods for filling a selection outline in Photoshop:

✔ To fill a selection with the foreground color, press Option-Delete.

✔ To fill a selection with the background color, press ⌘-Delete.

✔ In earlier versions of Photoshop, you could press Delete to fill a selection with the background color. You can still use that method in Version 4 *if* the selection exists on the background layer *and* hasn't been moved. Otherwise, pressing Delete gets rid of the selected area instead of filling it with the background color. So that you don't have to worry about the possibility of destroying your selection instead of filling it, get in the habit of always using ⌘-Delete instead of Delete to fill a selection.

✔ When you're working on a layer and want to fill the opaque part of a selection with the foreground color while leaving the rest of the selection transparent, press Shift-Option-Delete. Press ⌘-Shift-Delete to fill the opaque area with the background color. (And if all this makes no sense at all, read Chapter 15, which explains layers and transparency.)

✔ Choose Edit⇨Fill to display the Fill dialog box, which lets you fill the selection with translucent color or with the saved image or snapshot.

✔ Drag with the gradient tool to create a gradient (blend) between two or more colors.

Two of these options — Edit⇨Fill and the gradient tool — require more discussion than I have devoted to them so far, which is why the rest of this chapter is so filled to the gills with text.

Fill, I Command You!

Choose Edit⇨Fill to display the Fill dialog box shown in Figure 14-4. The Use pop-up menu lets you specify the color or stored image with which you want to fill the selection; the Blending options let you mix the filled colors with the colors already inside the selection. All these options are discussed in more detail in the upcoming paragraphs.

You can also display the Fill dialog box by pressing Shift-Delete.

Figure 14-4:
Specify how
you want to
fill a
selection by
using the
options in
the Fill
dialog box.

Fill
Contents
Use: [Foreground Color] [▼]
[OK]
[Cancel]
Blending
Opacity: [100] %
Mode: [Normal] [▼]
☐ Preserve Transparency

Select your stuffing

The most important part of the Fill dialog box is the Use pop-up menu. Here you select the stuff you want to use to fill the selection. The options are as follows:

- The Foreground Color option fills the selection with the foreground color, and the Background Color option fills it with the background color. I can see by your expression that you're not surprised by this news.

- The next option, Pattern, fills a selection with a repeating pattern. To use this option, you must first define the pattern by selecting a rectangular area and choosing Edit⇨Define Pattern. If no pattern has been defined, the Pattern option is dimmed. As I state in Chapter 10 when discussing the rubber stamp and will restate now, the Pattern option doesn't serve much of a practical purpose.

✔ Choose the Saved option to fill the selection with the saved version of that portion of the image. Using this option is just like reverting a selected area (as discussed in Chapter 11), except that Photoshop decided to stick it in this out-of-the-way place where no one would think to look for it. This is a great feature, and you'll use it often.

✔ Similarly, the Snapshot option lets you change the selection to the way it looked when you chose Edit➪Take Snapshot. For more about the Take Snapshot command, refer to Chapter 11.

✔ The last three options — Black, 50% Gray, and White — fill the selection with black, medium gray, or white. What's the point? Not much. If the foreground and background colors are set to blue and orange and you don't want to change them, I suppose that you might find these options useful. And pigs might fly. You just never know.

How not to mix colors

You can enter a value into the Opacity option box of the Fill dialog box to mix the fill color or saved image with the present colors in the selection. You can also mix the fill and the selected color using the options in the Mode pop-up menu, which include Multiply, Screen, Difference, and all those other wacky brush modes that you may remember from Chapter 8 (and Color Plate 8-2).

Notice that I said you *can* do these things, not that you should. The truth is, you don't want to use the Fill dialog box's Blending options to mix fills with selections. Why? Because the Fill dialog box doesn't let you preview the effects of the Blending options. Even seasoned professionals have trouble predicting the exact repercussions of Opacity settings and brush modes, and it's likely that you will, too. And if you don't like what you get, you have to undo the operation and choose Edit➪Fill all over again.

The better way to mix fills with selections is to copy the selection to a new layer, fill it, and experiment with the Opacity slider and mode options in the Layers palette. Naturally, you may have no idea what I'm talking about, but you will after you read the supremely insightful Chapter 15. Until then, take my valuable advice and be content to ignore the Opacity and Mode options in the Blending area at the bottom of the Fill dialog box.

The Preserve Transparency check box comes into play when you're working on a layer other than the background layer, as discussed in Chapter 15. If the check box is turned on, only the opaque pixels in a selection are filled when you apply the Fill command — the transparent areas remain transparent. If the check box is turned off, the entire selection is filled. The option is dimmed if the Preserve Transparency option in the Layers palette is turned on.

The Ever-Changing Color Sea

The third tool from the bottom on the right side of the toolbox, the gradient tool, lets you fill a selection with a fountain of colors that starts with one color and ends with another. By default, the two colors are the foreground color and background color.

But Photoshop 4 can do more than create simple two-color blends. You can now create custom gradients that blend as many as 32 colors and vary from opaque to transparent throughout the blend. The gradient tool has gotten a lot more powerful — and a lot more complex — in Version 4, which is why I've broken down the necessary information into the easily swallowed chunks of text that follow.

Checking out the gradient tool

The following steps provide one of those in-depth introductions to the gradient tool that folks find so helpful nowadays:

1. Select some portion of your image.

In Figure 14-5, I selected the jar again. I love that jar. It's so pristine, it just begs for me to mess it up.

If you don't select a portion of your image before using the gradient tool, Photoshop fills the entire image with the gradient. (Or, if you're working on a layer, as discussed in the next chapter, the gradient fills the entire layer.)

2. Select the gradient tool.

To do it quickly, just press the G key.

3. Select the Foreground to Background option from the Gradient pop-up menu in the Gradient Tool Options palette.

To display the palette, press Return. The Foreground to Background option is the default setting. It creates a gradient that begins with the foreground color and ends with the background color.

4. Set the foreground and background colors the way you want them.

This step is up to you. You can stick with black and white or select new colors with the eyedropper tool or Color palette. For purposes of the figure, I just set my colors to the defaults, black and white.

5. Begin dragging at the point where you want to set the foreground color.

In Figure 14-5, I began my drag at the bottom of the jar.

6. Release where you want to position the background color.

I released at the top of the jar. The result is a black-to-white gradation.

If you Shift-drag with the gradient tool, Photoshop constrains the direction of your drag to a horizontal, vertical, or 45-degree diagonal angle.

Gradient tool

Figure 14-5: I replaced the vegetables inside the jar with a black-to-white gradient.

Gradient preview

Changing the way of the gradient

You can muck around with the performance of the gradient tool by double-clicking on its toolbox icon or pressing Return to display the Gradient Tool Options palette shown in Figure 14-5.

Like the Opacity settings and brush modes available inside the Fill dialog box, the Opacity and brush mode options inside the Gradient Tool Options palette are best ignored. If you want to mix a gradation with the existing colors in a selection, create the gradation on a layer and select options inside the Layers palette, as discussed in Chapter 15.

Choosing between linear and radial

Number one on the Important Option Hit Parade is the Type pop-up menu. This wonderful little control lets you choose between two basic kinds of gradients, Linear or Radial:

✔ The Linear option creates a gradient in which colors blend in a straight line, as in the left examples in Figure 14-6.

✔ If you select Radial, the colors blend in concentric circles, from the center outward, as in the two examples on the right side of the figure.

✔ Note that in every example in Figure 14-6, the foreground color is white and the background color is black. You almost always want to set the lighter color to the foreground color when using the Radial option, because this creates a glowing effect. If the foreground color is darker than its background compatriot, the gradation looks like a bottomless pit.

✔ Next to the Type pop-up menu are two check boxes, Mask and Dither. The Dither check box is easy: When turned on, it helps eliminate a problem known as *banding,* in which you can see distinct bands of color in a printed gradient (that's a bad thing in nine out of ten households). Leave the check box turned on unless you're feeling especially contrary and want to create a banding effect.

Linear   Radial

Foreground to background

Foreground to transparent

Figure 14-6: Our jar filled with two different gradient types — Linear (left) and Radial (right) — as well as two different styles (top and bottom).

✔ The Mask check box is a little more complicated. Here's the scoop: Gradients can include areas that are partially or fully transparent. In other words, they fade from a solid color to a more transparent color. When the Mask check box is turned off, Photoshop creates the gradient using all opaque colors, ignoring the transparency information.

The best way to get a grip on what the Mask check box does is to try a little experiment. First, turn on the check box and press D to get the default foreground and background colors. Now choose the Transparent Stripes option from the Gradient pop-up menu and draw a gradient. You get a fill pattern that consists of a series of black and transparent stripes. Next, draw a gradient with the Mask check box turned off. You now get a series of solid black and white stripes. In most cases, you don't need to bother with the check box — just leave it turned on.

✔ If you upgraded from an earlier version of Photoshop, you may be wondering what happened to the Midpoint and Radial Offset sliders that used to live in the Gradient Tool Options palette. In Version 4, you adjust the offset and midpoint using the midpoint markers in the Gradient Editor dialog box, explained in the upcoming section "Becoming a gradient wizard."

Selecting your colors

The Gradient pop-up menu lets you change the way colors blend inside the gradation and select from a variety of prefab gradients:

✔ Normally, Foreground to Background is selected. This option does just what it sounds like it does, blending between the foreground and background colors, as in the two top examples in Figure 14-6.

✔ If you select one of the Transparent options, the gradient tool blends the foreground color into the original colors in the selection. Both bottom examples in Figure 14-6 were created with the Foreground to Transparent option selected.

✔ The remaining options in the Gradient pop-up menu create a variety of factory-made gradients, some involving just a few colors and others blending a whole rainbow of colors.

When you select a gradient from the pop-up menu, Photoshop displays it in the gradient preview at the bottom of the Gradient Tool Options palette, as labeled in Figure 14-5.

If none of the existing gradients suits your taste, you can create your own custom gradient, as I did in Color Plate 14-1. The next section explains the ins and outs of building your own gradients.

Becoming a gradient wizard

You can design your own custom gradient by editing an existing gradient or starting an entirely new gradient from scratch. To do either, display the Gradient Tool Options palette by double-clicking on the gradient tool icon in the toolbox or pressing return with the tool selected. Then click on the Edit button at the bottom of the Gradient Tool Options palette. The Gradient Editor dialog box, shown in Figure 14-7, appears. Uh-oh. Looks like you've ventured too far into geek space, doesn't it?

The Gradient Editor dialog box is a bit complex, and chances are you won't use it much. But I don't want you to feel as though you didn't get full value for your $19.99, so the following list gives you a brief introduction to the dialog box:

- ✓ The scrolling list at the top of the dialog box lists all the prefab gradients — the same ones in the Gradient pop-up menu in the Gradient Tool Options palette. Select the gradient you want to edit from this list. Then click on Duplicate to create a copy of the gradient and give it a new name. Now you can edit that gradient without worrying about wrecking the original.

- ✓ To create a new gradient that isn't based on an existing gradient, click on the New button.

- ✓ The two radio buttons, Color and Transparency, let you adjust, uh, the color and transparency of the gradient. When the Color button is selected, the fade bar (labeled in Figure 14-7) shows the gradient colors. You can then add, change, or delete colors from the gradient, as explained in the next section.

Figure 14-7:
The new Gradient Editor gives you complete control over your gradients.

✔ When the Transparency button is turned on, you can change the transparency of your gradient, as explained in the upcoming (and appropriately named) section "Changing the transparency." The fade bar displays the opaque colors in the gradient in black and the transparent areas in white. Gray areas represent colors that are partially transparent.

✔ The little house-shaped boxes underneath the fade bar are called color stops when the Color button is selected and transparency stops when the Transparency button is selected. You use these stops to change the colors and transparency of the gradient, as explained in the upcoming two sections.

✔ The preview bar at the bottom of the dialog box displays both the colors and transparent areas of your gradient. Transparent areas are represented by a gray-and-white checkerboard pattern.

✔ The Save button saves your gradient to a different location on disk. You don't need to save the gradient using this button unless you want to store your gradient in some spot other than where the rest of the gradients are located, however. After you edit a gradient and click on OK, the gradient is automatically added to the Gradient pop-up list in the Gradient Tool Options palette.

✔ To remove a gradient from the list, select the gradient in the Gradient Editor dialog box and click on the Remove button.

Changing, adding, and deleting colors

To change one of the colors in the gradient, first check to see whether the "roof" on that color's color stop is black. The black roof indicates the active color stop — the one that is to be affected by your changes. If the roof isn't black, click on the color stop to make it active.

After you activate the color stop, you can make one of three choices. Click on the leftmost stop type icon (labeled in Figure 14-7) to change the color to the one showing in the stop color preview box (also labeled in Figure 14-7). To change the color in the color preview box, you can either click on a color in your image, in the Color palette, or in the fade bar.

If you click on the F or B stop type icons, you change the color marked by the color stop to the foreground or background color, respectively. Keep in mind that if you change the foreground or background color, the color in the gradient changes automatically, too. The change doesn't affect any gradients you've already drawn, but does affect any future gradients you create.

Here's some more stuff you need to know about playing with the colors in your gradient:

✔ To add a color to the gradient, select a stop type icon and then click just below the fade bar at the point where you want the color to appear. You get a new color stop icon representing the color.

✔ To remove a color from the gradient, drag its color stop down away from the fade bar.

✔ If you drag a color stop to the right or left, you can change the position of the color in the gradient. Suppose that you have a gradient that fades from black to white. If you want more black and less white, drag the black color stop toward the white stop.

✔ The little diamonds on the top of the fade bar represent the midpoint between two colors. Using the example of a black-to-white gradient again, the midpoint marks the spot at which the gradient contains equal amounts of black and white. To move a midpoint, just drag the diamond.

✔ The Location option box shows the placement of the active color stop or midpoint marker. If you want to be terribly precise, you can enter a value into the Location box to position a color stop or midpoint marker instead of dragging the icons.

When a color stop is active, a value of 0 (zero) represents the very beginning of the gradient; 100 represents the very end. Midpoint values are always relative to the two color stops on either side of the midpoint. A value of 50 percent places the midpoint an equal distance from both color stops. For reasons unknown, the minimum and maximum Midpoint values are 13 and 87 percent. Just thought you might like to store that useless bit of information in your memory banks.

Changing the transparency

Hold on to your stomach — now we're really veering into the land of the propeller heads. Photoshop 4 lets you adjust the amount of transparency in a gradient. You can make a portion of the gradient fully opaque, completely transparent, or somewhere in between the two.

Suppose that you want to create a gradient that starts out white, gradually fades to completely transparent, and then becomes completely white again. In other words, you want to create a variation of the effect shown back in the bottom half of Figure 14-6. Here's how to create such a gradient:

1. **First, make white the foreground color.**

2. **Inside the Gradient Editor dialog box, choose the Foreground to Transparent gradient from the scrolling list.**

   The gradient you want to create is similar to one that already exists, so you may as well save yourself the trouble of starting from scratch.

3. **Click on Duplicate and give your new gradient a name.**

   Photoshop creates a copy of the Foreground to Transparent gradient for you to muck up.

4. Click on the Transparency radio button.

The fade bar now shows your gradient in terms of transparent and opaque areas. Black represents opaque areas; white represents transparent areas; gray areas represent everything in between. The preview bar at the bottom of the dialog box shows you the opaque areas in their actual colors and transparent areas in a gray and white checkerboard pattern.

When you have the Transparency button selected, the color stops become transparency stops, enabling you to change the opacity of different portions of your gradient. The midpoint marker represents the spot at which the gradient is 50 percent white and 50 percent transparent.

5. Click on the rightmost transparency stop.

In this example, the rightmost stop represents the completely transparent end of the gradient.

6. Change the value in the Opacity option box to 100.

You now have a gradient that fades from fully opaque white to fully opaque white. Wow, that's exciting, huh?

It's tempting to press Return after you change the option box value, but don't — pressing Return closes the dialog box. The value you enter into the option box takes effect without any press of the Return key. To switch to another option box, press Tab.

7. Click in the middle of the fade bar to create a new transparency stop.

By default, each new stop you create is 100 percent opaque.

8. Change the value in the Opacity option box to 0 (zero).

You now have a gradient that starts out fully opaque, becomes transparent in the middle, and becomes opaque again at the end. Apply it to an image to get a better idea of what you just created. Heady stuff, eh?

You can also add as many transparency stops as you want and set different Opacity values for each. To move a transparency stop, just drag it right or left; to delete a stop, drag it off the bar. To move a midpoint, drag it right or left.

The Mask check box in the Gradient Tool Options palette determines whether transparency settings are ignored or not when you apply a gradient. If the check box is turned off, your gradient is completely opaque. For example, if you turn off the check box when applying the gradient created by the preceding steps, you get a completely white gradient instead of one that fades from white to transparent and back again.

Your Image Needs Strokes, Too

The last item on today's agenda is Edit⇨Stroke, a command that traces borders around a selection. When you choose this command, Photoshop displays the Stroke dialog box shown in Figure 14-8. Enter the thickness of the border you want into the Width option box. This value is measured in pixels.

Figure 14-8:
Use the
Stroke
dialog box to
draw a
border
around a
selection.

Stroke

Stroke
Width: 1 pixels

OK
Cancel

Location
○ Inside   ● Center   ○ Outside

Blending
Opacity: 100 %   Mode: Normal ▼
☐ Preserve Transparency

In Figure 14-9, for example, I traced a 16 pixel-wide black border around the jar. (This is the maximum Width value, incidentally.) Then I swapped the foreground and background colors, chose Edit⇨Stroke again, and entered 8 into the Width option box. The result is a white border inside a black border. Slick, huh? (Oh, come on, say it is, even if it's just to make me feel better.)

How the border rides the track

The Location options in the Stroke dialog box determine how the border rides the selection outline. The border can cruise around fully inside or fully outside the selection, or it can sit astride (Center) the selection. Why might you want to change this setting? Well, take another look at Figure 14-9. Suppose that instead of the white border flanked on either side by black, which I created using the Center option, I want the two borders to sit beside each other. If I select the Inside option, the white border appears inside the selection and the black border inside that, as in the first example of Figure 14-10. If I select Outside, the white border traces the outside of the jar and the black border extends even farther out, as in the figure's second example.

Actually, I don't recommend selecting the Outside option. It has a nasty habit of flattening off the edges of curves, as you can see along the sides of the jar in the second image in Figure 14-10. For the best results, stick with Inside or Center.

Figure 14-9:
The classic double-border effect, so in demand at today's finer jar emporiums.

Figure 14-10:
Variations on the borders from our last figure using the Inside (left) and Outside (right) options.

Mix your stroke after you press Return

Like the Blending and Opacity options in other dialog boxes, the ones in the Stroke dialog box don't provide you with a preview of how the effect will look when applied to your image. So if you want to play with the blend modes or opacity of your stroke, ignore the options in the dialog box. Instead, create a new layer (as explained in Chapter 15) and do your selecting and stroking on that layer. You can then adjust the blend mode and opacity via the Layers option palette, also discussed in Chapter 15.

On the off chance that you're curious about the Preserve Transparency check box, it affects only images with layers. If you don't have any layers going, don't worry about it. (Again, layers are explained in Chapter 15.) Even if your image does contain layers, don't worry about this option. It just ensures that the transparent portions of layers remain transparent.

Color Plate 15-2:
The eight images I used to create Color Plate 15-1. The arrows show the layering order of the images, from the kelp (lower right) at the bottom of the heap to the planet Neptune (upper left) at the top.

Normal, 100% Opacity

50% Opacity

Fish: Multiply; Cathedral: Screen

Difference

Color Plate 15-3:
After positioning the cathedral on one layer, the fish on a layer beneath it, and the kelp in the Background layer (top left), I experimented with various Opacity settings and modes. First I changed the Opacity of both layers to 50 percent (top right). Then I returned the Opacity to 100 percent and applied the Multiply mode to the fish and the Screen mode to the cathedral (bottom left). Finally, I applied the Difference mode to both layers (bottom right).

Overlay

Fish: Soft Light; Cathedral: Hard Light

Color

Luminosity

Color Plate 15-4:
Continuing from Color Plate 15-3, I applied the Overlay mode to both fish and cathedral (top left). Then I applied Soft Light to the fish and Hard Light to the cathedral (top right). Finally, I tried out the Color (bottom left) and Luminosity (bottom right) modes on both layers.

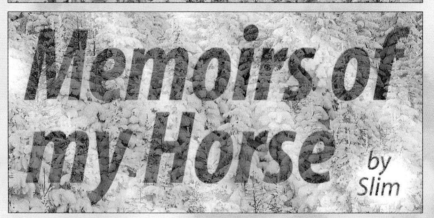

Color Plate 16-1:
Photoshop lets you create some wild type effects that are either difficult or impossible to produce in other programs. Some examples include double outline type (top), text with soft drop shadows (middle), and translucent text (bottom).

Color Plate 17-1:
Starting with the original inset image, I selected the dark portions of the image with Select⇨Color Range, applied the Add Noise filter with an Amount value of 100 and the Gaussian option selected, and then followed things up with the Motion Blur filter. The only difference between the top and bottom images was the setting of the Monochromatic check box in the Add Noise dialog box. In the top image, it was turned off; in the bottom image, it was on.

Color Plate 18-1:
Don't be surprised if you open up a scanned image and find it looking like the one on the left. The image isn't beyond redemption, it just needs some color correction. In fact, I was able to correct the colors using the Levels and Variations commands in about ten minutes (right).

Color Plate 18-2:
The results of adding blue (left) and yellow (right) to the image using Image⇨Adjust⇨Variations. Colors that have little or no blue or yellow in them — such as the reds in the bows and the greens in the packages and apples — remain virtually unaffected.

Color Plate 18-3:
Here I used the Levels command to correct the colors in a muted image. For reference, the histogram and Input Levels options from the Levels dialog box are inset with each step. Starting with the uncorrected Photo CD scan (top left), I adjusted the black slider triangle (top right), the white triangle (bottom left), and the gamma point (bottom right) to create a sound image with excellent color depth.

Color Plate 18-4:
The colors of paradise lost (left) and found again (right) by selecting the Saturation radio button inside the Variations dialog box and increasing the saturation.

Original

More Blue

More Blue

More Magenta

More Magenta

More Blue

Color Plate 18-5:
I fixed an image that had a preponderance of yellow and green (top left) by clicking on the labeled previews in the Variations dialog box. For example, to produce the top middle image, I clicked on the More Blue preview; to get the top right image, I clicked on that same preview again.

Part V

So, You Say You're Serious about Image Editing

The 5th Wave   By Rich Tennant

"...AND THROUGH IMAGE EDITING TECHNOLOGY, WE'RE ABLE TO RECREATE THE AWESOME SPECTACLE KNOWN AS TYRANNOSAURUS GWEN."

In this part . . .

One of the great legacies of Walt Disney — the man, not the company — was his insistence that animation take full advantage of its unreal medium. He and his staff perfected techniques, camera angles, and character movements that would have proven impossible had the studio been working with live actors and sets. Ironically, these very unreal techniques produced the effect of heightened realism, in which backgrounds shifted on multiple planes, cameras swooped and glided without regard for terrain, and characters moved more gracefully and far more expressively than their human counterparts.

Simply put, Walt figured that there was no point in creating cartoons if all you intended to do was slavishly adhere to the dictates of real life. The same argument can be made for digital image editing. What's the point of going to all the trouble of scanning an image to disk and opening it up in Photoshop if you're not going to take it beyond the boundaries of real life in the process? In a word, none. In a few more words, if you're going to use Photoshop, then there's no reason not to make every image you create more real than reality.

Chapters 15 through 18 show you how. Here you'll discover how to mix images to create breathtaking visual collages, add type to your images, automatically correct the focus of images, stamp images in metal and create other special effects, and bring out brilliant colors that you never knew were there. In other words, you discover how to turn your images into something much better than they were before.

Chapter 15
Layers upon Layers upon Layers

● ●

In This Chapter

▶ Working with layers

▶ Combining images

▶ Pasting an image inside a selection outline

▶ Dragging and dropping selections

▶ Scaling an image to fit the composition

▶ Converting a floating selection into a layer

▶ Adjusting the Opacity setting

▶ Applying blend modes

▶ Erasing holes in layers

● ●

*I*nsofar as "high art" is concerned, the heyday for surrealism was 60 to 70 years ago. But the problem with guys like Max Ernst, René Magritte, and even Salvador Dalí was that they never got around to learning how to use Photoshop. Oh, sure, Ernst and Magritte were long dead by the time Photoshop debuted, and Dalí might have had better things to do in his final days than learn a new piece of software. But still, think of what they could have done. A paint-brush is great, but it pales when compared to Photoshop as a means for merging photo-realistic images to create flat-out impossible visual scenarios.

Color Plate 15-1 shows what I mean. No matter how hard you work at it, you can never assemble these elements in a photo shoot. It's just so darn difficult to squeeze a giant fish, the Reims Cathedral in France, and the planet Neptune into the same room together. If you had talent streaming like fire-hydrant jets out your ears, you might be able to paint the image, but most of us would have thrown in the towel at the prospect of re-creating a High Gothic cathedral façade that took a team of thirteenth century masters 65 years to carve.

But we live in a sparkling modern age, filled with more dazzling masterworks of automation than we know what to do with. Thanks to one such masterwork — I speak here of Photoshop, naturally — I was able to throw together Color Plate 15-1 in a couple of hours. Altogether, the composition comprises eight separate images, but required not so much as a single stroke of a painting or editing tool. I simply selected the images, combined them, blended them together, and erased a few stray pixels that weren't doing the final study in surrealism a lick of good.

Because it might be difficult to distinguish every one of the eight images, Color Plate 15-2 shows each one on its own. The arrows indicate the order in which the images are stacked on top of each other. For example, the underwater kelp jungle in the bottom-right corner of Color Plate 15-2 lies at the bottom of the composition in Color Plate 15-1; the photo of Neptune in the upper-left corner of the second color plate rests at the top of the composition. It's as if I cut out a picture of the kelp and pasted it onto a page, cut out the fish and pasted it on the kelp, cut out the astronaut and pasted him in front of the fish, and so on.

Some images are blended together using the same brush modes I discuss in Chapter 8. For example

- ✔ Remember the Multiply mode, the one that darkens colors as if they were painted on top of each other with watercolors? I used Multiply to blend the nebula — the image just below the flower in Color Plate 15-2 — with the fish to create the black eye effect in Color Plate 15-1.

- ✔ The spray coming out of the fish's mouth is the comet from the upper-right corner of Color Plate 15-2. I blended the two using the Screen mode.

- ✔ I blended the Reims Cathedral and Neptune with the images behind them using modes I haven't discussed yet. Respectively, these modes are Luminosity and Hard Light. I explain more about them in the section "Playing around with blend modes," near the end of this chapter.

This is the point at which you ask, "Yeah, yeah, yeah, but how in the world do I pull off something like this?" Well, wouldn't you know it, that's what this chapter is all about. I tell you how to get different images into the same document, how to assign them to separate layers, and how to mix them together using modes and the eraser tool. And remarkably, it's all a lot easier than you'd think.

Pasting Images Together

Suppose that you want to paste the fish image from the bottom of Color Plate 15-2 into the neighboring kelp image, as in Figure 15-1. How do you go about it? Here's one approach:

1. Open the fish image and select the fish.

2. Press ⌘-C.

⌘-C is the time-honored keyboard shortcut for the Edit⇨Copy command, which places a copy of your selection onto the Clipboard. The *Clipboard* is a temporary storage area for image data. Any previous occupant of the Clipboard — sent there via Edit⇨Copy or its close cousin, Edit⇨Cut — is displaced by the fish.

3. Open the kelp image.

4. Press ⌘-V.

That's the shortcut for the Edit⇨Paste command, which dumps the current contents of the Clipboard into your image. Consider fish and kelp combined into one. The original fish image remains intact, because the fish you pasted into the kelp was merely a copy.

Figure 15-1:
The kelp image before (left) and after (right) pasting the fish image.

But these steps aren't the only way to combine images. You also have these options at your disposal:

✔ To cut a selection from one image and paste it into another, choose Edit⇨Cut and then Edit⇨Paste. The selection is removed entirely from the first image and planted in the second.

✔ You can clone a selection from one image to another by dragging the selection with the move tool. Or ⌘-drag with any tool except the hand or pen tool.

✔ This method of cloning between images is known in the computer world as *dragging and dropping,* by the way.

✔ To transfer an entire image into another image window, choose Select➪All (⌘-A) before dragging or using the Cut or Copy commands.

✔ For a weird but occasionally useful trick, use Edit➪Paste Into to paste an image inside an existing selection, as described in the upcoming section "Filling a selection with a selection."

When you use the Paste command, Photoshop places the pasted image on a new layer. When you drag and drop a selection between images, Photoshop puts the selection on a new layer as well. For more on working with layers, start reading at the section "Excuse me, But What's a Layer?" and keep going to the end of the chapter.

When you use the move tool to move or close a selection within the same image, Photoshop creates a *floating selection,* which has special properties similar to those offered by layers. For the lowdown on that topic, see the section "Exploring floating selections," which happens to come next.

Exploring floating selections

As I just mentioned, when you move or clone a selection using the move tool, Photoshop creates what's known as a *floating selection.* A floating selection hovers over the surface of the image, as if it lived on its own independent plane. This means that you can move the selection by dragging it or by pressing an arrow key without leaving a hole in the underlying image. Here are a few other things you can do with a floating selection:

✔ Delete part of a floating selection by Option-dragging around it with a lasso or marquee tool or Option-clicking with the magic wand. The part you Option-drag around or Option-click disappears entirely.

✔ You can blend the floating image with the underlying image using the Opacity slider and blend modes pop-up menu in the Layers palette, which I discuss a little later in this chapter. Or press any number key (1 through 0) to change the opacity in 10 percent increments. For example, press 1 to change the opacity to 10 percent. To enter a more specific percentage — say, 23 — just type the number quickly. (A selection tool must be active for this trick to work.)

✔ Fill it using the Delete key tricks discussed in Chapter 14.

In Photoshop 3, you could turn a selection into a floating selection by choosing the Select➪Float command (or pressing ⌘-J). Although the Select➪Float command is gone in Photoshop 4, you can still float a selection — albeit in a rather roundabout way. With the move tool selected, press Option-up arrow to clone the selection and move it one pixel north. Then press the down arrow once to move the clone back into its original position. You now have a clone that floats above the surface of the original.

Setting a floater down

If you defloat the selection, it becomes part of the underlying image. A defloated selection may remain selected, but you can't mix it with the underlying image and you can't move it without leaving a background-colored hole. The following operations defloat a selection:

- ✔ Shift-dragging in the image with a lasso or marquee tool or Shift-clicking with the magic wand. When you add to the selection outline, you defloat the selection.

- ✔ Applying a painting tool, filter, or other editing command, including Edit⇨Stroke.

- ✔ Cloning the selection by Option-dragging it with the move tool (or ⌘-Option-dragging with another tool). Option-dragging defloats the original; only the clone remains floating.

- ✔ Choosing Layer⇨Defloat or pressing ⌘-E.

- ✔ Deselecting the selection by clicking with the lasso or marquee tool, pressing ⌘-D, or by selecting a different portion of the image.

- ✔ Selecting a different layer in the Layers palette.

- ✔ Quitting the program.

Of course, one day you may have to perform one of these operations. Just make sure that you don't defloat the selection until you finish moving it around and otherwise adjusting it. The only way to preserve a floating selection forever is to assign it to its own layer, as described next.

Turning a selection into a layer

If you want a floating selection to retain its floating properties no matter what editing actions you take, you can turn it into a layer. Discussed in the second half of this chapter, layers are in essence permanent floating selections.

To turn a floating selection into a layer, press ⌘-Shift-J and name the layer in the resulting dialog box. Or, to create the layer without naming it, click on the new layer icon in the Layers palette (see the upcoming Figure 15-4). Photoshop gives the layer a name like Layer 1.

To send a regular (nonfloating) selection to its own layer, press ⌘-Shift-J. Or, if you want to name the layer, press ⌘-Shift-Option-J. In either case, the selection is removed from its original layer. If you want to keep the selection intact and place a copy on the new layer instead, create your layer by pressing ⌘-J.

When you turn a selection into a layer, the selection outline disappears. Not to worry; this is perfectly normal. Because the image sits on a layer by itself, you no longer need a selection outline to isolate it. If you apply a filter, for example, it affects the active layer only; none of the other layers are touched.

Filling a selection with a selection

The Edit⇨Paste Into command lets you insert an image into an existing selection outline. For example, I wanted to paste the fish behind some of the vegetation in the neighboring kelp image so that the fish would appear to be intertwined with his environment. In the first example of Figure 15-2, I selected an area inside the kelp stalks and feathered the selection by choosing Select⇨ Feather, as discussed in Chapter 13. Then I chose Paste Into (⌘-Shift-V) to create the fish-inside-the-kelp shown in the second example. (Note that I've hidden the selection outlines in the second example so that you can better see the transitions between fish and stalks.)

Photoshop pastes the selection to a new layer. You can then move and blend the pasted image just as if it were a floating selection. It's just that the pasted image is invisible outside the boundaries of the previous selection outline.

You can also paste into the deselected area of an image by pressing the Option key as you choose Edit⇨Paste Into. If I had done this with the image in Figure 15-2, for example, the fish would show through the exact opposite areas of the kelp bed as he does now.

Figure 15-2: After selecting an area of kelp (left), I chose the Paste Into command to introduce fish to his new kelpy home (right).

Resizing an Image to Match Its New Home

When you bring two images together, you always have to deal with the issue of relative size. For example, the fish that I've been having so much fun with is too large for its surroundings. Here's how to ensure that the two images you want to combine are sized correctly:

1. **Magnify the two images to the exact same zoom factor.**

   In order to see them side by side, a zoom ratio of 50 percent or smaller will probably be necessary.

2. **If either of the two images appears disproportionately large, scale it down using Image⇨Image Size.**

   In this case, you don't care at all about the dimensions or resolution of the image; all you care about is the file size — that is, the number of pixels comprising the image. If the image you want to copy or drag (Fish) is too large, scale it down just enough to fit inside the destination image. If the destination image (Kelp) is too large, reduce it as desired. Keep ⌘-Z ready in case you accidentally go too far. (Refer to Chapter 4 for more information about the Image Size command.)

   Be careful not to over-reduce! Remember that you're throwing away pixels and therefore sacrificing detail. If you go too far, you can always restore the original by choosing File⇨Revert, as discussed in Chapter 11.

3. **Combine the two images.**

   Copy and paste, drag and drop, or punt on fourth down.

4. **Position the image vaguely where you want it.**

   For my part, I stuck the fish in the upper-right corner.

5. **Choose Layer⇨Transform⇨Scale.**

   This command lets you fine-tune the relative size of the imported image with respect to its new home. A marquee with four corner handles surrounds the image.

6. **Drag a corner handle to scale the image.**

   Shift-drag a handle to scale the image proportionally. The first example in Figure 15-3 catches me in the act. After you release the handle, Photoshop previews how the resized image will look. Don't worry that the preview is a little choppy; the scaled image will be smooth.

   Don't scale the image up; only scale it down. Otherwise, Photoshop has to make up pixels, which is most assuredly not one of the program's better capabilities.

Figure 15-3:
Use the
Scale
command to
refine the
image size.

7. **Move your cursor inside the marquee and double-click.**

When you have resized the image as desired — you can drag the corner handles all you want — move your cursor inside the marquee. Double-click or press Return to accept the image's new size and tell Photoshop to work its magic. The resized image will appear perfectly smooth.

If the scaled image looks choppy after you double-click, you probably have a preference set wrong. Choose File⇨Preferences⇨General or press ⌘-K and then select the Bicubic option from the Interpolation pop-up menu.

If you decide that you don't want to scale the image before you double-click or press Return, press Esc to get rid of the marquee. If you already have double-clicked or pressed Return, you can restore the image to its original size by pressing ⌘-Z.

Excuse Me, But What's a Layer?

So far in this book, I've made about a bazillion references to layers. By now, you're probably getting fairly annoyed, wondering when the heck I'm going to explain just what the term means.

Well, here's a little analogy to get things rolling. Imagine that you had three sheets of acetate — you know, like folks used to slide into overhead projectors to bore audiences before the days of multimedia presentations. Anyway, on one sheet you draw a picture of a fish. On another, you draw a fishbowl. And on the third, you draw the table on which the fishbowl sits. When you stack all the sheets on top of each other, the images blend together to create a seamless view of a fish in his happy home.

Layers in Photoshop work just like that. You can keep different elements of your image on separate layers and then combine the layers to create a composite image. You can rearrange layers, add and delete layers, blend them together using different opacity values and blend modes, and do all sorts of other impressive things.

Another advantage of using layers is that you can edit or paint on one layer without affecting the other layers. That means that you can safely apply commands or painting tools to one portion of your image without worrying about messing up the rest of the image — and without having to bother selecting the element you want to edit.

Although layers were introduced in Photoshop 3, they play a much bigger role in Version 4. Photoshop now automatically creates a new layer any time you use the Paste command. Also, the old Float command, which used to turn a selection into a floating selection, is gone. If you press ⌘-J, the old keyboard shortcut for floating a selection, Photoshop sends the selection to a new layer. (I present a workaround to this change in the section "Exploring floating selections.")

You aren't restricted to the layers that Photoshop creates automatically, however. You can create as many new layers as your computer's memory will allow. In the case of the image shown in Color Plate 15-1, I kept kelp, fish, astronaut, nebula, cathedral, flower, comet, and Neptune on separate layers. Though they may appear to blend together along the edges, they are in fact as distinct as peas in a pod.

Photoshop 4 also lets you create a special kind of layer called an *adjustment layer.* An adjustment layer allows you to play with the color correction commands discussed in Chapter 18 without permanently affecting any of your image layers. For more on that juicy topic, see Chapter 18.

Finding your way around the Layers palette

The Layers palette, shown in Figure 15-4, is Grand Central Station for managing layers. To display the palette, choose Window➪Show Layers or just press F7.

Display layer

Blend mode

Figure 15-4:
The Layers
palette is
key to
managing
your layers.

Active layer   New layer   Trash

Here's what you need to know to navigate the Layers palette:

- ✓ The Background layer is the bottom layer in the image. Every image has a Background layer.

- ✓ The order of the layers in the Layers palette represents their order in the image. The top layer in the palette is the top layer in your image, and so on.

- ✓ You can edit only one layer at a time — the active layer. The active layer is the one that's highlighted in the Layers palette and has a little paintbrush icon to the left of the layer name. To make another layer active, just click on its name.

- ✓ Press Option-] to move up one layer; press Option-[to activate the next layer down. Press Shift-Option-] to move to the very top layer; press Shift-Option-[to move to the Background layer. (If you upgraded from Version 3, note that the old shortcuts for moving through layers, ⌘-] and ⌘-[, now change the order of the active layer, as discussed in the section "Moving and manipulating layers.")

✔ An eyeball icon next to a layer name means that the layer is visible. To hide the layer, click on the eyeball. To display the layer, click on the eyeball column to bring the eyeball back.

✔ To hide all layers but one, Option-click on the eyeball in front of the name of the layer you want to see. Option-click again to redisplay all the layers.

✔ If you hide the Background layer, you see a checkerboard pattern surrounding your images. The checkerboard represents the transparent areas of the visible layers.

✔ To find out how to use the blend mode pop-up menu and the Opacity slider at the top of the palette, read the upcoming section "Tending Your Many Splendid Blends" three times fast.

✔ To create a new, blank layer, click on the new layer icon at the bottom of the palette (labeled in Figure 15-4). To create a duplicate of an existing layer, drag the layer to the new layer icon.

✔ When you create a layer in the manner mentioned in the above paragraph, Photoshop gives the layer a name like Layer 1, Layer 2, and so on. If you want to name the layer, double-click on it in the Layers palette and enter a name in the Layer Options dialog box that appears.

✔ Alternatively, you can create the layer by choosing the New Layer or Duplicate Layer command from the Layers palette menu (click on the right-pointing arrow at the top of the palette). If you use this method of creating a layer, Photoshop prompts you to give the layer a name.

✔ If you create a floating selection, it appears in the Layers palette with the name Floating Selection (oddly enough). To turn the selection into its own layer, click on the new layer icon or press ⌘-Shift-J.

✔ When the Layers palette contains a Floating Selection, clicking on another layer name defloats the selection.

✔ To delete a layer, drag it to the Trash icon. Keep in mind that you're throwing away the layer along with the image on it.

✔ In Chapter 14, I mention that you can paint inside a selection outline to paint just the selection and leave the surrounding areas untouched. But when you send a selection to a layer, the selection outline disappears, so how do you just paint inside the image on a layer? For example, maybe I want to paint stripes on my fish without going outside the lines. The solution is to select the Preserve Transparency check box near the top of the Layers palette. The transparent areas around the fish stay transparent, allowing you to paint only inside the opaque and translucent fishy bits.

✔ For a quick way to turn the Preserve Transparency check box on and off, just press the forward slash key (/).

✔ Just in case you ever want to re-create that selection outline around the elements on a layer, though, Photoshop gives you an easy way to do it. Just ⌘-click on the layer name in the Layers palette.

Moving and manipulating layers

Layers are flexible things — you can move them, group them together, shuffle their order, and otherwise rearrange them as though they were a deck of playing cards. Here's a look at some of the more common layer-manipulation moves you might need to make:

- ✔ To move an image on a layer, drag it with the move tool or ⌘-drag with any other tool but the hand or pen tool. To move the layer in 1-pixel increments, press an arrow key with the move tool selected or press ⌘ plus an arrow key with any other tool selected but the hand or pen tool. To move the layer in 10-pixel increments, press Shift as you press the arrow key.

- ✔ Turn on the Pixel Doubling check box in the Move Tool Options palette (press Return with the move tool selected to display the palette). This option speeds up on-screen previews when you drag layers. The drawback is that Photoshop displays only every other pixel, making the preview a little blotchy.

- ✔ To link an active layer to another layer, click in the second column of the layers palette — just to the left of the layer name — next to the layer that's not active. A little link icon appears in the column. Now you can move, scale, and rotate both layers at once. To remove the link, click on the link icon.

- ✔ Can't figure out what layer holds the element you want to edit? With the move tool selected, Control-Option-click on the element. Or ⌘-Control-Option-click with any other tool but the hand or pen tool. Photoshop automatically activates the appropriate layer.

- ✔ After you get a few layers going, you can move one in front of or behind another by dragging it up or down in the list of layers in the Layers palette. A heavy black line shows where the layer will be inserted.

- ✔ Another way to rearrange layers is to use the commands in the Layer⇨Arrange submenu. Click on the layer that you want to move in the Layers palette. Then choose Layer⇨Arrange⇨Bring to Front (⌘-]) to make the layer the topmost layer; Bring Forward (⌘-Shift-]) to move the layer one level up; Send Backward (⌘-Shift-[) to move the layer one level down; and Send to Back (⌘-[) to move the layer to just above the Background layer.

- ✔ You can copy an entire layer to another image by selecting the layer in the Layers palette and dragging and dropping the layer to the new image. The layer is dropped at the spot where you release the mouse button and resides one layer above the active layer in the new image.

- ✔ You can even change the placement of a floating selection by dragging the Floating Selection item up or down in the list.

Flattening and merging layers

Sadly, layers aren't all fun and games. To put it bluntly, they come at a steep price and require some concerted management skills. First, if an image contains layers, saving it in any other format other than the Photoshop format (as discussed in Chapter 6) merges all the layers into one. The Photoshop format is the only format that preserves layers. Second, layers can really slow Photoshop down. To keep running at peak efficiency, it's best to juggle as few layers as possible at a time.

If you want to save your image for use in a different program but you're not willing to sacrifice your layers just yet, you can save the composition to a different file and flatten it — that is, smush all the layers together. To do this, choose File⇨Save a Copy. The familiar Save dialog box appears on-screen, but it includes an additional Flatten Image check box. No need to turn on Flatten Image; just select TIFF, JPEG, or some other option from the Format pop-up menu, and Photoshop selects Flatten Image for you. Then name the image and press Return. Photoshop saves the flattened image to a different file; the layers in the on-screen image remain intact. Even the name on the title bar remains unaffected, meaning that the next time you press ⌘-S, Photoshop saves to the original file in the Photoshop format, not the Save a Copy file in the new format.

But useful as that is, you're still going to want to merge layers every so often to keep your image manageable. Otherwise, operations slow to a snail's pace, and that's an insult to the snail. Slow is hardly the word. Watching your arm hair grow is action-packed compared with working in a 10-layer Photoshop image. We're talking slow like a potted plant here, and a dead potted plant at that. So here are your merging options:

✔ To merge several layers into one, hide all layers except the ones you want to merge. In other words, eyeball icons should appear in front of the layers you want to merge. Hide the eyeball if you don't want to merge the layer. Then choose Merge Visible from the Layers palette menu (by dragging from that right-pointing arrowhead in the upper right corner of the palette). Or just press ⌘-Shift-E.

✔ You can merge one layer into the layer below it by choosing Layer⇨Merge Down or pressing ⌘-E.

✔ If you want to flatten the entire image and get rid of all the layers, choose the Flatten Image command from the palette menu or from the Layer menu. You can undo the command right after you choose it, and you can revert to a saved version of the image that contains layers, but otherwise your layers are gone for good.

Tending Your Many Splendid Blends

Being able to segregate different portions of your image onto separate layers is a great way to edit one part of your image without harming another. But as image editing goes, this aspect of layers isn't terribly exciting. The real fun begins when you start playing around with different options that Photoshop gives you for blending all your various image layers together.

Fooling with layer opacity

One neat trick to try with a layer is to make it partially translucent using the Opacity slider in the Layers palette. In Figure 15-5, for example, I made the fish partially translucent by setting the Opacity to 70 percent. In the second example, I made him even more ghostly by lowering the Opacity to 30 percent. Whether the image is on its own layer or just temporarily floating, you can use the Opacity slider bar in the Layers palette to achieve this sort of effect.

Opacity: 70%   Opacity: 30%

Figure 15-5:
Hey, kids, it's Phantom Phish, the exciting translucent character whose merchandising will clutter markdown shelves any day now.

To change the Opacity setting for a layer or floating selection from the keyboard, make sure that a selection tool — marquee, lasso, wand, move, crop, or type — is selected and press a number key. Press 9 for 90 percent, 8 for 80 percent, and so on, down to 1 for 10 percent. To return to 100 percent, press 0.

To see Phantom Phish in color, turn to Color Plate 15-3. In the top-left example, both the fish and cathedral are positioned on their own layers, and both layers are fully opaque. In the top-right image, I changed the Opacity for both layers to 50 percent. Sends a chill down your spine, doesn't it?

Keep in mind that the Opacity setting only applies to floating selections and layers. You can't change the Opacity of the Background layer, Kelp, because nothing lies behind it. You'd be looking though the kelp into the empty void of digital space, a truly scary prospect. The same is true for the blend modes discussed in the next section.

Playing around with blend modes

The options in the blend mode pop-up menu in the top-left corner of the Layers palette correspond exactly to the brush modes in the Options palette, discussed in Chapter 8. You have Multiply, Screen, Overlay, and the rest of the gang. These options aren't called brush modes when they're applied to floating selections or layers because no brush is involved. You can call them overlay modes or blend modes; some folks call them calculations. But just plain modes is fine, too.

✔ Multiply burns the floating image into the images behind it, darkening all colors where they mix. Screen is just the opposite, lightening the colors where they mix.

✔ I love descriptions like that, because they make no sense. Pure wonderful computer gibberish. If you want sense, take a look at the bottom-left example in Color Plate 15-3. I applied Multiply to the fish and Screen to the cathedral. Imagine this: The kelp background is a poster on a wall. The fish is printed on a piece of transparent film and tacked in front of the kelp. The cathedral is a slide loaded in a projector and shined onto the poster. This is precisely how Multiply and Screen work.

✔ The Difference mode has no real-world analogy. It creates a photo negative — or inversion — of the blended images according to their colors. Where one of the images is black, no inversion takes place. Where the images are light, you find lots of inversion. In the bottom-right example of Color Plate 15-3, for example, the cathedral looks normal at its base because the kelp beneath it is black. The center of the kelp is white, however, so the fish's face changes from yellow to its opposite, blue, and the top of the cathedral changes from light brown to deep violet.

✔ Overlay, Soft Light, and Hard Light are very similar options. Overlay multiplies the dark colors and screens the light ones, as witnessed by the fish and cathedral in the top-left example of Color Plate 15-4. Soft Light — applied to the fish in the top-right example in the color plate — produces a more subtle effect. Hard Light is more dramatic than Soft Light or Overlay. You can still see the base of the cathedral in the top-right image in Color Plate 15-4 even though it overlaps the black area of the kelp. Meanwhile, the base of the Overlay cathedral is swallowed up in the murk.

✔ Like Multiply and Screen, the Color and Luminosity modes produce exactly opposite effects. The Color mode blends the color of the layer with the detail from the underlying images. Luminosity keeps the detail from the layer and mixes it with the colors of the underlying images.

✔ In the bottom-left image in Color Plate 15-4, for example, Color is applied to both fish and cathedral. The colors from the fish are bright; those of the cathedral are muted. But you can see each stalk of kelp clearly because Color doesn't obscure detail.

✔ In the bottom-right image, I applied the Luminosity mode to fish and façade. Now you can clearly see the fish pores and the cathedral carvings, but the color comes from the kelp.

✔ For some other interesting effects, experiment with the Color Dodge, Color Burn, and Exclusion modes, new to Photoshop 4. Suppose that you have two layers, a background layer and Layer 1. Color Dodge lightens the pixels in the background layer and infuses them with colors from Layer 1. Color Burn darkens the pixels and infuses them with color. Exclusion works similarly to Difference; it turns all black pixels white, all white pixels black, and all medium colors gray.

✔ You can skip the other blend modes — Dissolve, Lighten, Darken, Hue, and Saturation. They range from boring to duller than dull, and they rarely come in handy.

Two other blend modes — Behind and Clear — pop up when you have a floating selection on a layer. Few experienced users know what the heck these do, but because I'm such a swell guy, I'll tell you.

✔ The Behind mode slips the floater behind the nonfloating pixels in the layer, much like the fish-in-the-kelp image back in Figure 15-2.

✔ If you select Clear, Photoshop turns the floating selection into a floating hole in the layer. You can move the hole around to see through different parts. And you don't do any damage to the image unless you defloat the selection. If you decide not to carve a hole in the layer, just select a different mode or delete the floater.

Just so you know, you can mix a translucent Opacity setting with a blend mode. But you can't select more than one blend mode at a time. It might be fun to combine Luminosity with Multiply, for example — you know, to apply detail that only darkens — but you just can't do it. Oh well.

Erasing holes in layers

If a layer has a lot of weird little flecks in it or some other distracting gook, you can simply erase it away with the eraser tool. When you work on a layer, the eraser tool erases transparent holes in the layer, assuming the Erase to Saved check box in the Eraser Options palette is not turned on. If Erase to Saved is turned on, you can Option-drag with the eraser to make holes in the layer. Also, the Preserve Transparency check box must be deselected in the Layers palette. If the check box is turned on, the eraser paints in the background color.

Figure 15-6 shows examples of erasing parts of the fish layer. In the first example, I erased around the outside of the fish; in the second example, I erased inside the fish. In both cases, the eraser was set to the Airbrush mode, ensuring soft, subtle transitions between the opaque pixels in the layer and the transparent ones.

Figure 15-6:
Two ways to erase a fish layer, around the outside (left) and inside (right).

Creating an image like Color Plate 15-1

Assuming that you've read through the first part of this chapter and now have some vague idea about how layers work, take another look at Color Plate 15-1 just to make sure that everything gels. Here's the lowdown on each of the layers, starting at the bottom and working up to the top:

- The kelp was the base image — the one that I dropped the others into — so it served as the Background layer.

- I reduced the fish using Layer⇨Transform⇨Scale and erased some of the gook around its edges. The blend mode was Normal and the Opacity was 100 percent.

- In the original astronaut image, the astronaut is missing his right arm and parts of his left hand and leg. So I erased these areas away to create a soft transition. I also tinted the image yellow using the Variations command (discussed in Chapter 18). As with the fish, the blend mode was Normal and the Opacity was 100 percent.

- I rotated the nebula 90 degrees counterclockwise by choosing Image⇨Rotate Canvas⇨90° CCW. Then I scaled it to fit the fish's eye and assigned the Multiply mode to it. I erased the center of the nebula to reveal the white of the fish's eye. The Opacity setting was 100 percent.

- I shrunk the height of the cathedral, increasing the appearance of perspective. Then I applied the Luminosity mode with the usual Opacity of 100 percent. I erased the tops of the towers slightly so that they merged with the fish.

- Not much happened to the flower. I changed the Opacity to 80 percent, but the overlay mode is Normal.

- All those little white sparkles come from the comet. I applied the Screen mode to it so that it lightened the image and used an Opacity of 100 percent. Then I erased the tip of the comet to fit it in the fish's mouth. That's Halley's comet again, by the way, but this time it's a 1986 version.

- Good old Neptune. I reduced this planet to little more than a circle of color by positioning it in the lower-left corner and applying the Hard Light mode to it. The Opacity remained set to 100 percent. I love the way those deep blue columns show through from the cathedral.

Keep in mind that I selected every one of the images before dragging and dropping it inside the composition, so none of the black, blue, or multicolored backgrounds from the original images shown in Color Plate 15-2 were included.

Naturally, I didn't create the image in exactly this order. I'm not that organized, and I might suggest that the artistic process doesn't benefit from such organization. The idea is to just experiment, experiment, experiment, until you get what you want. Hopefully, this chapter has paved the way a little, but you can expect to still be in for a lot of pleasant and amazing surprises.

Chapter 16

Digital Graffiti

● ●

● ●

*C*hapters 12, 13, and 14 — known collectively as Part IV — lead you on a merry tour of the various tools and commands for selecting a part of your image. But in those chapters I skip over one other type of selection outline you can create in Photoshop, and you are never going to guess what it is. Not in a million years. Give up? The answer is text. That's right, Photoshop lets you build a selection outline out of numbers, vowels, consonants, and any other character you can tap in from your keyboard.

Check out Figure 16-1 if you're having trouble believing me. In the top example, I created two lines of text using the type mask tool, which is a variation of the old type tool from earlier versions of Photoshop. Notice that dotted outlines surround the letters, showing that they're selected. The letters are filled with the foreground color, black. As with any selection outline, I can fill the text with a different color, stroke it, or even paint inside it, as demonstrated in the bottom example of the figure.

The Photoshop approach to text makes it an ideal program for subjecting large letters to special effects. On the other hand, you shouldn't mistake Photoshop for a word processor. After text is on the page, you can't select and edit it with the type tool as you can in other programs. So don't attempt to use Photoshop to create large chunks of text or even medium-sized chunks of text; instead, use a desktop publishing program like PageMaker.

Figure 16-1:
Text created
with the
type mask
tool is just a
bunch of
selection
outlines
stamped
into the
shapes or
recognizable
letters.

To make sure that you understand the gist of the message I seek to convey, take this little quiz.

Photoshop is great for creating text that is

    A. Large.

    B. Enormous.

    C. Gargantuan.

    D. All of the above, only bigger.

The great thing about this quiz is that there are no wrong answers. Everyone's a winner, except you folks who went and wrote in your own answers like "Miserably small and peculiar looking" or "Itsy-bitsier than a single-celled organism." So long as you understand that the bigger your text, the better it looks, you're mentally prepared to create text in Photoshop.

Two, Two, Two Types of Text

Photoshop 4 provides two tools for creating text: the standard type tool, whose toolbox icon looks like a big letter *T;* and the new type mask tool, which resides on the same flyout menu as the regular type tool and is represented in the toolbox by a dotted outline of the letter *T.* To select the type tool that's visible in the toolbox, press T. Press T again to select the other type tool. Isn't it great when icons and keyboard shortcuts make so much sense?

Here's the lowdown on the type tools:

✔ The standard-issue type tool creates foreground-colored text on a new layer. (Layers are explained in excruciating detail in Chapter 15.) As with any other element on a layer, you can paint, edit, and otherwise abuse the text without worrying about touching the underlying image. You can make the text more or less translucent by playing with the Opacity slider in the Layers palette, and you can blend the text with the underlying layers using the blend modes pop-up menu. And, perhaps most important, you can replace or update your text as needed without affecting the rest of the image.

✔ The new type mask tool creates your text as a selection outline. You can manipulate, edit, paint, and otherwise play with the selection outline as you would any other selection outline. And because the type mask tool works like any other selection tool, you can use it to add or subtract from an existing selection outline, as described in Chapter 13. (Shift-click with the tool to add character-shaped outlines to the existing selection; Option-click to subtract character-shaped outlines from the existing selection; and Shift-Option-click to find the intersection between the text selection and the existing selection.)

So, which tool do you use when? It depends upon what sort of effect you're trying to create. If you want opaque type, obviously, use the regular type tool. If, on the other hand, you want to create character outlines such as those shown in the top example in Color Plate 16-1, use the type mask tool and then simply stroke the selection outline using Edit⇨Stroke. If you want to soften the edges of your letters — for example, to create a fuzzy shadow behind your letters, as in the middle example in the color plate — you can use the type mask tool and soften the selection outline using Select⇨Feather. (I give the how-tos for creating both these examples later in this chapter.)

The truth is, though, that you can create both of these effects using the regular type tool, too. It just involves a few more steps and a slightly different approach. Similarly, if you want to create opaque type, you can just as easily use the type mask tool and then fill the selection outline by using Option-Delete.

In other words, either tool can get you where you want to go. So just remember that the basic difference between the two tools is that one creates foreground-colored type on a new layer; the other simply gives you a selection outline in the shape of your characters. Pick the tool that gives you the quickest route to the effect you're trying to achieve.

The biggest disadvantage of the type mask tool is that when you deselect the text selection, it becomes permanently fused to the underlying image, making editing difficult. But you can get around this problem by creating a new layer before you click with the type mask tool. Now any text effects you create exist on their own layer.

Putting Your Words on Screen

To type out a few letters in Photoshop, select either of the type tools and click inside the image. It doesn't really matter where you click, by the way. Photoshop positions your text at the spot you click, but you can always move the text after you create it. (However, if a selection outline is active and you click inside it with the type mask tool, Photoshop simply deselects the current selection. You need to click again to create your text.)

Rather than responding with a little blinking cursor or some other subtle doohickey that you may have come to expect from working in other programs, Photoshop goes all out and displays the Type Tool dialog box shown in Figure 16-2. This dialog box is where you enter your text, format it, and otherwise get it ready for its debut inside the image window.

Actually, when you first click with the type tool, Photoshop may display a message telling you that it's building some kind of font list. This just means that it's trying to load all the typefaces available to your system into memory. Just wait the message out. It goes away soon enough, after which the dialog box appears in all its glory.

All-important text-entry box   I-beam cursor

Figure 16-2:
To create
text, enter it
into this
dialog box.

Typing what must be typed

When you first enter the Type Tool dialog box, the text-entry box — labeled in
Figure 16-2 — is active. Here's where you enter the text that you want to add to
your image. If this is the first time you've entered text in Photoshop, a little
vertical line called an *insertion marker* blinks away next to the left side of the
box. If you've entered text before, the previous text appears highlighted, as in
the figure, thus allowing you to edit the text or enter new text. You can do a
number of things inside the text-entry box:

✔ Start typing away to create the text you want to add to your image. If any
existing text in the box was highlighted, Photoshop replaces it with the
new text.

✔ After entering your text, you may find that you've made a mistake or two.
To delete a letter, click in front of it and press the Delete key. To add text,
click at the point where you want to insert it and enter the new text from
the keyboard.

✔ When you move the cursor inside the text-entry box, it changes to an
I-beam, as labeled in Figure 16-2. To replace text, drag over it with the
cursor to highlight it and then start whacking those keys. To delete more
than one letter, highlight the letters and press Delete.

- You can highlight a whole word by double-clicking on it. To highlight multiple words, hold the mouse button down on the second click and drag.

- Press the arrow keys to move the insertion marker one letter to the left or right or one line up or down. Press Shift with an arrow key to select letters and lines.

- To move the insertion marker one whole word in a given direction, press Option along with the left or right arrow key. Shift-Option-left arrow or right arrow selects whole words.

- Photoshop automatically wraps words to the next line when it reaches the right boundary of the text-entry box. But it places all words on a single line in the image unless you insert a paragraph return by pressing the Return key. In Figure 16-2, for example, I typed **Poems**, Return, **by Slim**.

- If the text is too long to fit entirely inside the text-entry box, you can use the scroll bar to see hidden text above or below the visible text.

When inside the Type Tool dialog box, you can access the Cut, Copy, Paste, and Undo commands under the Edit menu. These commands enable you to move text around and undo mistakes. For example, to move some letters from one place to another, follow these steps:

1. **Highlight the text you want to move.**

   Drag over the text with the I-beam cursor, double-click to select words, or use the arrow keys as I described a moment ago.

2. **Choose Edit⇨Cut.**

   Or just press ⌘-X. Photoshop removes the text and puts it in a special location in your computer's memory called the Clipboard.

3. **Click at the point where you want to move the text.**

   Your click repositions the insertion marker.

4. **Choose Edit⇨Paste.**

   Or press ⌘-V. Photoshop retrieves the text from the Clipboard and inserts it at the desired spot.

If you want to duplicate a word, you can highlight it, choose Edit⇨Copy (⌘-C), reposition the insertion marker, and choose Paste. You can also undo the last edit by choosing Edit⇨Undo or by pressing ⌘-Z.

Changing how the type looks

The remaining options inside the Type Tool dialog box determine how your text looks. These options control the typeface, the type size, the amount of space between lines, and all that other rigmarole. When all these characteristics get together in the same room, they're usually called *formatting attributes.* You can, of course, make additional enhancements to the appearance of your text after you return to the image window, but the formatting options let you set up the fundamental stuff.

In Photoshop, all text in the text-entry box is formatted the same. For example, you can't highlight a single word and assign it a different typeface than you assign to its neighbors. Therefore, the following formatting options affect each and every character in the text-entry box equally and without prejudice:

✔ Select a typeface and type style from the Font pop-up menu. Assuming that you installed Photoshop correctly — as I tell you to in Appendix A — type styles such as bold and italic appear in their own submenus. But if they don't, no biggie. Just select a typeface from the pop-up menu and set the style using the check boxes above the text-entry box.

✔ In order to successfully use a typeface in Photoshop, you must be using ATM (that's Adobe Type Manager, not Automatic Teller Machine or Arbitrary Toaster Molester) and you must have all the important font data — including both screen and printer fonts — in your Fonts folder inside the System folder. If your text comes up smooth and beautiful, not to worry. If your text is so jagged that it looks like you drew it on an Etch a Sketch — as in the case of Bad type in Figure 16-3 — something's wrong. Either use a different font or consult with your local computer know-it-all to figure out the problem.

Figure 16-3:
If your text looks smooth (top), super. If not (bottom), try a different font or ask someone smart for help.

Good type
Bad type

✔ Enter the size of the text into the Size option box. The Size value is measured in points (one point equals $1/72$ inch) or pixels, depending on the setting in the pop-up menu to the right of the option box.

- The size of a point on-screen depends on the Resolution setting in the Image Size dialog box (discussed back in Chapter 4). If the Resolution value is 400 ppi, a 36-point letter is 200 pixels tall. If the Resolution is only 72 ppi, that same type is only 36 pixels tall. Talk about confusing! To remain sane, I always set the pop-up menu to Pixels, because a pixel is a pixel the world around.

- To hop from one option box to another, press Tab. Pressing Tab jumps your cursor from the text-entry area to the Size option box, from the Size option box to the Leading option box, and so on. To go backward, press Shift-Tab.

- The Leading value controls the amount of space between lines of type. It's called *leading* (pronounced *ledding*) because back in the old days — we're talking anywhere from the 1600s to the 1950s — printers used to stick pieces of lead between lines of type. Of course, Photoshop doesn't do anything like that, but old terms die hard.

- If you don't enter a Leading value, Photoshop assigns spacing equal to 120 percent of the Size value. If you do enter a value, I recommend that it be equal to at least 90 percent of the Size value to keep the lines from overlapping. In Figure 16-4, for example, the Size value was 144 pixels and the Leading value was 130 pixels.

Figure 16-4:
Here's how the Size (dark gray) and Leading (light gray) values are measured.

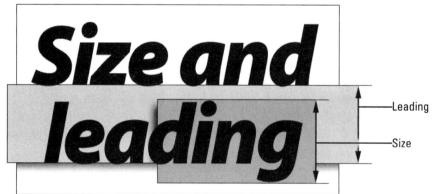

- A positive Spacing value adds space between each letter of text. A negative Spacing value tightens the space between letters. No Spacing value — or a value of 0 — just spaces the letters normally.

- Like the Size value, both the Leading and Spacing values are measured in points or pixels, depending on the pop-up menu setting.

- Select one or more Style check boxes to assign different type styles. Bold makes the text thicker; Italic makes it slanted or cursive; Underline — well, you know what that does.

✔ Don't select the Outline or Shadow styles. They produce unspeakably ugly results that will inspire your family to disinherit you, your friends to alienate you, and your business associates to bar you from all future staff parties and reindeer games. I tell you some better ways to outline text and create shadows later in this chapter.

✔ Always select the Anti-aliased check box. If you turn it off, your text has tiny jagged edges, and you don't want that. (This check box doesn't cure big, huge jags created by the font problems I mentioned earlier.)

✔ Select an Alignment option to determine whether multiple lines of text are aligned by their left edges, right edges, or centers. Don't select any of the options along the right side of the dialog box. They create vertical text, which is just as ugly as the Outline and Shadow styles I warned you away from a moment ago.

Previewing a few formatting attributes

The two check boxes underneath the text-entry box — Font and Size — control how text looks inside the dialog box. See, in Photoshop 2.5, the letters in the text-entry box always appeared in the standard Macintosh system font, 12-point Chicago. But Adobe decided that people might like to actually see what they're doing, so you now have the choice of previewing the specified Font and Size settings or seeing them in 12-point Chicago as in the old days.

The effects of the Leading, Spacing, Anti-aliased, and Alignment settings are not reflected in the text-entry box, regardless of which check box you select.

Bringing text and image together

To instruct Photoshop to create your text, click on the OK button or press the Enter key on the keypad. If you press Return, you run the risk of wiping out the letters in the text-entry box because the Return key adds a paragraph return. (Okay, a few of you may have noticed that the Return key does activate the OK button when you're editing the Size, Leading, or Spacing values, but it's best to get in the habit of pressing Enter just to be safe.)

Photoshop then creates your text in the image window. If you notice a misspelled word or some other typographical gaffe, don't attempt to drag over the text with a type tool and edit it. Instead, press ⌘-Z to undo things and then click again with the type tool to revisit the Type Tool dialog box. Photoshop displays your previous settings and even retains the text in the text-entry area. You're right back at the spot you last left off.

If you created text with the type mask tool and you notice an incorrect character at the end or beginning of a word, you can Option-drag around the blooper with the lasso tool to eliminate the character from the selection outline. For example, if you typed *Bye* when you meant to type *by*, you can Option-drag around the *e*. You probably won't find yourself in this particular pickle very often, but it's nice to know all the possible ways to clean up your messes, don't you think?

If the bottoms of some of your characters that dip down low — like *g, p,* and *y* — are getting cut off, you need to change a setting inside ATM. To open the ATM control panel, choose the Control Panels command from the Apple menu and then double-click on the ~ATM file name. (Or choose Apple⇨Control Panels⇨ ~ATM if you use System 7.5.) Next, select the Character Shapes radio button, spotlighted in Figure 16-5. Click in the close box to close the control panel and restart your computer by choosing Special⇨Restart at the Finder. (Be sure to save any open images in Photoshop before you restart your machine.)

Figure 16-5:
Select the
Character
Shapes
option in the
ATM control
panel to
keep letters
from getting
cut off in
Photoshop.

Declaring Open Season on Type

If you've created your type and it's sitting there selected inside your image, you can do all kinds of things with it, including the following:

- You can move the text around. If you created your text with the regular type tool, select the move tool and then drag the text or press the arrow keys to move the text, as you would any other element on a layer. (Press ⌘ to drag or nudge the text with any of the other tools except the hand or pen tool.)

- To move a text selection outline created with the type mask tool, drag with the type mask tool or one of the other selection tools. Or press the arrow keys to nudge the selection outline this way or that.

To move or clone the text selection itself, use the same techniques you use to move or clone any other selection (refer to Chapter 13 for a refresher). Drag with the move tool to move the text; Option-drag to clone the text.

In other words, selections that you create with the type mask tool work just like any other selection.

✔ You can paint inside the text as demonstrated back in Figure 16-1. After you paint inside the letters, you can use the edit tools to smear the colors, blur them, lighten them, and so on.

✔ You can fill the text with the foreground color by pressing Option-Delete. To fill text with the background color, press ⌘-Delete. To fill the text with a blend of colors, just drag across the text with the gradient tool. It just couldn't be easier.

✔ You can apply a border around your type by choosing Edit➪Stroke.

✔ Before you fill or stroke a selection outline, be sure that your text is positioned where you want it. You can't move the stroked text after you create it without leaving a hole in your image. Ditto with any other painting or editing commands you apply to a text selection outline.

✔ Remember that if you created the text with the regular type tool, the text exists on its own layer. If the Preserve Transparency option in the Layers palette is selected, you can't paint or apply editing commands outside the confines of your text. If you want to alter the appearance of the background on the text layer, deselect the check box. (For example, if you want to apply a stroke around the outside edges of your character, you need to deselect the check box.)

✔ To delete text that was created with the regular type tool, just drag the text layer to the trash icon in the Layers palette (for help, refer to Chapter 15). Or just click on the layer name and then the trash icon. If you want to delete text that was created with the type mask tool — and you didn't take my earlier advice to create that text on its own layer — you may be able to choose File➪Revert, discussed in Chapter 11, to bring your image back to its pre-text appearance.

Every one of these techniques can achieve some truly remarkable effects. Just to show you what I mean, I provide some step-by-step examples that show you how to create outline type and text with shadows, as I promised earlier. I also show you how to create translucent type. For full-color demonstrations of these techniques, see Color Plate 16-1.

Tracing outlines around your letters

Off we go. Today's first set of steps tells you how to create genuine outline type, like the stuff shown in Figure 16-6 and the top example in Color Plate 16-1. You can see through the interiors of the letters and you can make the borders as thick as you please. What more could you ask from life?

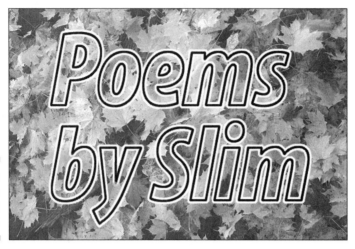

Figure 16-6:
Outline type
created the
right way.

1. **Create a new layer.**

   You don't have to put your text on its own layer, but doing so makes it simpler to edit the text later on if necessary. To create a layer, click on the new layer icon in the Layers palette, as discussed in Chapter 15.

2. **Use the type mask tool to create your text.**

   Click with the tool, type away into the text-entry area, format to your heart's content, and press Enter. Then move the text selection outline into the desired position by dragging it or nudging it with the arrow keys.

3. **Set the foreground color to white.**

   You can do this quickly by pressing D to get the default colors and then X to swap them.

4. **Make sure that the Preserve Transparency check box in the Layers palette is deselected.**

   In the next step, you apply a stroke to the center of your selection outline (that is, with half the stroke appearing on the inside of the outline and half appearing on the outside). If you don't deselect the Preserve Transparency check box, Photoshop doesn't let you paint outside the selection outline.

5. **Choose Edit⇨Stroke, select the Center radio button, and enter** 12 **as the Width value.**

   After making your selections in the Stroke dialog box, press Return. You now have a 12-pixel thick, white outline around your type.

6. **Make black or some other dark color the foreground color.**

   To create the top example in Color Plate 16-1, I changed the foreground color to red.

7. **Choose Edit⇨Stroke and enter 4 as the Width value.**

Then press Return. Congratulations, you have now arrived at the effect shown in Figure 16-6 and the top of Color Plate 16-1. If you created your text on a layer, as I heartily recommended back in Step 1, you can use the move tool to reposition the text if needed. (Press ⌘-D to deseelct the text first.) You can also play with the blend modes and Opacity slider in the Layers palette to change how the text blends with the underlying image.

Adding shadows behind your letters

In these steps, you create letters with shadows, as shown in Figure 16-7 and the second example in Color Plate 16-1. These kinds of shadows are commonly called drop shadows because they don't extend away from the letters; instead, they merely rest behind the letters.

1. **Create a new layer.**

Always a good step when creating text with the type mask tool.

2. **Create and format your text using the type mask tool.**

Blah de blah de blah. (In other words, do what needs to be done, Bucko.)

3. **Position the outline where you want the text shadow to appear.**

Figure 16-7: Drop shadows help to set text off from the background and otherwise make it look way cool.

Put the outline a little down and to the right of where you want the foreground text.

4. **Choose Select⇨Feather.**

The Feather command softens the selection outline to give your shadow a fuzzy, shadowlike effect. Use a fairly high Feather value, such as 10. Press Return to exit the Feather dialog box.

5. Set the foreground color to black.

To do it quickly, press D.

6. Press Option-Delete.

Photoshop fills the selection with black.

7. Click with the type mask tool again.

Up pops the Type Tool dialog box again. You want to use the same text as before, so don't change anything. Just press Enter.

8. Use the arrow keys to position the selection outline with respect to the shadow.

Position the outline above and to the left of the shadow.

9. Change the foreground color to white.

Press X to get there quickly.

10. Press Option-Delete.

Photoshop fills the selection with white.

11. Change the foreground color to medium gray or some other medium color.

In Color Plate 16-1, I used purple. This color is for the soft shading inside the letters. If it helps to hide the marching ants around the letters, press ⌘-H.

12. Paint a couple of streaks across the letters with the airbrush tool.

You now have something resembling the image shown in Figure 16-7 and in the middle of Color Plate 16-1.

Turning your letters into ghosts of their former selves

This last set of steps explains how to create translucent letters, which are just the ticket for creating ghosted or tinted text, as shown in Figure 16-8 and the third example in Color Plate 16-1. You might think that this effect would be rather difficult, but in truth, it's way easier than the previous techniques.

1. Start with a light background.

I lightened my leaves a little to achieve Figure 16-8. (I explain how to adjust the colors in your image in Chapter 18.)

2. **Change your foreground color to something dark.**

   In Figure 16-8, I used black, one of your darker colors. In Color Plate 16-1, I opted for dark orange.

3. **Select the regular type tool and create your text.**

   Photoshop creates type in the foreground color and places it on a new layer.

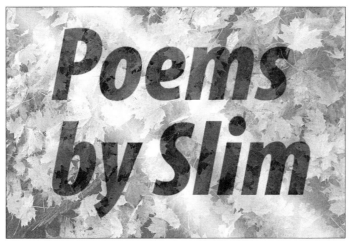

Figure 16-8: Translucent text is the picture of subtlety and good taste, especially when you're creating the title for a book of cowboy poetry like this one.

4. **Drag or nudge the text into position using the move tool.**

5. **Press a number key.**

   When you're working with a layer, pressing a number key changes the opacity of the layer. Higher numbers make the selection more opaque; lower numbers make it more transparent. Chapter 15 explains all of this in more detail, but for now, just press the number keys until you get the effect you want. (You can also drag the Opacity slider in the Layers palette, if you prefer.)

6. **Deselect the Preserve Transparency check box in the Layers palette.**

   This allows you to paint the areas around the letters on the text layer, which you do two steps from now.

7. **Select the airbrush tool and set the brush mode to Behind.**

   Press A to get the airbrush, press Return to open the Airbrush options palette, and select the Behind mode from the brush mode pop-up menu in the palette. The Behind mode lets you paint behind the existing elements on a layer, which you do one step from now.

8. Set the foreground color to white and take a couple of swipes at the background with the airbrush.

Ooh, isn't that pretty. I can't decide whether it looks more like the title for a wedding invitation, a soap opera, or a wake, but it sure is pretty.

Keep in mind that you can apply any of the techniques in the preceding three sets of steps to any layer as well as to text created with the type tools.

Moving and Deleting Characters

I would be remiss in my duties if I failed to pass along one last tip before I tuck in this chapter and tell the bed bugs not to bite. After you exit the Type Tool dialog box, Photoshop lets you manually adjust the amount of space between letters. This kind of letter spacing adjustment is sometimes called *kerning* by folks who have enough time on their hands to go around inventing new and weird-sounding words.

You can only kern characters in text that exists on its own layer. In other words, if you used the type mask tool to create your text and you didn't create that text on a new layer, as I advise earlier in this chapter, you're stuck. Moving the characters will leave a background-colored hole in your image. So does deleting the characters.

If your text does exist on its own layer, kerning is a cinch. First, select the characters you want to kern with the lasso tool. Shift-drag to add additional characters to the selection. Then ⌘-drag the letters (pressing ⌘ activates the move tool, which enables you to drag the text). Alternatively, you can press ⌘ and press the arrow keys to move the characters in 1-pixel increments. Press Shift as you press the arrow keys to nudge the selected characters in 10-pixel jumps.

If you want to delete characters instead of moving them, use the lasso tool to select the characters to be terminated and just press Delete. Those characters vanish in a puff of electronic smoke. Remember that you only want to delete characters in this way when they exist on an independent layer — otherwise, you end up cutting holes in your image.

Chapter 17

Forays into Filters

· ·

· ·

*I*f you're a photographer or you've taken a photography course or two, you know how photographic filters work. They refine or refract light to modify the image as it comes into the camera. A daylight filter strains some of the blue out of the image; a polarization lens eliminates reflected light; a fish-eye lens refracts peripheral imagery into the photo.

But real-life filters present a couple of problems. First, they're a nuisance. They take up a ton of room in your camera bag, they generally bang around and get scratched, and you never know when you're going to contract a sudden case of butterfingers and drop a lens on a marble floor. Second, you have to decide which filter you want to use while shooting the photo. Not only is it difficult to experiment through a viewfinder, whatever decision you ultimately make is permanent. If you go with a fish-eye lens, you can't go back and "undistort" the image later.

The Photoshop filters are another story entirely:

✔ All filters reside under a single menu (called Filter, surprisingly enough).

✔ You can immediately undo a filter if you don't like the results.

✔ You can preview the outcome of the most common filters.

✔ You can apply several filters in a row and even go back and revisit a single filter multiple times.

✔ Most Photoshop filters have no real-world counterparts, which means that you can modify images in ways that simply aren't possible inside a camera.

If you're a photographer, you may want to forego a few of your camera's filters and take up Photoshop filters instead. Granted, you may still want to use corrective lenses to adjust color and keep out reflected light, but avoid any special-effects filter that makes the image look like more than what your eyes can see. Such filters merely limit the range of effects you can apply later inside Photoshop.

If you aren't a photographer, filters open up a whole new range of opportunities that no other Photoshop function quite matches. They apply changes automatically, so there's no advantage to being an artist (although an artistic vision certainly comes in handy). Filters can make poor images look better and good images look fantastic. And you can use them to introduce special effects, such as camera movement and relief textures. Frankly, filters turn Photoshop into a lean, mean, photo-munching machine. In a good way, of course.

Photoshop 4 brings you 48 new filters, for a whopping total of 90 filters altogether. (The new effects formerly were available as a stand-alone product, Adobe Gallery Effects.) This chapter doesn't even start to cover all the Photoshop filters, just those that you're likely to use on a regular basis. To see some of the others in action, check out Chapter 20.

A Few Fast Filter Facts

Before I launch into explanations of Photoshop filters, I thought I would share a few introductory facts:

✔ If some portion of your image is selected, the filter affects the selection and leaves the rest of the image unmodified. If no portion of the image is selected, the filter affects the entire image.

✔ To create smooth transitions between filtered and unfiltered areas in an image, blur the selection outline by choosing Select⇨Feather, as discussed in Chapter 13.

✔ After you apply a filter, you can reapply it in the very same manner by choosing the first command in the Filter menu or by pressing ⌘-F.

✔ Some filters display a dialog box so that you can control how the filter is applied. If the last filter was one of these, press ⌘-Option-F to redisplay the dialog box and apply the filter again using different settings.

✔ The section "Previewing the filter effects" in Chapter 10 explains how to use the preview options and other controls inside filter dialog boxes.

✔ Some filters take a few seconds or even minutes to apply. You can cancel such a filter in progress by pressing ⌘-period. The name of the previous filter remains at the top of the Filter menu, so you can't press ⌘-F to apply a canceled filter.

✔ To undo the last filter, press ⌘-Z. Unlike a canceled filter, the undone filter remains at the top of the Filter menu, so you can later apply it by pressing ⌘-F.

✔ Before applying two or more filters in a row, save your image just to be safe. You can restore the saved image if you don't like the results.

✔ In Photoshop 3, you could blend a filtered image with the unfiltered original by taking advantage of the Float command. The Float command is gone in Photoshop 4, as I discuss in Chapter 15. But Version 4 offers the Fade command, which is designed specifically for blending a filtered image with its unmolested twin. If you choose Filter⇨Fade immediately after applying a filter, the dialog box shown in Figure 17-1 appears, enabling you to play with the Opacity and blend mode of the filtered image. This command enables you to create all sorts of variations on a filter, as illustrated in Figure 17-2.

✔ Again, you have to apply the Fade command *immediately* after you apply the filter. If you choose another command or apply a painting or editing tool to the image, you can't use the Fade command.

Figure 17-1:
The new Fade command lets you blend a filtered image with the unfiltered original.

Figure 17-2:
A dapper gentleman takes on a new look after I apply the Fresco filter once. Applying the Fade command with a 60 percent Opacity setting and with the Darken blend mode creates variations on the effect.

Original   Fresco

Opacity 60%   Opacity 60%, darken

How to Fortify Those Wishy-Washy Details

No matter how you acquired an image or how good it looked before you scanned it, chances are better than even that it appears a little out of focus on-screen. Not necessarily blurry, but a bit soft.

The image in Figure 17-3, from which I captured a subject for Figure 17-2, is an exaggerated example. Snapped around the time Stonehenge was built — well, around the time of the Magna Carta, then — this photo has suffered the cruel scourges of time. It probably wasn't that sharply focused in the first place, but lo these many years later, it looks so soft you'd swear that it was sculpted out of Jell-O.

The solutions to softness are the four commands under the Filter⬄Sharpen submenu. The following sections explain how these filters work and when — if ever — to apply them.

Figure 17-3:
Antique
images such
as this
one are
notoriously
soft on
focus.

The single-shot sharpeners

The first three sharpening filters — Sharpen, Sharpen Edges, and Sharpen More — are what I call single-shot filters. You choose them, and they do their work without complex dialog boxes or other means of digital interrogation. These filters, with their straightforward names, are a breeze to use.

Unfortunately, when it comes to Photoshop, you get back what you put in — mentally, that is. In other words, if you don't have to work at it, it's liable to deliver rather mediocre results. As demonstrated in Figure 17-4, all three of these Sharpen filters sharpen, but none satisfactorily remedies the image's focus problems.

Figure 17-4 shows the results of applying each of the three single-shot sharpeners to a detail from the image. In each case, I applied the filter once — as shown in the middle row — and then a second time — as shown in the last row. For the record, here's what each of the filters do:

  ✔ Filter➪Sharpen➪Sharpen enhances the focus of the image very slightly. If the photo is already well focused but needs a little extra fortification to make it perfect, the Sharpen filter does the trick. Otherwise, forget it.

Sharpen   Sharpen more   Sharpen Edges

Original

Filtered once

Filtered twice

Figure 17-4: The effects of applying each of the single-shot sharpeners are shockingly shabby.

✔ The Sharpen More filter enhances focus more dramatically. Although it's easily the most useful of the three single-shooters, it's still fairly crude. For example, the center image in Figure 17-4 is not sharp enough, while the bottom image is so sharp that little flecks — called artifacts — are starting to form in the woman's dress. Boo, hiss.

✔ The Sharpen Edges filter is a complete waste of time. It sharpens the so-called edges of an image without sharpening any of the neutral areas in between. In the figure, for example, the filter sharpens the outline of the guy's face but ignores the interior of his jacket. The result is an inconsistent effect that eventually frays the edges and leaves non-edges looking goopy by comparison.

As you may have gathered by now, I'm not a big fan of these filters. Still, you may want to go ahead and apply Sharpen or Sharpen More to an image to see whether it does the trick or not. If a single-shot sharpener turns out to be all you need, great. If not, undo the effect (press ⌘-Z) and try out the Unsharp Mask command, explained next. It's a little scarier, but it works like a dream.

Supersharpen!!!

Figure 17-5:
Experts
agree that
the Unsharp
Mask dialog
box really
should be
called the
Supersharpen
dialog box.

Unsharp Mask: The filter with a weird name

If the Photoshop programmers had been in charge of naming Superman, they would have called him "Average Guy from Krypton." Rather than describing what the guy does, the programmers describe his origins. I say this because that's exactly what they did with Filter⇨Sharpen⇨Unsharp Mask. Rather than calling the filter "Supersharpen," which would have made a modicum of sense and may have even encouraged a few novices to give it a try, they named it after a 40-year-old stat camera technique that a few professionals in lab coats pretend to understand in order to impress members of the opposite sex.

So forget Unsharp Mask and just think "Supersharpen." To use the "Supersharpen" command, choose Filter⇨Sharpen⇨Unsharp Mask. The "Supersharpen" dialog box appears, as shown in Figure 17-5.

Inside the "Supersharpen" dialog box

Like the Dust & Scratches dialog box that I discuss in Chapter 10, the one from Figure 17-5 allows you to preview what happens when you change the values in the three option boxes. You can preview the filter both inside the dialog box and in the main image window. If you can't quite remember how these previewing functions work, skim through the bullets in the "Previewing the filter effects" section of Chapter 10.

From the people who brought you the uncola nut . . .

For those of you who are the least bit interested, an unsharp mask is not a fuzzy disguise that you wear on Halloween. Here's how it used to work: A negative version of an image was shot out of focus — hence, the "unsharp" part. The negative was then used to mask off portions of the original image, much like a stencil. Believe it or not, this soft mask sharpened the edges of the

original without significantly sharpening the graininess — just the ticket for Figure 17-3.

Any technique that makes this little sense must have been an accident, and unsharp masking was no exception. It was developed to prevent alignment problems; the sharpening effect was pure coincidence.

To sharpen an image, use the three slider bars like so:

✔ Change the Amount value from 1 to 500 percent to change the amount of sharpening. This may strike you as obvious, but just to be sure, higher Amount values produce more sharpening.

✔ Adjust the Radius value to specify the width of the edges you want to sharpen. If the image is generally in good shape, use a Radius of 0.5. If the edges are soft and syrupy, like the ones in Figure 17-3, use a Radius of 1.0. And if the edges are almost nonexistent, go with 2.0. Generally speaking, you won't want to go any lower than 0.5 or any higher than 2.0 (though 250.0 is the maximum).

✔ You don't have to enter 1.0 or 2.0 into the Radius option box. A simple 1 or 2 will suffice. It's just that you can enter $^1/_{10}$ values — such as 1.1 and 1.9 — if you're in a particularly precise mood.

✔ As with the Threshold option in the Dust & Scratches dialog box, the Unsharp Mask Threshold option determines how different two neighboring pixels must be to be considered an edge. (See Chapter 10 for a review of this concept.) The default value of 0 tells Photoshop to sharpen everything. By raising the value, you tell Photoshop not to sharpen low-contrast pixels.

✔ This is a great idea, but the implementation by Photoshop leaves something to be desired. The filter creates an abrupt transition between sharpened and ignored pixels, resulting in an unrealistic effect. Therefore, I recommend that you leave Threshold set to 0.

Some sharpening scenarios

Figure 17-6 demonstrates the effects of several different Amount and Radius values on the same detail to which I applied the piddly little Sharpen More command in Figure 17-4. Throughout Figure 17-6, the Threshold value is 0.

Figure 17-6 is organized into two rows. To create the images in the top row, I started with an Amount value of 200 percent and a Radius of 0.5. Then I halved the Amount value and doubled the Radius in each of the next two images. Though the effect is similar from one image to the next, you can see that the right image has thicker edges than the left image. (The differences are subtle; you may have to look closely.)

Figure 17-6:
The effect of a whole bunch of Amount and Radius values on detail from an ancient photo.

200%, 0.5   100%, 1.0   50%, 2.0

500%, 0.5   250%, 1.0   125%, 2.0

The bottom row of the figure features more pronounced sharpening effects. Again, I started with one set of Amount and Radius values — 500 percent and 0.5 — and progressively halved the Amount and doubled the Radius. Notice that not only are the edges in the right image thicker, but the left image contains more *artifacts* (those little flecks in the jacket and hat).

After experimenting with a few different settings — hey, you don't have to know what you're doing to experiment — I decided that my favorite setting was an Amount of 250 percent and a Radius of 1.0. The final image sharpened with these settings is shown in Figure 17-7. Not bad for an image as old as the pharaohs.

Figure 17-7:
The image
from
Figure 17-3
sharpened
with an
Amount
value of 250
percent and
a Radius
value of 1.0.

Myopia Adds Depth

If you want to make a portion of your image blurry instead of sharp, you can apply one of the commands under the Filter⇨Blur menu. Right off the bat, you quick thinkers will be thinking to yourselves, "Blurry? Why would I want my image to be blurry?" This is a classic problem. You're thinking of blurry as the opposite of sharp. But blurry and sharp can go hand in hand inside the same image. The sharp details are in the foreground, and the blurry stuff goes in the background.

Take Figure 17-8, for example. In this image, I selected and blurred the background. The scene becomes a little more intimate, as if the background were far, far away. It also has the effect of making the foreground characters seem more in focus than ever.

To make the effect complete, I selected the lower-right corner of the image, which represents the ground coming toward us. I feathered the selection (using Select⇨Feather set to a value of 30) and then blurred it. The result is a gradual blurring effect, as if the ground were becoming progressively out of focus as it extends beyond our field of vision.

For the most part, then, blurring is a special effect. Unlike sharpening, which has the effect of correcting the focus, blurring heightens reality by exaggerating the

Figure 17-8:
Blurring the background as well as a small tip of the foreground (bottom right) brings the family up close and personal.

depth of an image. In other words, you never have to blur an image — and you probably won't do it nearly as frequently as you sharpen — but it's a lot of fun.

Choosing your blur

The first two commands under the Filter⇨Blur submenu — Blur and Blur More — are the Dumb and Dumber of the blur filters. Like their Sharpen and Sharpen More counterparts, they produce predefined effects that never seem to be quite what you're looking for.

The "Superblur" command — the one that offers the powers you need to get the job done right — is Filter⇨Blur⇨Gaussian Blur. The filter is named after Karl Friedrich Gauss, a dusty old German mathematician who's even older than the photograph from Figure 17-3. But just think "Superblur" — or, as Mr. Gauss would have put it, "Ueberblur."

When you choose Filter⇨Blur⇨Gaussian Blur, Photoshop displays the dialog box shown in Figure 17-9. The Radius value determines the number of pixels that get mixed together at a time. You can go as high as 250.0, but any value over 10.0 enters the realm of the legally blind. In Figure 17-8, I blurred the background with a Radius value of 4.0 and the lower right patch of ground with a Radius of 2.0.

Ueberblur!!!

Figure 17-9:
Specify the exact amount of blur you want in the Ueberblur dialog box, a.k.a. the Gaussian Blur dialog box.

Creating motion and puzzle pieces

The Filter⇨Blur submenu contains three additional filters — Motion Blur, Radial Blur, and Smart Blur — all of which are exclusively special-effects filters. The Motion Blur filter makes an image appear to move in a straight line; the Radial Blur filter can be used to either move the selection in a circle or zoom it outward toward the viewer.

The Smart Blur option, new to Photoshop 4, finds the edges in your image and then blurs only between the edges — it's as if Photoshop was carving your image up into puzzle pieces and then blurring each piece. If you apply the effect in heavy doses, the result is an image that resembles a watercolor painting and isn't too far removed from the effect created by the Filter⇨Artistic⇨Watercolor filter.

Of the three filters, Motion Blur is the filter you're more likely to use. First, the dialog box offers the standard previewing options, making it accessible and predictable. Second, it's much easier to use. Finally, when compared with Radial Blur, it takes a lot less time to use; Radial Blur is one of the slowest Photoshop filters.

When you choose Filter⇨Blur⇨Motion Blur, Photoshop displays the dialog box in Figure 17-10. The filter smears pixels at a specified angle and over a specified distance. Enter the angle and distance into the appropriately named option boxes. You can also drag the spoke inside the circle on the right side of the dialog box to change the Angle value.

Figure 17-10:
The Motion Blur filter wiggles pixels back and forth to create the illusion of movement.

Figure 17-11:
Two unlikely applications of the Motion Blur filter.

By way of example, Figure 17-11 shows a couple of discrete applications of the Motion Blur filter. To blur the boy, I selected him, feathered the selection, and applied the Motion Blur filter with an Angle value of 90 degrees — straight up and down — and a Distance of 30 pixels. To blur sister's arm — the one nearest her beaming brother — I used an Angle of 45 degrees and a Distance of 6 pixels. As you can see, Distance values over 20 smear the image into oblivion; smaller Distance values create subtle movement effects.

Filter Potpourri

The Filter⇨Sharpen and Filter⇨Blur submenus contain the filters you use most often. In fact, if you like, you can blow off the rest of the chapter without being much the poorer for it. But if you have five minutes or so to spare, I'd like to show you a few other interesting commands scattered throughout the Filter menu.

Giving your images that gritty, streetwise look

For starters, there's the Add Noise command. Not to be confused with the as-yet uncompleted Adenoids filter, Add Noise randomizes the colors of selected pixels. The result is a layer of grit that gives smooth images a textured appearance.

Choose Filter⇨Noise⇨Add Noise to display the Add Noise dialog box shown in Figure 17-12. Here's how to use the options found therein:

Figure 17-12:
This filter adds "noise" to your image to give it a gritty texture.

▱ Drag the Amount slider triangle or enter a value between 1 and 999 to control how noisy the image gets. Low values — such as the default value 32 or lower — permit a small amount of noise; high values permit more. Anything over 100 pretty much wipes out the original image.

✔ Select a Distribution radio button to control the color of noise. The Uniform option colors pixels with random variations on the shades it finds in the original image; the Gaussian option — which should be labeled High Contrast — colors pixels with more exaggerated light and dark shades. Therefore, Gaussian produces a noisier effect, about twice as noisy as Uniform. For example, an Amount value of 32 combined with Gaussian produces a similar visual effect to an Amount value of 64 combined with Uniform.

✔ The Monochromatic check box adds grayscale noise to full-color images. When the option is turned off, Photoshop adds all colors of noise. (The option has no effect on grayscale images except to shift the pixels around a little.)

To rough up the dark areas in the mom and son detail shown on the left side of Figure 17-13, I used Select⇨Color Range to select the dark areas in the image and then applied the Add Noise filter. By changing the Amount value to 100 and selecting Gaussian, I arrived at the effect shown in the middle example in the figure. To achieve the right-hand image, I applied Filter⇨Blur⇨Motion Blur with an Angle value of 45 degrees and a Distance of 6 pixels. Photoshop creates an etched metal effect that suits these two characters to a tee.

Color Plate 17-1 shows the same Add Noise and Motion Blur effect applied to the dark portions of a full-color image. But there's a slight twist. In the top image, I applied the Add Noise filter with the Monochromatic check box turned off; in the bottom image, the check box is turned on. As a result, the top image contains color streaks, and the bottom image contains black-and-white streaks. I prefer the black-and-white streaks for this particular image — they give it a more rustic look — but you, of course, are free to do as you see fit.

Original   Add Noise   Motion Blur

Figure 17-13: I selected the dark portions of the image on the left and applied the Add Noise filter (middle) followed by Motion Blur (right).

Stamping your image in metal

Another intriguing and sometimes useful filter is Emboss. It makes your image appear as if it were stamped in metal. The edges in the image appear in relief, and the other areas turn gray.

When you choose Filter⇨Stylize⇨Emboss, Photoshop displays the dialog box shown in Figure 17-14. You enter the angle of the light shining on the metal into the Angle option box. The Height value determines the height of the edges, and the Amount value determines the amount of contrast between blacks and whites.

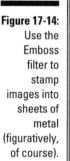

Figure 17-14: Use the Emboss filter to stamp images into sheets of metal (figuratively, of course).

I'm breezing over these options because they aren't the most useful gang in the world. In fact, they can be big time wasters. From personal experience, I can tell you the following about the Emboss dialog box:

- ✔ It doesn't matter how you set the Angle value. Feel free to drag the spoke on the circle around until you get what you want, but don't expect big differences between one angle and another.

- ✔ Set the Height value to 1 or 2. Any value over 2 has a habit of impairing detail.

- ✔ Okay, the Amount value is useful. Enter 50 percent for a very subtle effect, 100 percent for a medium Emboss effect, and 200 percent for added drama. You can go as high as 500, but higher values make the contrast between blacks and whites too abrupt (in my humble opinion).

Sharpening the blur

After you read about Figure 17-15, your reaction may be one of, "Whoa, hold up a minute here. First you blur and then you sharpen? What kind of crazy logic is that?" Well, pretty sound logic, actually.

After I applied Gaussian Blur, the image turned overly gray, as you can see in the second example in the figure. Luckily, one of the properties of Unsharp Mask is that it increases the amount of contrast between dark and light pixels. So to bring the blacks and whites back from the dead,

I set the Radius value inside the Unsharp Mask dialog box to the exact value I had used inside the Gaussian Blur dialog box — that is, 2.0. Using this value ensured that Unsharp Mask was able to correctly locate the blurred edges and boost their contrast.

If you can figure it out, it's a great technique. If not, you can use the Auto Levels or Levels command to change the contrast, as I describe in the next chapter.

Like Add Noise, Emboss isn't the kind of filter you go around applying to an entire image. I mean, after you've done it once or twice, it gets a little old. Rather, you want to apply it to selected areas.

In the first example of Figure 17-15, I selected the dark areas in the mother/son image and applied the Emboss filter with an Angle of 45 degrees, a Height of 2, and an Amount of 200 percent. In the middle example, I blurred the selection using the Gaussian Blur filter set to a Radius of 2 pixels. Then I applied Unsharp Mask with an Amount of 500 percent and a Radius of 2 pixels, arriving at the thrilling mottled metal effect on the far right.

Emboss   Gaussian Blur   Unsharp Mask

Figure 17-15: After selecting the dark portions of the image, I embossed it (left), blurred it (middle), and sharpened it (right), creating a soft relief.

Merging colors in flaky images

The last two filters I cover in this chapter — Facet and Median — average the colors of neighboring pixels to create areas of flat color. Both throw away detail, but they're great for smoothing out the imperfections in old, cruddy images such as the one that keeps popping up in this chapter.

Filter⇨Pixelate⇨Facet is a single-shot command that roams the image looking for areas of similarly colored pixels and then assigns the entire area a single color. In Figure 17-16, I started with the elder daughter from way back in Figure 17-3, before she got sharpened. In the middle example, I applied Filter⇨ Pixelate⇨Facet. See how the image is now divided up into a bunch of globby areas of color? To make it more clear, I applied the Unsharp Mask filter to the right-hand example, using an Amount value of 250 percent and a Radius value of 0.5.

Original   Facet   Unsharp Mask

Figure 17-16: Starting with the original image (left), I applied the Facet filter (middle) and then reinforced the edges with Unsharp Mask (right).

Filter⇨Noise⇨Median averages the colors of so many neighboring pixels. To tell Photoshop the "so many" part, choose the Median command and enter a value from 1 to 16 into the Radius option box.

Figure 17-17 shows the result of applying various Radius values to the elder daughter. The top row shows the effects of the Median command; the bottom row shows what happened when I applied Unsharp Mask to each image. Notice how higher values melt away more of the image's detail. A Radius value of 3 makes the image gooey indeed; any higher value is pure silliness.

Radius: 1   Radius: 2   Radius: 3

Figure 17-17: I applied the Median filter at three different Radius settings (top row) and then sharpened the results (bottom row).

You can use Facet and Median to blur background images, just as I did earlier with Gaussian Blur. Or you can combine them with the Add Noise and Emboss filters to create special effects.

Keep in mind that the real beauty of these more specialized filters is in combining them and applying them to small, selected portions of your image.

Chapter 18

Drawing Color from a Dreary Wasteland

*H*ere's a common scenario for you: You get some pictures or slides back from the photo developer — I'm talking regular photos here, not the digital kind — and one of them catches your eye. The color is great, the composition is fantastic, everyone's smiling; it ranks among the best pictures you've ever shot. It's not 100 percent perfect, but you figure you can fix the few glitches inside Photoshop.

A few days later — after you've had the photo scanned to Photo CD — you open the image inside Photoshop, and your heart sinks to the pit of your stomach. The image is dark, colorless, and generally a big, fat disappointment. That little picture on the cover of the CD jacket looks better than this murky mess on-screen.

In a perfect world, this would never happen. The service bureau that scanned the image would have corrected the colors so that they would look the way they did in your photo. But in practice, even the best service bureaus let a few duds fall through the cracks, and some don't bother with color correction at all. It's a pickle.

Take Color Plate 18-1, for example. The original slide looked something like the example on the right, but when I opened the image in Photoshop, it appeared as shown on the left. Sure, it's an old slide — that's me in the striped shirt, so you know that a couple of years have passed — and the composition leaves something to be desired. (I have a fake tree growing out of my shoulder and my sister seems to be balancing a flower-adorned globe on her head.) But, come on, it didn't look this bad. I mean, are we auditioning for the remake of *20,000 Leagues Under the Sea* here or what?

If you run into a similar problem, never fear — you have cause to be optimistic. The colors may not look like much now, but chances are better than even that you have enough colors to get by. Though it may be hard to believe, your image very likely contains a few million colors; it's just that they're all squished toward the dark end of the spectrum. Your job is to bring these colors back to life.

Want proof? The image on the right side of Color Plate 18-1 isn't a different scan, it's just a color-corrected version of its neighbor on the left. In fact, I revived the color using only two commands — Levels and Variations. I didn't touch a painting or editing tool, I didn't draw a selection outline, I didn't do anything to add colors to the image. I merely took the existing colors and stretched them across the spectrum.

Photoshop offers several color-correction commands, but you only need three of these — at the most — to get the job done. In this chapter, I show you how these miracle commands work and encourage you to ignore the rest. I also explain how to use Version 4's new adjustment layers, which let you do some of your color correcting on an independent layer, providing you with extra flexibility and safety.

The Color-Correction Connection

The Photoshop color-correction commands are located in one central spot, under the Image⇨Adjust submenu. Of these commands, only three should be of the least concern to you at this stage in your mastery of Photoshop: Levels, Auto Levels, and Variations.

Your friends Auto Levels, Levels, and Variations

Choose Image⇨Adjust⇨Auto Levels or press ⌘-Shift-L to automatically correct the contrast of an image. For example, Figure 18-1 shows a typically low-contrast image composed entirely of cheerless grays. The inset squares show the lightest and darkest colors in the image as well as some sample shades in between. If I apply the Auto Levels command, Photoshop automatically makes the lightest gray white, the darkest gray black, and stretches out the colors in between. Figure 18-2 shows the result.

Figure 18-1: What a dismal scene: Come to this gas station and get your tank filled with depression. The grim reaper will change your oil.

Figure 18-2: The Auto Levels command brings out some strong blacks and whites, but the grays remain dark and dreary.

Unfortunately, Auto Levels doesn't always do the trick. Figure 18-2, for example, contains strong blacks and whites, but the grays appear overly dark (as witnessed by the shades in the inset squares). The solution is Image⇨Adjust⇨Levels, which you can access from the keyboard by pressing ⌘-L. The Levels command takes some getting used to, but it lets you adjust the darkest and lightest colors as well as the medium gray. (I explain the command in detail later in this chapter, in the section "Leveling the Contrast Field.") Figure 18-3 shows the Gulf station running in tip-top condition, thanks to the Levels command. See how much clearer the details in the cars now appear?

Figure 18-3: A nice, even transition of grays makes a day at the gas station seem like a walk through the park.

Unlike Auto Levels and Levels, which serve grayscale and color images equally well, Image⇨Adjust⇨Variations is specifically designed to correct full-color images. (You can use the command on grayscale images, but it merely duplicates some of the options inside the Levels dialog box.) You can increase or decrease the intensity of colors or tint the image to remove a color cast. For example, if an image is too yellow, you can add blue to it, as in the first example in Color Plate 18-2. If the image is too blue, add yellow, as in the second example. In both cases, Variations preserves nonblue and nonyellow colors. Throughout, for example, the Christmas tree remains true to its natural color of pink.

Upcoming sections explain how to use Levels, Auto Levels, and Variations in detail. But just for the record, here's the general approach to take when color correcting an image in Photoshop:

1. **Apply the Auto Levels command.**

   Regardless of whether you're editing a grayscale or color image, this is a good first step.

   If you like what you see, you can skip all the other steps. If you think some more tweaking might be in order, proceed to Step 2.

2. **Apply the Levels command.**

   Use this command to change the contrast of the image and to lighten or darken the medium colors.

   If you're editing a grayscale image, this command is the end of the line. If your full-color image looks a little drab, however, keep correcting.

3. **Choose the Variations command and select the Saturation radio button.**

   The options inside the Variations dialog box let you boost the intensity of colors in an image, as discussed in this chapter in the section "Variations on a Color Scheme."

   If the colors now look the way you want, press Return and get on with your life. Continue only if you want to tint the image with a certain color or remove a color cast.

4. **Still inside the Variations dialog box, select the Midtones radio button and adjust the colors in the image.**

   The section "It sure feels good to remove that color cast" at the end of this chapter tells all.

The other color correctors (boo, hiss)

The other color-correction commands in the Image⇨Adjust submenu range from useful but very complex to simple but completely inept. Just in case you're chock full of curiosity, here's the rundown:

- ✔ The Curves command is even more capable than the Levels command, allowing you to change every one of the possible 16 million colors to a different color. Unfortunately, this feature is also very difficult to use.

- ✔ The Brightness/Contrast command is utterly and completely worthless. I'm serious. If you've never used it, don't start. If you have used it, stop — you're hurting your images.

- ✔ Color Balance is another loser. You keep thinking that it's going to produce some kind of useful results, but it never does. Worthless and irritating — what a combination.

- ✔ Hue/Saturation is good, but not great. It lets you change the color, intensity, and lightness of an image using three slider bars. However, the Variations dialog box provides these same controls and does a better job.

✔ Desaturate is just the thing for draining the color from a selected area and leaving it black and white. But if you want to convert an entire image to grayscale, refer to the "The road to grayscale" section in Chapter 5.

✔ The Replace Color command is a combination of Select⇨Color Range and the Hue/Saturation command. What's the point?

✔ The Selective Colors command lets you modify a range of colors using CMYK slider bars. Not a terrible command, but not a particularly useful one either.

✔ The other commands on the Adjust menu — Invert, Equalize, Threshold, and Posterize — are typically used for creating special effects. Invert, for example, makes all white pixels black and all black pixels white, creating a photo-negative effect. Fun to play with, but not the sort of tool you can use to brighten up a dingy gas station.

Leveling the Contrast Field

Not one image in this book — except the gloomy-looking Figure 18-1 — has escaped a thorough going-over with the Levels command. I consider this command to be one of the most essential functions inside Photoshop. In fact, if an image displays any of the following symptoms, you can correct it with Levels:

✔ The image is murky, without strong lights and darks, like the one in Figure 18-1.

✔ The image is too light.

✔ The image is too dark.

✔ The image is gaining weight, losing hair, and developing bags under its eyes.

Whoops, that last item sneaked in by mistake. If an image gains weight, loses hair, and develops baggy eyes, you have to send it on a three-week cruise of the Caribbean.

Leveling on a layer

Photoshop 4 offers a new feature to use in conjunction with the Levels command (and, in a roundabout way, the Auto Levels command): adjustment layers. Adjustment layers are just like the layers discussed in Chapter 15, except that you use them expressly to apply color correction commands.

At any rate, adjustment layers offer several advantages:

✔ The color correction affects all the underlying layers in the image. If you don't use an adjustment layer, the color correction affects the active layer only.

✔ You can create as many different adjustment layers as you want. So if you want a few layers to use one set of color correction settings and the rest of the image to use another set, you just create two different adjustment layers.

✔ Because the color correction "exists" on its own layer, you can experiment freely without fear of damaging the image. If at some point you decide that you don't like the effects of the color correction, you can edit the adjustment layer or just delete it entirely and start fresh.

✔ You can blend the adjustment layer with the other layers using the Opacity and blend mode controls in the Layers palette, just as you can with any layer. This feature gives you even more control over how your image appears.

To create an adjustment layer, do the following:

1. **In the Layers palette, click on the top layer you want to color correct.**

When you create an adjustment layer, Photoshop places it directly on top of the active layer in the Layers palette. The adjustment affects the layer or layers underneath, depending on what setting you choose in the New Adjustment Layer dialog box in Step 2.

If you select a portion of your image before creating the adjustment layer, the color correction affects the selected area across all underlying layers.

2. **Choose Layer⇨New⇨Adjustment Layer or ⌘-click on the new layer icon at the bottom of the Layers palette.**

The dialog box shown in Figure 18-4 appears. Here's a field guide to your options: If you want to give your adjustment layer a specific name, enter the name into the top option box. The Type pop-up menu lists all the different color correction commands you can select — the only one you need to worry about is Levels, which is selected by default.

Although the Auto Levels command isn't available in the Type pop-up menu, you can apply the Auto Levels command on an adjustment layer by choosing the Levels option from the pop-up menu. The option leads you to the Levels dialog box, which has an Auto button that works just like the Auto Levels command.

Skip the Opacity and Mode pop-up menus; if you want, you can change these settings later, in the Layers palette. Skip the Group with Previous Layer check box, too.

Figure 18-4:
The New
Adjustment
Layer dialog
box enables
you to do
your color
correcting
on an
independent
layer.

New Adjustment Layer

Name: Levels

Type: Levels

Opacity: 100 % Mode: Normal

☐ Group With Previous Layer

OK

Cancel

3. Press Return.

Photoshop adds the adjustment layer to the Layers palette and displays the Levels dialog box, which is explained in the next section.

Remember that an adjustment layer works just like any other layer in the Layers palette. You can vary the effects of the adjustment by playing with the Opacity slider and blend modes; you can move the layer up or down in the layers palette to affect different layers; and you can merge the layer with an underlying layer to permanently fuse the color correction to the image. (You can't, however, merge an adjustment layer with another adjustment layer.)

If you ever want to change the color-correction settings for an adjustment layer, just double-click on the adjustment layer name in the Layers palette. Photoshop redisplays the Levels dialog box, where you can modify the settings. To delete the adjustment layer, drag it to the trash icon in the Layers palette.

You can flip back and forth between a view of your corrected image and your uncorrected image by simply clicking on the eyeball icon next to the adjustment layer name in the Layers palette. When the eyeball is present, the layer is visible, showing you the color-corrected image. When the eyeball is hidden, so is the layer, giving you a "before" view of your image.

Making friends with the Levels dialog box

To apply the Levels command, you can either create a new adjustment layer, as described in the preceding section, or choose Image➪Adjust➪Levels or press ⌘-L. If you choose the command from the Image menu or press the keyboard shortcut, the color correction is applied directly to the image and affects the active layer only.

Histogram

Figure 18-5:
The
complicated-
looking
Levels
dialog box
contains a
lot of
options that
you don't
need to
worry about.

Either way, the dialog box shown in Figure 18-5 appears. Luckily, you don't need to address all the options that inhabit this dialog box. So before you break into a cold sweat, shriek at the top of your lungs, or do whatever it is you do when you see terrifying sights like Figure 18-5, let me try to distinguish the important options in this dialog box from the stuff you won't use in a month of Sundays:

- ✔ The options in the Channel pop-up menu let you adjust one color channel in a full-color image independently of the others. These options are helpful if you know what you're doing, but not terribly important.

- ✔ The three Input Levels option boxes control the settings of the darkest, medium, and lightest pixels in your image, in that order. These options are important, which is why I cover them thoroughly in the next section.

- ✔ That black birthmark in the middle of the dialog box is called a *histogram*. It shows you how the colors in your image are currently distributed. It also rates the Seal of Importance.

- ✔ The slider bar beneath the histogram provides three triangles, one each for the darkest, medium, and lightest pixels in your image. These triangles are the most important options of all.

- ✔ The Output Levels option boxes and the accompanying slider bar let you make the darkest colors lighter and the lightest colors darker, which is usually exactly the opposite of what you want to do. Mark these options Not Particularly Important.

- ✔ The OK and Cancel buttons are as important as always. One applies your changes, the other doesn't. No news here.

- ✔ Press the Option key to change the Cancel button to a Reset button. Click on the button while pressing Option to reset the settings to the way they were when you entered the dialog box. Very helpful.

✔ Click on the Save button to save the settings in this dialog box to disk. Click on the Load button to later load and reapply them. Unless you're color correcting about 20 images in a row, all of which require exactly the same treatment, these buttons are about as important to your health and well-being as lava lamps. Ignore them.

✔ Click on the Auto button to automatically change the darkest pixels to black and the lightest ones to white, exactly as if you had chosen Image⊸Adjust⊸Auto Levels. The only time you need to use this button is when you want to apply the Auto Levels command on an adjustment layer, as discussed earlier. Otherwise, just choose the command from the Image⊸Adjust menu or press ⌘-Shift-L and save yourself some work.

✔ When you press the Option key, the Auto button changes to an Options button. I only tell you about this feature because I'm afraid that you may notice it for yourself when you press the Option key to access the Reset button. But whether you notice it or not, the Options button is totally unimportant.

✔ The three eyedropper icons let you click on colors in your image to make them black, medium gray, or white. If I were you, I'd steer clear of these icons except to stamp them Not Important, Ditto, and Doubly So.

✔ The Preview check box lets you view the effect of your edits inside the image window. It's very important that you turn this option on.

Figure 18-6 shows the Levels dialog box as it appears after you strip it down to its most important components. As you can see, the Input Levels options — which include the three option boxes, the histogram, and the slider bar — represent the core of the Levels command. The other options are just icing on the cake.

Figure 18-6: When you strip the Levels dialog box of its excessive regalia, it becomes far less daunting.

Brightness and contrast as they should be

The histogram in Figure 18-6 is a graph of the color in the uncorrected image in Figure 18-7. (I didn't even choose the Auto Levels command.) The graph is organized from darkest colors on the left to lightest colors on the right. The peaks and valleys in the histogram show the color distribution. If the darkest colors were black, the histogram would start on the far left edge of the slider bar. If the lightest colors were white, it would continue to the far right edge. But as it is, the left and right edges taper off into flatlands. This means that the darkest and lightest pixels in the image are not as dark or light as they could be.

Figure 18-7:
Though they lived in a time when Photoshop was not available, these uncorrected characters still managed to find something to smile about.

If some of that information went a little over your head, not to worry. Some folks understand graphs, while other folks think that they're in a board meeting and start to nod off the second they see anything resembling a graph. Either way, remember that the histogram is provided for your reference only. All that matters is how you adjust the slider triangles underneath the histogram:

✔ To make the darkest pixels black, drag the left slider triangle to the right so that it rests directly under the beginning of the first hill in the histogram. Figure 18-8 shows the dragged triangle and its effect on the image.

✔ To make the lightest pixels white, drag the right-hand triangle to the left so that it lines up directly under the end of the last hill in the histogram, as in Figure 18-9.

Figure 18-8:
Dragging the first triangle affects the darkest pixels in the image.

Figure 18-9:
The image lightens up when I drag the white triangle to the left.

✔ If you already chose the Auto Levels command or the Auto button in the Levels dialog box, you most likely won't have to change either the left or right slider because Photoshop has already done this automatically. (You may want to adjust the sliders slightly, but that's up to you.) Instead, just concentrate on positioning the middle slider, described next.

✔ The most important triangle is the middle one. Called the *gamma point* — just in case you get stuck in an elevator with the guys from R&D and find yourself scraping for something to talk about — this triangle lets you change the brightness of the medium colors in your image. Drag to the right to make the medium colors darker. But more likely, you want to drag to the left to make the medium colors lighter, as demonstrated in Figure 18-10.

Figure 18-10: Dragging the middle triangle brings out the detail in an image.

The values in the three option boxes above the histogram update as you drag the slider triangles. The left and right values are measured in color levels. Just like the values in the Color palette — where you define colors (refer to Chapter 5) — 0 is black and 255 is white. So if the left value is 45, as it is in Figures 18-8 through 18-10, any pixel that is colored with a level of 45 or darker becomes black. The gamma value — the middle one — is measured as a ratio . . . er, forget it, it doesn't make any sense and it matters even less. The point is, a value of more than 1 lightens the medium colors; a value less than 1 darkens them.

The old stock photo featured in Figures 18-7 through 18-10 is a wonderful example of a work of art that takes on new meaning the more you look at it. Three of the subjects are proudly displaying unlighted tobacco products, the fourth guy is using a paper cup for a megaphone, and all four have feathers in their caps (figure that one out). Meanwhile, you can see their shadows on the wall in back of them. Call me picky, but it sort of ruins the illusion that they might be outdoors enjoying a chilly sporting event.

If you'd like to see the effect of the Levels command on a full-color image, you need look no further than Color Plate 18-3. Nestled in this quiet corner of the book is a homemade Italian gate. Starting with the uncorrected image in the upper-left corner, I adjusted each of the slider triangles, eventually arriving at the much superior color balance shown in the lower-right image. It just goes to show you, Levels is bound to do any image good.

If you notice a loss of color in your image after you apply the Levels command, don't worry. You can get that color back by using the Variations command, discussed in the next section.

Variations on a Color Scheme

One negative effect of the Levels command is that it can weaken some of the colors, particularly if you lighten the medium colors by dragging the gamma point in the Levels dialog box to the left. To bring the colors back to their original intensity, call on Image⇨Adjust⇨Variations.

The Variations command can also cure color casts, in which one color is particularly prominent in the image. A photograph shot outdoors, for example, may be overly blue; one shot in an X-rated motel room may be a shade heavy in the reds. Whatever color predominates your image, the Variations command can tone it down with elegance and ease.

Turning plain old color into Technicolor

To bolster the intensity of colors in your image — for what it's worth, color intensity is called *saturation* in image editing vernacular — follow these pleasant steps:

1. **Choose Image⇨Adjust⇨Variations.**

   The enormous Variations dialog box erupts onto your screen, filled with about a million small previews of your image.

2. **Select the Saturation radio button in the upper-right corner of the dialog box.**

   Most of the small preview images disappear. Only five remain, as shown in Figure 18-11. The three previews in the middle of the dialog box represent different color intensities. The top two previews show the image as it appeared before you chose the Variations command and how it looks now, subject to the changes in the Variations dialog box.

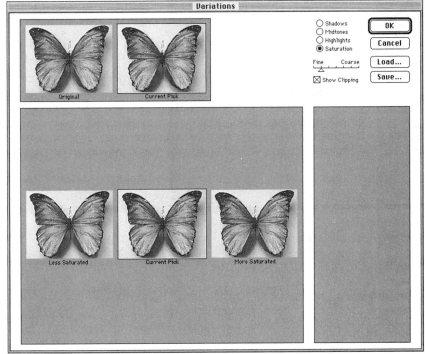

Figure 18-11:
Click on
the More
Saturated
preview to
boost the
intensity of
the colors in
an image.

3. Drag the slider triangle in the upper-right corner to the left, toward Fine.

This slider controls the extent of the changes made inside the Variations dialog box. If you drag the triangle toward Coarse, the changes become more drastic; drag it toward Fine, and they become more gradual. The setting is reflected inside the left and right previews in the middle of the dialog box, which become more subtle.

Because color intensity is a very sensitive function inside Photoshop, it's best to set the slider to one of the first two notches so that you can make gentle, incremental changes.

4. To increase color intensity, click on the preview labeled More Saturated.

Clicking once increases the intensity by a gradual amount, owing to the slider bar setting. To add more intensity, click again. Each time you click, the Current Pick previews — one in the middle and one at the top — update to reflect your latest change.

If inconsistently colored pixels begin to emerge, Photoshop is telling you that these colors are outside of the CMYK color range and will not print. Don't worry about it until the weird pixels take over a third or more of your image. (If you don't care whether the colors will print correctly or not, turn off the Show Clipping check box to view the pixels normally.)

If at any time you want to reset the Current Pick preview to the original image, just click on the preview labeled Original in the upper-left corner of the dialog box.

5. **When you're satisfied with the increased color intensity, press Return.**

Photoshop applies your settings to the original image, just as they were shown in the Current Pick preview. No surprises with this dialog box.

Changes you make via the Variations dialog box affect the active layer only. Unfortunately, you can't apply the Variations command using an adjustment layer as you can the Levels and Auto Levels commands.

Color Plate 18-4 shows the difference between a butterfly whose splendor I completely destroyed using the Levels command and that same butterfly restored to its original luster and brilliance via the Variations command. To achieve this radical transformation, I set the slider bar inside the Variations dialog box to the second notch over from the left and clicked on the More Saturated preview a total of six times.

It sure feels good to remove that color cast

Images are like people in that they hate to wear casts. When your image is encumbered by a color cast, it becomes uncomfortable and downright crotchety. Take the first image in Color Plate 18-5, for example. To the inexperienced eye, this image may appear happy and at peace with itself. But in truth, its life is a living heck, made miserable by a decidedly yellow color cast.

To remove the color cast once and for all, revisit the Variations command:

1. **Choose Image⇨Adjust⇨Variations.**

The Variations dialog box takes over your screen.

2. **Select the Midtones radio button in the upper-right corner of the dialog box.**

This option lets you edit the medium colors in your image. (You can also edit the dark or light colors by selecting Shadows or Highlights, but these options produce extremely subtle effects and have little impact on your image.)

After you select Midtones, the central portion of the dialog box fills with seven previews, as shown in Figure 18-12. These previews let you shift the colors in the image toward a primary color — green, yellow, red, magenta, blue, or cyan. As usual, the Current Pick preview in the center of the cluster updates to show the most recent corrections applied to the image.

Figure 18-12:
Click on the More Blue preview to add blue and remove yellow in an image. Click on More Magenta to add magenta and remove green.

The three previews along the right edge of the Variations dialog box let you lighten and darken the image. But because they're less capable than the gam-ma point control in the Levels dialog box, you can feel free to ignore them.

3. **Click on one of the More previews to shift the colors in the image toward that color.**

   First, identify the color cast. Then click on the preview opposite to that color. In the case of the horse image from Color Plate 18-5, the cast is clearly yellow and, to a lesser extent, green. To eliminate the yellow cast, I clicked on More Blue. To eliminate the green cast, I clicked on More Magenta.

   Remember Color Plate 5-3, which shows that yellow ink filters out blue light and magenta ink filters out green light? This means that yellow and blue are direct opposites, as are magenta and green. Such opposite colors are termed *complementary*. I'm not sure why. I guess it's like a marriage of opposites in which each spouse complements the other. If they don't kill each other first, of course.

4. If you go too far toward one color, just click on the opposite color to step backward.

In Color Plate 18-5, for example, I clicked on the More Blue preview twice, clicked on More Magenta twice, and then clicked on More Blue again. But after some concerted soul searching, I decided that I had gone too far. The resulting image — shown in the bottom-right corner of the color plate — was too blue and too magenta. So I clicked on the More Yellow button to remove the last application of blue and clicked on More Green to remove the last application of magenta. The bottom-left example in the color plate shows the result.

As when you adjust color saturation, you can vary the impact of the previews on the image by dragging the slider triangle toward Fine or Coarse. The images in Color Plate 18-5 were all created with the triangle set right in the center, as it is by default.

If your image has more than one layer, your color-cast manipulations affect the active layer only.

Part VI
The Part of Tens

The 5th Wave   By Rich Tennant

ATTEMPTING TO SAVE MONEY ON FAMILY PHOTOS, THE DILBRANTS SCAN THEIR NEWBORN INTO A PHOTO IMAGING PROGRAM WITH PLANS OF JUST DITHERING THE CHILD INTO ADOLESCENCE.

In this part . . .

Some say that there's magic in the number three. Bears, pigs, Musketeers, and Stooges regularly cavort about in groups of three. But I say that the real magic is in tens. The Ten Commandments, the ten amendments that make up The Bill of Rights, and the ten ingredients in a Big Mac — if you count both all-beef patties and the three sesame seed buns — are items that we can count on the ten fingers of our hands (or the ten toes of our feet when we're at the beach). Top ten lists abound in newspapers, magazines, books, and late-night TV shows. And I say, why buck a trend? If everyone else is doing it, I for one am happy to mindlessly follow along.

But then I thought, "What ho, if there's magic in threes and in tens, why not do both?" So that's what I did. This part contains three chapters, each of which contains ten factoids. Ten great shortcuts that you'll want to assign to memory, ten great ways to wreak havoc on a loved one's face, and ten things you can do with your image after you finish messing it up in Photoshop.

As if that's not enough, the last chapter of this book — Chapter 21 — is divisible not only by 3, but also by the lucky number 7. We are talking major number magic at work here, the kind of stuff that numerologists, fortune tellers, and lottery fanatics would give their eye teeth for. And it only cost you $19.99, a number whose only claim to fame is that it's slightly cheaper than $20.

Chapter 19

Ten Tricky Techniques to Assign to Memory

· ·

In This Chapter

▶ Hiding the toolbox and palettes

▶ Changing the way a tool works

▶ Scrolling and zooming

▶ Changing the brush size

▶ Changing the opacity of a brush, layer, or floating selection

▶ Creating straight lines

▶ Adding to and subtracting from selection outlines

▶ Nudging and cloning

▶ Filling a selection

▶ Making, switching, and selecting layers

· ·

Some guy named Odell Shepard said, "Memory is what makes you wonder what you've forgotten." I don't know anything about this Odell fellow — he was just lucky enough to get picked up by one of those books of quotations that are supposed to make you sound like a halfway intelligent human being without really trying. Not having met Odell — Odie, we call him — I can only hazard the guess that he was talking about that feeling you get — usually, when you're in bed, trying to sleep, or when you're on the way home from work and it's too late to turn back — that you've forgotten something that's pretty much going to send your life spinning into a state of absolute chaos. In fact, I believe that feeling is known as the Odie Syndrome.

Well, I can't help you with every aspect of your life, but I can help you with Photoshop. Say, for example, that you wake up at 2 a.m. one morning with the dread suspicion that you've forgotten an important Photoshop shortcut. Normally, of course, your life would be forfeit. You'd just have to give up on your technological pursuits and take up beet farming. But thanks to this chapter, people like you can again live happy and productive lives because all of the most important Photoshop shortcuts are contained in these pages. A few minutes of reading, and order is restored.

Displaying and Hiding the Toolbox and Palettes

Tab

I'm ashamed to admit this, but there was a time when I wanted to view an image on-screen all by itself, without the toolbox. I had no idea how to do it. I even called the Photoshop product manager and asked him how to do it. He told me it was impossible.

Naturally, he was wrong. It was possible then, and it's possible now. Just press the Tab key. The toolbox and all the palettes disappear, leaving just you and the image. To bring the toolbox and palettes back, press Tab again. To make the toolbox and palettes flash crazily on-screen and off, press Tab over and over again until your finger gets numb. I'm not sure why you'd want to do this, but I like to spell out all the options.

If you want to hide the palettes but keep the toolbox visible, by the way, press Shift-Tab. Press Shift-Tab again to bring the palettes back.

If you have a dialog box open or an option in a palette is active (highlighted), Tab and Shift-Tab take you to the next option box or move you back one option box, respectively. But after you close the dialog box or press Return to apply the palette option, Tab and Shift-Tab control your palettes and toolbox once again.

F5, F6, F7, F8

Press F5 to hide or display the Brushes palette; F6 to hide or display the Color palette; and F7 to hide or display the Layers palette. To display the Navigator palette, press F8, which brings up the Info palette. Then click on the Navigator palette tab. Press F8 twice to hide the palette.

Changing the Way a Tool Works

Return

After selecting a tool in the toolbox, press Return to bring up the Options palette for that tool. If the palette contains an option box, the value inside the option box becomes highlighted, allowing you to change it.

Up arrow, down arrow

Enter a new value in the option box or use the up or down arrow key to raise or lower the value by 1. Press Shift-up arrow or Shift-down arrow to raise or lower the value by 10, respectively. Then press Return again to accept the new value.

Scrolling and Zooming

Spacebar

Press the spacebar to temporarily access the hand tool. As long as the spacebar is down, the hand tool is available. Spacebar-drag to scroll the image.

⌘-spacebar, Option-spacebar

To get to the zoom in cursor, press both ⌘ and spacebar. Pressing Option-spacebar gets you the zoom out cursor. This means that you can magnify the image at any time by ⌘-spacebar-clicking. To zoom out, Option-spacebar-click. You can also ⌘-spacebar-drag to marquee an area and magnify it so that it takes up the entire image window.

⌘-plus, ⌘-minus

Another way to magnify or reduce the image is to press ⌘-plus to zoom in or ⌘-minus to zoom out.

Double-click on the hand icon

To zoom the image so that you can see the whole thing on your monitor, double-click on the hand tool icon in the toolbox. Or press ⌘-0 (zero).

Double-click on the zoom icon

To restore the image to the 100 percent (Actual Pixels) zoom factor, double-click on the zoom tool icon or press ⌘-Option-0 (zero).

Shift-Return

When you change the zoom factor using the magnification box in the lower-left corner of the image window, press Shift-Return instead of Return after you enter a new zoom value. That way, the option box remains active after Photoshop zooms your image. If you need to further magnify or reduce your image, just press the up or down arrows or enter a new zoom value from the keyboard. When you have the image at the magnification you want, press Return to finalize things.

This trick also works when you're using the magnification box in the Navigator palette.

Changing the Brush Size

Left bracket ([ )

Press the left bracket key to reduce the brush size to the next smallest one in the brushes palette. If you're using the smallest fuzzy brush, pressing the left bracket selects the largest smooth one.

Right bracket ( ])

Press the right bracket to select the next brush size up. If you're using the largest smooth brush, pressing the right bracket selects the smallest fuzzy one.

Shift-[, Shift-]

Shift-left bracket selects the first brush size in the Brushes palette, which is the single-pixel brush. Shift-right bracket selects the last brush size. By default, this is the 100-pixel fuzzy brush, but if you've created some custom brushes of your own, Photoshop selects the last one in the Brushes palette.

Changing Opacity

1, . . . , 9, 0

To change the Opacity setting for a selected painting or editing tool, just press a number key — 1 equals 10 percent Opacity, 9 equals 90, and 0 equals 100 percent. To enter a more specific value — say, 82 — just type the number quickly.

If a selection tool or the move tool is active, pressing a number key changes the opacity of the active layer or floating selection.

Creating Straight Lines

Shift-click

To create a straight line with any of the painting or editing tools, click at one end of the line and Shift-click at the other. Photoshop connects the two points with a straight line.

Click with polygon lasso, Option-click with regular lasso

The new polygon lasso creates straight-sided selections; you just click to set the first point in your selection and keep clicking to create additional points.

When working with the regular lasso tool, you can temporarily switch to the polygon lasso by Option-clicking. Option-click to set the first point in the selection and keep Option-clicking until you finish drawing the desired outline.

However, don't use this approach when you want to add or subtract from an existing selection marquee. When you have an active selection marquee, pressing Option subtracts from the selection instead of switching you between lasso tools. So use the polygon tool to add or subtract straight-sided areas from a selection.

Adding to and Subtracting from Selection Outlines

Shift-drag, Shift-click

To select an additional area of your image without deselecting the part that is currently selected, Shift-drag around the new area with a lasso or marquee tool or Shift-click with the magic wand. You can also Shift-choose Select⇨Color Range.

Option-drag, Option-click

To deselect an area of the selection, Option-drag around it with a lasso or marquee tool or Option-click with the magic wand. You can also Option-choose the Color Range command.

Shift-Option-drag, Shift-Option-click

To retain the intersection of the existing selection and the new outline you draw with a lasso or marquee tool, Shift-Option-drag with the tool. To retain an area of continuous color inside a selection, Shift-Option-click with the magic wand.

Moving, Nudging, and Cloning

⌘ key

In Photoshop 4, you use the move tool to move selections and layers. To temporarily access the move tool, press and hold ⌘ while any tool except the pen or hand tool is active.

Arrow key

To nudge a selection one pixel, press one of the arrow keys with the move tool selected. Or press ⌘ and an arrow key with any tool except the hand or pen tool.

Shift-arrow key

To nudge a selection ten pixels, select the move tool and press Shift with an arrow key. Or select any tool but the pen or hand tool and press ⌘-Shift with an arrow key.

Option-dragging, Option-arrow key, Shift-Option-arrow key

To clone a selection and move the clone, Option-drag the selection with the move tool. You can also press Option with an arrow key to clone a selection and nudge it one pixel or press Shift-Option-arrow key to clone and nudge ten pixels.

When any other tool but the hand or pen tool is selected, you can accomplish the same cloning feats by pressing and holding the ⌘ key with the other keys. (Pressing ⌘ temporarily accesses the move tool, remember?)

Drag with a selection tool

To move a selection outline without moving anything inside the selection, just drag it with a marquee tool, lasso tool, or the magic wand. You can also press the arrow key or Shift-arrow key to nudge the selection outline in 1-pixel and 10-pixel increments, respectively.

Filling a Selection

⌘-Delete

To fill a selection with the background color, press ⌘-Delete. If the selection is nonfloating and exists on the Background layer, you can also press Delete to accomplish the same thing. However, if the selection is on a layer or is floating on the Background layer, pressing Delete wipes out the selection instead of filling it. So it's a good idea to always press ⌘-Delete instead of Delete to fill your selections.

Option-Delete

To fill any selection — floating or not — with the foreground color, press Option-Delete.

Shift-Delete

Press Shift-Delete to bring up the Fill dialog box, which lets you fill a selection with all kinds of stuff, including the saved version of that portion of the image.

Making, Switching, and Selecting Layers

⌘-J, ⌘-Shift-J

To clone a selection and place the clone on a new layer, press ⌘-J. To move a nonfloating selection and place the selection on a new layer, press ⌘-Shift-J.

Click on new layer icon, ⌘-Shift-J

To assign a floating selection to its own layer, click on the new layer icon in the Layers palette or press ⌘-Shift-J.

Option-[, Option-]

To activate the layer below the one that is currently active, press Option-[. To activate the next layer up, press Option-].

Control-Option-click with the move tool

To activate the layer belonging to a certain image, Control-Option-click on that image with the move tool. Or ⌘-Control-Option click on the image with any other tool except the pen or hand tool.

⌘-click on layer name

To generate a selection outline from the contents of a layer, ⌘-click on the layer name in the Layers palette. You can use any tool to do the job.

So Many Shortcuts, So Little Time

The preceding tips don't address all of the many Photoshop shortcuts. For some additional time-savers, be sure to check out the Cheat Sheet at the front of this book.

Chapter 20

Ten Amusing Ways to Mess Up a Loved One's Face

*N*ormally, we're all pretty fond of our loved ones. Friends and family members make life a real treat 364 days of the year. But on that one day when a loved one gets kind of pesky — or two days during leap years — it's nice to have Photoshop within easy reach.

Mad at your boyfriend for going on that trip to Paris with a childhood sweetheart? Just scan his face and while away the hours modifying it in a way he won't soon forget. Peeved at your sister for snagging all of Aunt Rowena's multimillion-dollar inheritance? Open Sis in Photoshop and distort her as you please. No need to get angry. Just warp your loved one's face, print it out, and send it off to your local newspaper or tack it up on neighborhood telephone poles.

This chapter — considered by many as an essential step toward utter Photoshop fulfillment — supplies an assortment of delightful recipes for making a digital mess of the one you love. Build understanding, facilitate dialog, and establish bonds that will last a lifetime by mucking up the kissers of those near and dear to your heart.

If I could, I would make a show of solidarity by applying these techniques to a loved one of my own. Alas, I am one of those rare people who has never experienced anger or resentment in my life. I read about these feelings once in *Boy's Life,* but that was as close as I've come.

So instead, I am going to take a stab at the absolute strangers shown in Figure 20-1. As I understand it, both women were actresses, captured in the moment of auditioning for a commercial. Though the line of dialog was the same — "Goodness, don't tell me my toilet bowl cleanser isn't working!" — the two women took opposite artistic approaches. Obviously, neither of them was cast in the part, but in tribute to their stirring performances, I'm going to trod heavily upon them in the following sections.

Figure 20-1:
Two faces that cry out, "Muck me up in Photoshop!"

If you're the kind who's a stickler for detail, you may have noticed that the introductory list to this chapter actually includes 11 items. Please don't let this fact upset your equilibrium — just think of this chapter as a buy 10, get one free sort of deal. Where else are you going to get that kind of value for your money?

Pinching the Face Inward

Here's how to get the effect applied to the surprised character in Figure 20-2:

1. **Select the face with the elliptical marquee tool.**

   You can use some other tool, but an oval selection outline produces the best results. No need to be very precise; an approximate selection is entirely adequate.

2. **Feather the selection.**

   Choose Select⇨Feather, enter **6** or thereabouts as the Feather Radius value, and press Return. This step ensures a smooth transition between the distorted and undistorted areas.

3. **Choose Filter⇨Distort⇨Pinch.**

   The Pinch dialog box appears, allowing you to collapse the selected image toward its center.

4. **Enter** 50 **as the Amount value and press Return.**

   The face pinches slightly, as shown in the first example in Figure 20-2. This is a dangerous step in the process because the face may actually look better. Typically, the forehead, jaw, and chin grow, while the nose shrinks — all ingredients that might be misconstrued as indications of beauty. So whatever you do, don't stop now.

Figure 20-2: Pinch the face once (left) and then pinch again (right).

    5. Press ⌘-F to reapply the filter.

    The second example in the figure shows the result. Now we're looking at some extreme distortion.

You may be wondering why I didn't just tell you to raise the value in Step 4 rather than applying the filter twice. After all, the Pinch dialog box accepts values as high as 100. However, thanks to the way the filter works, it's better to apply it multiple times using a low value than once with a high value.

Bending the Face Outward

The opposite of the Pinch filter, Filter⇨Distort⇨Spherize bends the face outward, as shown in Figure 20-3. Here's how to create a similar effect:

    1. Select the face with the elliptical marquee tool.

    Make your selection just as instructed in the preceding steps.

    2. Feather the selection.

    Again, you're just doing the same thing you did before.

    3. Choose Filter⇨Distort⇨Spherize.

    Now this part is different. The Spherize filter brings up the Spherize dialog box, which reflects the image on the back of a spoon so that it curves outward. (Remember staring sleepily at your spoon before diving into the Lucky Charms or Count Chocula? Even in those remote years, the Spherize filter was at work.)

    4. Enter 100 and press Return.

    Unlike the Pinch filter, Spherize works just fine at the maximum setting. (Better algorithm, don't you know.) The first example in Figure 20-3 shows the nose-expanding, chin-contracting results.

    5. Select a different area inside the first selection.

    One swipe of the Spherize filter is never enough, but you can't apply the filter twice to the same area without losing detail. The eyes may start sliding off the face, for example. So select an area inside the first selection to do more damage. (Shift-Option-drag with the elliptical marquee tool to get the job done.)

    6. Feather the selection.

    Choose Select⇨Feather or press ⌘-Shift-D and hit Return. Whatever value you use the first time does well the second time around.

Figure 20-3:
Bend the
face once
(left) and
then select
a different
area and
bend it
outward
some more
(right).

7. **Press ⌘-F to reapply the Spherize filter.**

Ooh, isn't that nice? The second example in Figure 20-3 shows what happened to my image. A couple of swipes more, and I bet we can see right up her nostrils.

Twisting the Face around a Taffy Pull

To twist a face so that it looks like it's being put through a blender — as demonstrated in Figure 20-4 — follow these steps:

1. **Select the face with the rectangular marquee tool.**

   For this effect, a rectangular selection outline works best.

2. **Choose Filter⇨Distort⇨Twirl.**

   The Twirl dialog box lets you do the twisting.

3. **Enter an Angle value between 100 and 200 and press Return.**

   The first example in Figure 20-4 shows the effect of a 100-degree twist; the second example shows a 200-degree twist. Any value over 200 eliminates too much detail for our purposes. Negative values between –100 and –200 are also acceptable.

Figure 20-4:
The Twirl filter applied at 100 degrees (left) and 200 degrees (right).

4. Sharpen the image.

The Twirl filter tends to blur the detail. To make it sharp again, choose Filter⇨Sharpen⇨Unsharp Mask. Enter an Amount value of 50 percent, a Radius between 0.5 and 1.0, and press Return.

Melting the Face into a Heap of Goo

No matter how long you use Photoshop, you are likely to never come up with this technique without at least some help. It's just too weird. But even so, it results in the awesome melted face effect shown in Figure 20-5. Don't try to understand it, just do it.

1. Press ⌘-D.

⌘-D deselects everything in your image. You have to apply the technique I outline here to the entire image, so you can't have any active selection outlines.

2. Choose Filter⇨Distort⇨Polar Coordinates.

The Polar Coordinates dialog box appears, giving you the power to turn an image inside out. Not a trick for the squeamish.

3. Select the Polar to Rectangular radio button and press Return.

The first image in Figure 20-5 shows the result. It's hard to see what's going on, but there's some good stuff there.

Figure 20-5:
A face subjected to the Polar Coordinates filter (left) and then flipped and offset (right).

4. **Choose Image⇨Rotate Canvas⇨Flip Vertical.**

   The image turns upside down, which makes it a little more recognizable.

5. **Press the Option key and press and hold on the page preview box in the bottom-left corner of the window.**

   You remember the file size box — from Chapter 3, right? It's that thing that says 379K/379K or 1.8M/3.6M or whatever. When you Option-click on it, you see the dimensions of your image.

6. **Write down the Width value (in pixels) and then divide that value by 2.**

   My image is 360 pixels wide; 360 divided by 2 is 180.

7. **Choose Filter⇨Other⇨Offset.**

   Up comes the Offset dialog box, which moves the pixels in an image around. An incredibly obscure feature, Offset is useful only for the occasional special effect.

8. **Enter your special divided-by-2 value into the Horizontal option box.**

   I entered 180.

9. **Select the Wrap Around radio button and press Return.**

   That's it; you're done. By offsetting the image half its width and wrapping the excess around to the other side of the image, you center the image inside the window, as shown in the second image in Figure 20-5.

Giving the Face a Bath

If you're only slightly piqued at your loved one, you may want to make the face appear under water, as shown in Figure 20-6. Here's how to submerge the image:

1. **Select the image any which way you want.**

   No special constraints this time.

2. **Choose Filter⇨Distort⇨Ripple.**

   I bet you're beginning to think that all the great face-mucking features are under the Filter⇨Distort submenu. As it turns out, Ripple is the last one that is.

3. **Select Medium from the Size pop-up menu in the Ripple dialog box.**

   The Small option isn't enough, and the Large option is too much. As with the baby bear in the famous story — I believe Snow White and the three little pigs is the one— Medium is just right.

4. **Enter any old Amount value you want and press Return.**

   In Figure 20-6, I applied an Amount of 300 to the first image and 999 — the maximum setting — to the second image.

Figure 20-6:
What happens when you apply the Ripple filter with an Amount of 300 (left) and 999 (right).

Stretching the Face This Way and That

Why don't you and I take a break from the commands under the Filter⇨Distort submenu and try out some manual distortion techniques? Figure 20-7 shows how you can distort an image using the new Photoshop 4 Transform and Free Transform commands. The following steps tell you what the figure leaves out.

1. Select something.

Again, select what you want. I can't make all the decisions for you. But you have to select something or you can't access the command I'm about to instruct you to use. If you want to apply the command to your entire image, press ⌘-A or choose Select⇨All.

2. Press ⌘-H.

Photoshop hides the selection outline. Otherwise, the outline just gets in your way.

3. Choose Layer⇨Free Transform or press ⌘-T.

The Free Transform command surrounds the selection with a marquee and displays square handles on the sides and at the corners. With the Free Transform marquee, you can resize, rotate, skew, distort, and apply perspective effects to your selection.

To scale (resize) the selection, drag any handle. Shift-drag to scale proportionately, and Option-drag to scale symmetrically around the center of the selection. To rotate the selection, move the cursor outside the marquee until you see a curved, double-headed arrow, and then drag. To move the selection, drag inside the marquee.

But to really have some fun, use the following techniques: ⌘-drag any handle to distort the image freely. ⌘-Shift-drag a side handle to skew the image. And ⌘-Shift-Option drag a corner handle to apply perspective effects.

Be patient when working with the Transform command — it sometimes takes Photoshop a while to generate the effects of your drags. If you don't like the outcome of a drag, just press ⌘-Z to undo it.

4. When you've distorted the image to your satisfaction, press Return.

Figure 20-7 shows two lovely effects created by tugging this way and that on my crying woman. In the left example, I skewed and distorted the image, giving Miss Crocodile Tears shoulders that a linebacker would envy. In the right example, I ⌘-Shift-Option-dragged to create an infant-looking-up-from-a-crib view.

The Layer⇨Transform submenu contains individual commands for distorting, skewing, scaling, rotating, and adding perspective to the image. When you choose one of these Transfrom commands, you get the transform marquee as you do when using Free Transform. Just drag the handles to apply the effect — no Option, ⌘, or Shift key combinations required. If you want to apply a different effect, you have to choose the desired effect from the Layer⇨ Transform submenu. I usually prefer the Free Transform command — it's one-stop-shopping for transforming.

You can choose the Flip Horizontal and Flip Vertical commands, also found in the Transform submenu, when you are in the process of transforming your image using the Free Transform command.

Figure 20-7:
The Free Transform command lets you bend, pull, rotate, and otherwise stretch a selection in whatever way you please.

Applying the Nuclear Sunburn Effect

Phew, that's enough of that manual stuff. You're entitled to automation, and automation is exactly what you're going to get. This next effect takes a different approach. Rather than moving the pixels around, the Nuclear Sunburn effect relies on commands that change the pixels' colors. As you can see in Figure 20-8, the face becomes lighted with a kind of eerie luminescence.

1. **Select your image.**

   Make your selection as detailed or as imprecise as you like.

2. **Choose Filter⇨Stylize⇨Solarize.**

   Sounds like an exciting command, huh? Actually, by itself, Solarize is pretty dull. It makes the black pixels black, the medium pixels medium, and the white pixels black again. Big whoop. But have no fear, we're going to spruce things up a little.

3. **Choose Image⇨Adjust⇨Auto Levels.**

   Photoshop lightens the gray pixels and makes them white, as shown in the first example in Figure 20-8. The areas that were previously either dark or light are now dark; the medium areas are now light.

Figure 20-8:
Choose the
Solarize
filter and
the Auto
Levels
command
(left) and
then
press ⌘-I.

4. **Choose Image⇨Adjust⇨Invert or just press ⌘-I.**

   This command inverts the image, turning the black pixels white and the white pixels black, as in a photo negative (kind of like a simplified version of the Difference mode). The finished result is shown in the second example of Figure 20-8.

Applying the I-Don't-Know-What-It-Is Effect

I really don't know what to make of this effect. Each time I look at it, a metaphor flashes into my head and then I lose it. It's like a face riddled with protozoa or some kind of crazy, impossible X ray. "The Face under the Electron Microscope" — maybe that's it. Well, whatever it is, you can check it out in Figure 20-9.

1. **Select your image.**

   What a fresh step for you.

2. **Choose Filter⇨Stylize⇨Find Edges.**

   The left example in Figure 20-9 shows how the Find Edges filter traces the contours of the selected face. Moderately cool, but not killer.

Figure 20-9:
The Find Edges filter on its own (left) and after sharpening the image to its utmost limit (right).

3. **Press ⌘-Z to undo the effect.**

   We can do better than that.

4. **Choose Filter⇨Sharpen⇨Unsharp Mask.**

   If you can bring out some additional edges, you give the Find Edges command more to work with. And nothing brings out the edges like Unsharp Mask.

5. **Enter the maximum Amount value, 500 percent, and the very high Radius value of 10.**

   Such a high Radius value takes you into the realm of special-effects sharpening. It really sharpens the holy heck out of the image.

6. **Press Return.**

   That caps off the Unsharp Mask filter.

7. **Again choose Filter⇨Stylize⇨Find Edges.**

   The result appears in the second example in Figure 20-9. Now that's what I call killer. I don't know what else to call it, of course, so I guess killer will have to do.

Stamping the Face in a Marble Haze

Again, this is a fairly weak name for a wonderful effect. The following steps alternatively lighten and darken the image utilizing a cloud pattern that ends up looking a lot like marble, as you can see in Figure 20-10.

1. **Select your image.**

   Yeah, yeah, yeah.

2. **Choose Filter⇨Render⇨Difference Clouds.**

   Of the two Clouds filters, this one is the more exciting. It blends Photoshop-generated clouds with the selected image using the Difference mode. The first example in Figure 20-10 shows the result of this single-shot filter.

3. **Press ⌘-F to reapply the Difference Clouds filter.**

   Photoshop blends the clouds with the image. Things are getting more mottled.

4. **Repeat Step 3 three times.**

   That's right. Press ⌘-F, ⌘-F, and yet another ⌘-F.

5. **Choose Image⇨Adjust⇨Auto Levels.**

   Looking a little dark? Auto Levels brings the colors back to life.

6. **Apply the Unsharp Mask filter.**

   An Amount value of 50 percent and a Radius of 0.5 should bring back some of the detail. The second example of Figure 20-10 shows how the face now appears emblazoned on a dense, marble wall. At least, that's what the image looks like to me. Feel free to draw your own conclusions.

Figure 20-10:
The result of choosing the Difference Clouds command once (left) and five times (right).

Effecting a Total Molecular Breakdown

This technique reduces your image to a bunch of colored shapes and then blends them with the original image to form something truly other-worldly, as shown in Figure 20-11.

1. **Select your image.**

   Admit it, you'd miss this step if it weren't here. You've seen it so many times, it seems like an old friend.

2. **Choose Filter⇨Pixelate⇨Crystallize, enter** 30, **and press Return.**

   Nice words, Pixelate and Crystallize, but what do they mean? Like most of the commands under the Filter⇨Pixelate submenu, Crystallize subdivides the image into blocks of color. In this case, the blocks resemble little particles of stained glass, as in the first example in Figure 20-11.

3. **Choose Filter⇨Fade.**

   The Fade command, new to Version 4, lets you mix the filter effect with the unfiltered original by using the same blending modes and Opacity slider you find in the Layers palette.

4. **Choose the Difference option from the Mode pop-up menu and press Return.**

   Photoshop uses the stained-glass pattern to invert the face.

5. **Press ⌘-L and use the options in the Levels dialog box to lighten the image.**

Figure 20-11: After applying the Crystallize command to my image, I used the Fade command to mix the new image with the original using the Difference mode (right).

As things stand now, the image is way too dark to print. I lightened the image on the right side of Figure 20-11 by setting the three Input Levels values to 0, 2.30, and 170 respectively. Press Return to apply the changes.

6. **Apply the Unsharp Mask filter.**

   I used an Amount value of 100 percent and a Radius of 0.5, but I encourage you to sharpen according to your personal tastes.

Framing the Goofy Pose

Sometimes, you're lucky enough to dig up a photograph of your unruly loved one that's embarrassing all on its own — no special effects required. In that case, all you need to do is add a little finishing touch, such as the drop shadow or vignette effect shown in Figure 20-12.

In Photoshop 4, the new Actions palette contains prerecorded macros (sets of commands) that apply the effects shown in Figure 20-12. Here's how to create the drop shadow effect using the Actions palette:

1. **Save your image.**

   After you apply the effect, you can't use Edit⇨Undo if you don't like the result. Photoshop actually applies a series of commands to generate the effect, and Edit⇨Undo only reverses the last command in the chain, which doesn't get you back to your original image. But if you save your image before you apply the effect you can use File⇨Revert to return to your original image if necessary

2. **Choose Window⇨Show Actions to display the Actions palette.**

3. **Click on the Drop Shadow (full image) item.**

   Photoshop sets about applying a drop shadow to your image.

4. **When you see a dialog box appear, press Return.**

   As Photoshop applies the drop shadow effect, two dialog boxes are presented enabling you to alter the effect a little. Just press Return to accept the default settings. Photoshop places the shadow on a separate layer.

To create a rectangular vignette, as shown in the right-hand example in Figure 20-12, follow the same steps, only choose the Vignette (full image) item in the Actions palette. This time, Photoshop doesn't present you with any dialog boxes, so you can skip Step 3.

Photoshop places the drop shadow or vignette effect on a separate layer. If you don't like what you see, drag the layer to the trash icon in the Layers palette. You can't undo the shadow or vignette using ⌘-Z or Edit⇨Undo, because Photoshop has actually applied a series of commands to create the effect. You can undo only the last command in the series, which doesn't get you back to your original image.

I applied the drop shadow and the vignette effects in Figure 20-12 to the same original image. As you can see from the figure, the drop shadow effect enlarges your overall image size a little — Photoshop adds the shadow around the outside of your original image. But the vignette effect eats away at your image, because the vignette is applied from the edges of the image inward. If you want more control over how your vignette is applied, you may prefer the method I explain back in Chapter 13, in the section "Making the selection fuzzy around the edges."

Well, that should do it. If you don't have the anger worked out of your system by now, I suggest counseling. Or better yet, you kids kiss and make up. That's what my wife and I always do. (Oh, dang, there goes my *Boy's Life* story!)

Figure 20-12:
You can easily create a drop shadow or vignette effect using the Actions palette in Photoshop 4.

Chapter 21

Ten Things to Do with Your Photoshop Masterpiece

*A*fter you finish creating your image in Photoshop, you may experience a hint of letdown. I mean, now that you're done with the image, what do you do with it? You can't just sit there and look at it on your screen for the rest of your life.

Well, that is an option, I suppose, but it's certainly not your only option. Photoshop is one of the key programs used by graphics professionals, and only a few of said professionals create images just to sit around and stare at them all day. More often, these images have specific purposes and are used in very specific ways.

This chapter examines a few options. Some of them cost money, and some involve the use of other programs that I don't explain in this book. All of the following options provide food for future thought.

Printing and Dispersing

Just about everyone who has a computer also owns a printer. Assuming that you do too, make sure that the image fits onto a sheet of paper and print it out (refer back to Chapter 7 if you need help). Then you can photocopy the image and hand it out to everyone you know or stick it in an envelope and mail it to your grandmother. Digital images are a welcomed gift any time during the year.

Framing Your Work of Art

Okay, that option was obvious. This one isn't, and it's expensive to boot. If you've created just about the best-looking image you could possibly imagine, you can actually print it out and frame it. The image needs to have a resolution of at least 150 ppi, and you probably want it to be fairly large to justify the expense (although many classic works of art are only a few inches tall). And, of course, the image should be full color, RGB.

When the image is ready to go, call around to a few service bureaus in your neck of the woods and find one that can print to a dye-sublimation printer. A dye-sub printer creates images that look just like photographs — no little dots, like you see in newspaper photos, just smooth colors. You can't reproduce from dye-sub prints, but they look great. (Professionals use them for proofing to make sure that the colors in the printed image look the way they want.)

A dye-sub printout will probably cost you around $20. But provided the image looks good, the results can be fantastic.

When you go to get the image framed, make sure to ask for UV-protected glass, which also runs around $20 to $30. Dye-sub prints can fade when exposed to direct or even indirect light, so hang the piece away from a window.

Placing the Image into PageMaker or QuarkXPress

Adobe PageMaker and QuarkXPress are two popular page-layout programs. They allow you to combine text and graphics to create multipage documents such as newsletters, reports, catalogs, even books. This book, for example, was laid out in PageMaker; the color plates were laid out in XPress.

If you want to use a Photoshop image in one of these programs, save it in the TIFF format with LZW compression. Then import the file from disk into PageMaker by choosing File⊃Place (⌘-D) or into XPress using File⊃Get Picture (⌘-E). (Both commands are found inside the respective programs, not inside Photoshop.)

Whatever you do, don't copy the image in Photoshop and paste it into PageMaker or XPress. To do so is the same as importing the image in the PICT format, and neither PageMaker nor XPress works very well with PICT.

You can change the dimensions of the image, move it on the printed page, run text around it, and print the final pages, all inside PageMaker or XPress. So unless you want to further modify the image, you have no reason to return to Photoshop.

Placing the Image into Illustrator or FreeHand

Adobe Illustrator and MacroMedia FreeHand are graphics programs like Photoshop, but instead of enabling you to edit images, they let you create smooth-line artwork. Information graphics, maps, architectural plans, general artwork, and single-page documents such as flyers are all projects ideally suited to Illustrator and FreeHand.

Both programs let you import images. In the case of Illustrator, save your Photoshop image in the EPS format. Then import it from disk by choosing File⊃Place Art from inside Illustrator. For FreeHand, go ahead and save the image as a TIFF file. Then choose File⊃Place (⌘-Shift-D) from inside FreeHand. Again, do not copy the image in Photoshop and paste it into either program.

After placing the image, you can combine it with smooth-line artwork or integrate it into a single-page document. The IDG Books production staff used FreeHand to label Figure 2-1 and the other figures that required labels in this book. It's not possible to label the figures inside Photoshop — which is where they all originated — because small text in Photoshop is jagged and illegible. PageMaker, meanwhile, is great for creating long text documents but not so good at handling little bits of text here and there.

Here's how labeled figures such as Figure 2-1 got onto their respective pages:

1. **I saved the image in the TIFF format.**

   Then I copied the TIFF file to disk and sent them to IDG Books Worldwide, Inc., in Indiana.

2. **A member of the IDG crackerjack production staff placed the images into FreeHand.**

   A production artist then created all the labels and saved the FreeHand document in the EPS format. EPS is the best format for smooth-line artwork and high-resolution text. It also retains the image.

3. **Inside PageMaker, another production artist imported the FreeHand EPS graphic.**

   The layout artist then positioned the EPS graphic and ran the text around it, as you see the page now.

4. **The final PageMaker document was saved to disk and shipped to the commercial printer.**

   The printer printed the pages and reproduced the pages onto the paper you're reading now.

How's that for a start-to-finish examination of how this process works? And just in case you thought I was spilling out some trade secrets, just about every publisher creates books this way these days. It's a desktop world.

Pasting the Image into Persuasion or PowerPoint

Adobe Persuasion and Microsoft PowerPoint are a couple of popular presentation programs used for creating slides and on-screen presentations for board meetings, product demonstrations, and kiosks. Photoshop is a great tool for creating backgrounds for these presentations or refining head shots that may appear on the slides.

Because Persuasion and PowerPoint do most of their work on-screen, it's perfectly acceptable to transfer the image from Photoshop via the Clipboard. While inside Photoshop, just select the portion of the image you want to use, copy it by pressing ⌘-C, switch to Persuasion or PowerPoint, and paste the selection by pressing ⌘-V.

As you can in PageMaker, you can move the image around, change the dimensions, and wrap text around it. If you plan on displaying the presentation on-screen, you want to give some thought to the file size of the image. For example, if you intend for the image to serve as a background for a presentation that takes up an entire 13-inch monitor, the image should be 640 pixels wide by 480 pixels tall. A good size for a head shot may be 300 pixels tall by 200 pixels wide. Experiment to find the file sizes that work best for you.

Making a Desktop Pattern

You know that pattern that appears in the background behind all the icons at the Finder? It may be plain gray or some kind of colored dot pattern. Well, using Photoshop and System 7.5, you can change this pattern.

First, go to the Finder and check which version of the system you're using (if you don't already know). Choose the About This Macintosh command from the Apple menu. A dialog box appears, listing the version number of your system. If it says System 7.5 (or later), you're in luck. Here's what you do:

1. **Find the Desktop Patterns program.**

   This program could be anywhere on your hard disk. If you're having problems finding it, press ⌘-F, enter Desktop Patterns, and press Return.

2. **Double-click on the Desktop Patterns program.**

   This displays a window with a scroll bar that lets you scroll through various predefined patterns.

3. **Switch to Photoshop.**

4. **Open an image.**

5. **Crop it down to 128 by 128 pixels.**

   Use Image⇨Canvas Size or the crop tool. This file size — 128 pixels by 128 pixels — is the maximum size of desktop patterns in System 7.5.

6. **Press ⌘-A, ⌘-C.**

   This selects the image and copies it.

7. **Switch back to the Desktop Patterns program.**

8. **Press ⌘-V to paste the image from the Clipboard.**

   If you get an insufficient-memory error, you have to increase the amount of memory devoted to Desktop Pattern, like so: Quit the program and select the program icon at the Finder level. Next, press ⌘-I to display the Info dialog box and enter a higher value in the Preferred Size option box. Close the Info dialog box and relaunch the Desktop Patterns program by double-clicking on it. Then press ⌘-V again.

9. **Click on the Set Desktop Pattern button.**

   The background fills with the pattern.

You may want to return to Photoshop and work on making the left edge of the image match with the right edge and the top edge match with the bottom. This feat takes some experimenting, of course, but it helps to eliminate the harsh edges that divide one tile from the next. If you decide to edit the image in Photoshop, just repeat Steps 6 through 9 to reapply it to the Finder background.

Making a Start-Up Screen

Another way to modify your working environment is to create a start-up screen. The start-up screen is the image that displays when your computer is starting up. Normally, you see a little box that says "Welcome to Macintosh," but you can make it say anything you want. Here's how:

1. **Create a screen-size image.**

   Again, if you're working on a 13-inch monitor, make sure that the image measures 640 by 480 pixels. The resolution doesn't matter.

2. **Choose File⇨Save As.**

   Up pops the Save dialog box.

3. **Select the PICT Resource from the Format pop-up menu.**

   The PICT Resource format is designed especially for start-up screens.

4. **Navigate to the System Folder.**

   If you've forgotten how to motor around your hard disk from inside the Save dialog box, check out the "Opening a non-Photo CD image" section in Chapter 3.

5. **Name the image StartupScreen and press Return.**

   Be sure the literal name is StartupScreen. A second dialog box, PICT Resource Options, appears.

6. **Enter SCRN into the Name option box.**

   It's very important that you exactly enter SCRN in all caps.

7. **Select None from the Compression radio button.**

   Oh, my goodness, is this step ever important. If you select any of the JPEG options, you really mess things up.

8. **Press Return.**

   Photoshop saves the file to disk.

9. **Quit Photoshop and restart your computer.**

   As the computer starts up, you get to see your awesome start-up screen. Kind of fun, huh?

Engaging in Tag-Team Editing

Just because you're an electronic artist doesn't mean that you have to work alone. If you'd like to give another artist or a friend a whack at one of your images, copy it to disk and mail it off. Then have the associate/friend mail the disk back when she is done. Or just send the file back and forth using e-mail, if you're hooked into the Internet or some other online service that offers e-mail.

You didn't have nearly this range of give-and-take editing options back in the days before computers. I mean, you can keep trading images for years. It's like a long-distance chess game — whoever comes up with the craziest editing trick wins.

Posting the Image over the Internet or an Online Service

Both the CompuServe and America Online electronic information services have Photoshop forums, and subscribers can connect to either service using a modem. You can then upload images to the forums to make them available to other subscribers. You have to pay for the time it takes to upload the image — and so does the person who downloads the image — so keep the images fairly small and save them in the JPEG format or CompuServe GIF.

If you happen to have your own Web page — or know someone who does — you can also add your image to the page, thereby making it available to Web surfers worldwide. As discussed in Chapter 6, you can use JPEG or the CompuServe GIF format to post images on the Web.

Just in case you haven't gotten enough of me through the course of reading this book, by the way, you can check out my Web page at the following URL: www.DekeMC.com. It offers some Photoshop tips and tricks along with a bunch of other stuff, including lots of shameless self-promotion. But hey, what's the point of having a Web page if you can't brag a little, right?

Adding It to Your Private Collection

No one says that you have to produce artwork for public consumption. I do plenty of stuff just for my own amusement and edification. What you see in the book, for example, represents about half of what I came up with; the other images are working files, experiments, or just too hideous for publication.

So share the stuff you're proud of, keep the random experiments to yourself, and try to learn from your inevitable mistakes. Oh, yeah, and don't beat the computer when it crashes.

Appendix A
How to Install Photoshop

●●●

*P*rograms like Photoshop don't magically appear on your hard drive. You have to go out and get them, bring them home, and install them by unwrapping and inserting disks. I know, such manual activities should be illegal in a computer-run economy like ours — I, for one, was led to believe that the 1990s would be a time when servo-robots catered to my every whim, so that the atrophy of my body would allow me to evolve into a floating brain — but, sadly, these things still require a lot of driving about, signing checks, ripping apart cellophane, and other laborious tasks. *Quel bummerre,* as the French say.

Now, of course, I could just tell you, "If you haven't yet installed Photoshop, read the Getting Started manual included with the program." But you didn't pay $19.99 of your hard-earned cash along with a nickel that you found on the street for me to tell you that. So without any further ado — I just love to say "ado," don't you? — here's how to install Photoshop.

Putting Photoshop on Your Hard Disk

Start by inserting the CD that came inside your package or the disk labeled *Installer—Disk 1.* Then do the following:

1. **Double-click on the CD icon on the desktop.**

   This opens the CD so that you can see its contents. (If you're installing from disk, skip this step.)

2. **Double-click on the Install Adobe Photoshop icon.**

   The installation program launches.

3. **When the splash screen comes up, press Return.**

   The splash screen — that thing that contains the Continue button — just tells you that you're entering the installer program. Pressing Return gets the show on the road. The Install Adobe Photoshop dialog box appears on-screen.

4. Select Custom Install from the pop-up menu in the upper left corner of the dialog box.

A list of check boxes becomes available.

5. If you own a Power Macintosh, select the Adobe Photoshop 4.0 Power Macintosh check box.

Look at your computer. It should actually say Power Macintosh on it. If it does not, select the first check box, Adobe Photoshop 4.0 68K.

If you aren't sure what kind of computer you own and you just don't want to make a mistake, select the Adobe Photoshop 4.0 Universal check box. (Whatever you do, don't select more than one of these three check boxes.)

6. Now select the following check boxes:

❏ Plug-ins

❏ Kodak Photo CD Support

❏ Adobe Type Manager

❏ QuickTime 2.1

❏ Adobe Type Reunion 1.2

If you have tons of free space on your hard drive, you can select some of the other items as well, but those listed above are the essential ones. (To find out about any item, click on the I (for Information) button to the right of the item that sparks your curiosity.)

7. Click on the Install button.

If any programs are running, the installer asks to quit them. Press Return to continue.

After that, the program sets about installing Photoshop. If you're installing from the CD, you may want to take a break for a few minutes while the installer does its stuff. If you're installing from disk, stick around; the program periodically spits out one disk and asks you to stick in another.

8. When the process is finished, click on the Restart button.

This restarts the computer so that it can load the ATM, QuickTime, and Type Reunion utilities.

The installer program may complain that you don't have enough space on your hard disk to hold Photoshop. There's only one solution: Quit the installer and delete some stuff from your hard disk. I can't tell you what to delete — I can't quite see your computer from this angle — so you have to decide for yourself. Or ask the advice of friends who have more experience than you, and see whether they can help out.

Appendix B
Photo Credits

· ·

*T*he following pages list every figure and color plate that features a photograph (or partial photograph) and the collection or photographer from which the photograph comes. My sincere thanks to the generous folks who contributed photos for inclusion in this book.

Figures	*Photographer/Product*	*Company*
Figure 1-1 (frame)	Signature Series #4, "The Painted Table"	PhotoDisc
Figure 1-2 (text)	Kent Knudson, Signature Series #2, "Urban Perspectives"	PhotoDisc
Figure 1-2 (eyes & mouth)	Vol. 11, "Retro Americana"	PhotoDisc
Figures 1-3 through 1-6	Vol. 11, "Retro Americana"	PhotoDisc
Figure 1-7	Vol. 13, "Italian Fine Art, Prints, & Photographs"	PhotoDisc
Figures 2-2, 2-3 (flower)	"Natural World"	Digital Stock
Figure 3-2	"Southern California"	Digital Stock
Figure 3-3	"Active Lifestyles 2"	Digital Stock
Figures 3-4, 3-5	"Children & Teens"	Digital Stock
Figure 3-6	"Active Lifestyles 2"	Digital Stock
Figure 3-8	"Southern California"	Digital Stock
Figure 4-1	"Children & Teens"	Digital Stock
Figures 4-3, 4-4, 4-5	Frederick Shussler, Signature Series #3, "Children of the World"	PhotoDisc
Figures 5-2, 5-6, 7-6,	"Indigenous Peoples" Color Plates 5-1, 7-1	Digital Stock
Color Plates 5-1, 7-1 (background)	"Natural Textures"	Digital Stock
Color Plates 5-2, 5-3 (background)	"Conceptual Backgrounds"	Digital Stock
Figure 5-3	"Natural World"	Digital Stock

Figures	*Photographer/Product*	*Company*
Figure 7-2	"Space Exploration"	Digital Stock
Color Plates 8-1, 8-2 (background)	"Conceptual Backgrounds"	Digital Stock
Figure 8-9	Robert Yin, "Undersea Textures"	Digital Stock
Figures 9-1, 9-2, 9-3	"Space Exploration"	Digital Stock
Figures 9-5, 9-6, 9-7, 9-10, 9-11, and Color Plate 9-1	"Undersea Life"	Digital Stock
Color Plate 9-1 (background)	"Urban Textures"	Digital Stock
Figures 10-1 through 10-4, 10-6 through 10-8	"Space & Spaceflight"	Digital Stock
Color Plate 10-1	"Indigenous Peoples"	Digital Stock
Color Plate 10-1 (background)	"Urban Textures"	Digital Stock
Figures 11-1, 11-2, 11-3	"Undersea Life"	Digital Stock
Figures 12-2, 12-4, 12-5	Eric Wunrow, "Sampler One"	ColorBytes
Figure 12-3	"Cyberstock"	Digital Stock
Figure 12-7	"Animals"	Digital Stock
Figures 12-8, 12-9,	"Animals" Color Plates 12-1, 12-2, 12-3	Digital Stock
Color Plate 12-1 (background)	"Urban Textures"	Digital Stock
Color Plates 12-2, 12-3 (background)	"Conceptual Backgrounds"	Digital Stock
Figures 13-1, 13-3	"Buildings & Structures"	Digital Stock
Figure 13-4	Frederick Shussler, Signature Series #3, "Children of the World"	PhotoDisc
Figure 13-5	"Skylines of North America"	Digital Stock
Figures 14-1, 14-2, 14-3, 14-5, 14-6, 14-9, 14-10, Color Plate 14-1	Signature Series #4, "The Painted Table"	PhotoDisc
Color Plate 14-1 (background)	"Conceptual Backgrounds"	Digital Stock
Figures 15-1, 15-2, 15-3, 15-5, 15-6	"Undersea Life"	Digital Stock

Figures	*Photographer/Product*	*Company*
Color Plates 15-1 through 15-4 (fish and kelp)	"Undersea Life"	Digital Stock
Color Plates 15-1 through 15-4 (cathedral)	"Buildings & Structures"	Digital Stock
Color Plates 15-1, 15-2 (Neptune, comet, astronaut, and nebula)	"Space & Spaceflight"	Digital Stock
Color Plates 15-1, 15-2 (lily)	"Flowers"	Digital Stock
Color Plates 15-1, 15-2 (background)	"Antistock"	Digital Stock
Color Plates 15-3, 15-4 (background)	"Natural Textures"	Digital Stock
Figures 16-1, 16-6, 16-7, 16-8 (leaves)	Hans Wiesenhofer, Signature Series #1, "Colors"	PhotoDisc
Color Plate 16-1 (trees)	Hans Wiesenhofer, Signature Series #1, "Colors"	PhotoDisc
Color Plate 16-1 (background)	"Natural Textures"	Digital Stock
Figures 17-2 through 17-17	Vol. 13, "Italian Fine Art, Prints, & Photographs"	PhotoDisc
Color Plate 17-1	"Western Scenics"	Digital Stock
Color Plate 17-1	"Tranquility" (background)	Digital Stock
Figures 18-1, 18-2, 18-3	Vol. 11, "Retro Americana"	PhotoDisc
Figures 18-7 through 18-10	Vol. 11, "Retro Americana"	PhotoDisc
Color Plates 18-1, 18-2	Daniel McFarland	
Color Plates 18-1, 18-2 (background)	"Conceptual Backgrounds"	Digital Stock
Color Plate 18-3	Denise McClelland	
Color Plate 18-3 (background)	"Antistock"	Digital Stock
Figure 18-11, Color Plate 18-4	"Animals"	Digital Stock
Figure 18-12, Color Plate 18-5	"Animals"	Digital Stock
Color Plates 18-4, 18-5 (background)	"Conceptual Backgrounds"	Digital Stock
Figures 20-1 through 20-12	Vol. 11, "Retro Americana"	PhotoDisc

Index

....

• M •

12 Free Photo CD Scans...

Not All Photo CD Scans Are Equal

Quality, excellent service and support... just a few of the reasons Photoshop users, artists, designers, photographers, and publishers from around the United States choose PALMER'S for their Photo CD scanning. Your image is taken seriously whether you need one scan or thousands.

Introduce yourself to the PALMER'S difference. We'll scan 12 negatives or slides for free* (a $36 value) with an order of $36 (12 Repro scans) or more. That's it! You'll find PALMER'S is America's premier Photo CD service.

PALMER'S

MOUNTAIN VIEW	**SACRAMENTO**
650 Castro Street	2313 C Street
415 969 1950	916 441 3305
415 969 1956 *fax*	916 441 1157 *fax*

SMART SOLUTIONS
800 735 1950
pcd@palmers.com

Yes! *I Want 12 Free!*

Name _____ Title _____

Company _____ Telephone _____

Address _____ Fax _____

City _____ Business Type _____

State/Zip _____ Scans Per Month _____

How did you hear about us? _____

*This offer is good for **35mm film** and **one time only**, although pass it along to your friends.
(does not include disc and offer subject to change)

IDG

Notes

Notes

Notes

Notes

Notes

Notes

WWW.DUMMIES.COM

YOUR ONLINE RESOURCE

Discover Dummies Online!

The Dummies Web Site is your fun and friendly online resource for the latest information about ...*For Dummies*® books and your favorite topics. The Web site is the place to communicate with us, exchange ideas with other ...*For Dummies* readers, chat with authors, and have fun!

Ten Fun and Useful Things You Can Do at www.dummies.com

1. Win free ...*For Dummies* books and more!
2. Register your book and be entered in a prize drawing.
3. Meet your favorite authors through the IDG Books Author Chat Series.
4. Exchange helpful information with other ...*For Dummies* readers.
5. Discover other great ...*For Dummies* books you must have!
6. Purchase Dummieswear™ exclusively from our Web site.
7. Buy ...*For Dummies* books online.
8. Talk to us. Make comments, ask questions, get answers!
9. Download free software.
10. Find additional useful resources from authors.

Link directly to these ten fun and useful things at **http://www.dummies.com/10useful**

For other technology titles from IDG Books Worldwide, go to
www.idgbooks.com

Not on the Web yet? It's easy to get started with *Dummies 101*®: *The Internet For Windows*®*95* or *The Internet For Dummies*®, 4th Edition, at local retailers everywhere.

Find other ...*For Dummies* books on these topics:

Business • Career • Databases • Food & Beverage • Games • Gardening • Graphics • Hardware
Health & Fitness • Internet and the World Wide Web • Networking • Office Suites
Operating Systems • Personal Finance • Pets • Programming • Recreation • Sports
Spreadsheets • Teacher Resources • Test Prep • Word Processing

The IDG Books Worldwide logo and Dummieswear are trademarks, and Dummies Man and ...For Dummies are registered trademarks under exclusive license to IDG Books Worldwide, Inc., from International Data Group, Inc.

IDG BOOKS WORLDWIDE
BOOK REGISTRATION

Register This Book and Win!

We want to hear from you!

Visit **http://my2cents.dummies.com** to register this book and tell us how you liked it!

- Get entered in our monthly prize giveaway.
- Give us feedback about this book — tell us what you like best, what you like least, or maybe what you'd like to ask the author and us to change!
- Let us know any other ...*For Dummies*® topics that interest you.

Your feedback helps us determine what books to publish, tells us what coverage to add as we revise our books, and lets us know whether we're meeting your needs as a ...*For Dummies* reader. You're our most valuable resource, and what you have to say is important to us!

Not on the Web yet? It's easy to get started with *Dummies 101*®*: The Internet For Windows*® *95* or *The Internet For Dummies*,® 4th Edition, at local retailers everywhere.

Or let us know what you think by sending us a letter at the following address:

...*For Dummies* Book Registration
Dummies Press
7260 Shadeland Station, Suite 100
Indianapolis, IN 46256-3945
Fax 317-596-5498

BUSINESS AND GENERAL REFERENCE BOOK SERIES FROM IDG

COMPUTER BOOK SERIES FROM IDG